S0-BIP-400

WITHDRAWN
College of St. Scholastica
Duluth, Minnesota 55811

Introduction to Gaming:
*Management Decision Simulations*

*The Wiley Series in*

MANAGEMENT AND ADMINISTRATION

ELWOOD S. BUFFA, *Advisory Editor*
*University of California, Los Angeles*

John G. H. Carlson
Michael J. Misshauk

# Introduction to Gaming: Management Decision Simulations

JOHN WILEY & SONS, INC.
New York • London • Sydney • Toronto

658.403
C28

Copyright © 1972, by John Wiley & Sons, Inc.

All rights reserved. Published simultaneously in Canada.

No part of this book may reproduced by any means,
nor transmitted, nor translated into a machine lan-
guage without the written permission of the publisher.

Library of Congress Catalogue Card Number: 73-175790

ISBN 0-471-13485-6

Printed in the United States of America

10  9  8  7  6  5  4  3  2  1

# Preface

We have designed this textbook to meet the needs of students in several areas: (1) introductory simulation and gaming courses, (2) management decision gaming techniques, (3) model design and decision processing, and (4) management laboratories.

Simulation and gaming is currently a part of the integrative, capstone or summary courses for many undergraduate as well as graduate programs. As more schools attempt to provide an opportunity for students to test their newly acquired skills in the classroom, simulation techniques will become increasingly popular.

Decision gaming is being considered by many for incorporation into introductory courses in business in order to illustrate management decision techniques. In this area the text might be used in conjunction with a management principles text. This text is especially well suited for small colleges that would like to employ simulation and gaming techniques, but that lack the large computer facilities usually required for this purpose.

Courses in model design and decision process appear to be increasing in most business programs. In courses of this type this text could stand as the only book utilized in order to provide the students with an understanding of simulation concepts as well as a guide to developing their own skills in model building.

At the undergraduate level, many schools are currently using the management laboratory to increase student involvement in the learning process. This book meets the requirements of courses dealing with management training or behavioral understanding.

LIBRARY
College of St. Scholastica
Duluth, Minnesota 55811

MANAGEMENT DECISION SIMULATIONS

We have provided here many of the advantages of the case method and, in addition, the games give feedback to the students concerning the success of their decisions. The games also provide "experience" in the functional areas of business and are extremely helpful in tying together concepts among various functional areas.

John G. H. Carlson
Michael J. Misshauk

# Contents

# Introduction to Gaming

## INTRODUCTION

The business student and his counterpart in industry, unlike people in the sciences, have little chance of testing their ideas before making major decisions. A means must be made available to better predict and evaluate the overall effects of changes and decisions on our business systems. We seek representations or models that will simulate the interaction of men, machines, and materials in a system. Trial and error methods in real life are too disruptive and too costly. Ideas must be tested, risks calculated, uncertainty experienced, and results predicted by a less expensive method. Decision Games or Decision Simulations is an economical and effective method of imparting and testing knowledge and ideas by pretesting decisions.

This text may be used in conjunction with several areas of education and training curriculum for business. It encourages and services a type of business laboratory environment in which the member can learn more about the nature of various areas of the business world, compete in dynamic and competitive situations, discover the adequacy of his analysis regarding the game itself and, finally, gain valuable insights into his own behavior within task-oriented groups.

### The Gaming Methodology

Business gaming is a teaching vehicle or technique that makes use of situations specifically designed to represent the actual environmental conditions in the business world. The difference between conventional teaching techniques and gaming lies in the fact that most conventional methods concentrate on imparting definitions and explanations of certain variables or situations within a given area. Gaming, on the other hand, is most effective in providing the participant with a method for self-discovery of the variables and the relationships that exist between these variables. To the greatest extent possible, gaming enables the participant to become involved in the situation and to interact by making decisions about those variables that will optimize some criteria.

Because the participant is expected to bring a certain basic knowledge, vocabulary, or familiarity into most gaming situations, gaming might not be as effective as other methods at the first level of training or education within a given field. On the other hand, gaming in elementary and secondary education is evolving at a rapid pace including the teaching-learning experience through simulation and role playing in subject areas such as American history. At intermediate and advanced levels of education, gaming provides a unique opportunity for the participant to put his knowledge "to the test," enabling him to consider a total situation with its many complex variables, interactions, and relationships—to sort through this maze, selecting those variables that are critical, those that are useful and, finally, eliminating those that may be irrelevant to a particular problem.

Simulation gaming, representing as nearly as possible real-world conditions, is equivalent to a laboratory in which the participant can put into practice theories, rules, and equations that have been part of his education. Many bits of prior knowledge will be of use to him in analyzing, calculating, and evaluating variables and conditions in order to reach an optimum

decision within a given area. It enables the participant to test his decisions within a realistic and often competitive environment since most games make use of teams or individuals competing against one another to increase sales, cut costs, improve profit, and so on. Often the participant has the opportunity to function within an environment that is not fixed, that is, the responses of the other individuals or teams will depend on their own perception of the variables involved. The value of this educational method appears exceptional because it provides a training ground in which participants can test knowledge and skills in competition with others. They focus on the relationships among variables instead of on just the variables themselves. They make decisions based on their analysis but, in contrast to the case method, they receive feedback as to the correctness or worth of their decisions; and, finally, they discuss the reasons for the success or failure within the game situation. The objective is to improve performance with each future decision within the game and, more importantly, in the real world of business and decisions.

**Business Gaming**

Business games have become recognized both as a valued core or supplement to management development and in the educational processes of a school or university. These games are usually designed to familiarize the participants with some of the problems faced by administrators in real life. They are often used to assist in teaching management analysis, control techniques, and the understanding of some fundamental management concepts.

The objective of any game is for the player to manipulate effectively the system to find an optimum or near optimum solution. He should find this optimum only if he *understands* or *learns* the interrelationships inherent in the system, can see the effect of his past decisions, and can develop a rationale for making future decisions that will bring further improvements in the system operations.

Most real-life decisions deal with the discovery of the economic "trade-off" of two or more cost factors, such as the exchange of the cost of machine failure versus the cost of a preventive maintenance program. Most games recognize the complexity of these trade-offs and demonstrate the necessity for iterative or simulated trial-and-error method toward a solution. An analytical solution model is often difficult if not impossible to develop because of the complexity of the interactions involved or the generally abstract nature of the mathematics required.

With the above considerations in mind this text was designed to focus on the following objectives:

1. To provide a set of games that will help the participant gain additional insight into several functional areas of business, their decision variables, and the relationships among these variables with which these functions operate.

2. To provide realistic situations in which quantitative models such as linear programming can be applied or tested for application as decision aids, thereby developing understanding and practice in these techniques.

3. To provide a basis from which participants can acquire some basic techniques or tools necessary to develop their own models or simulations of realistic situations, thereby testing the participants' ability to comprehend relationships for business decision making.

4. To provide the environment in which the participant can gain understanding of his own behavior patterns, group behavior, and the impact of his own behavior on those with whom he is interacting.

## Cautions Concerning Gaming

Utilization of the gaming methodology presents some difficulties. In some cases the participant may become involved in ways of "beating the game" instead of in focusing on the variables of the game. The individual or team may try to establish ways of short-cutting the game's procedures or devoting less effort to areas within the game in which they may not be sufficiently penalized. In real life these same areas or variables can be of critical significance.

A second drawback may occur if the game is considered too easy—if variables are not complex enough to actually represent real life situations; or too difficult— if calculations or relationships are so complex that the participant will merely guess rather than get involved in sincere analysis. Game construction must present enough detail to gain involvement through realism, but should not be so complex as to frustrate the player attempting a rational decision.

Another factor to be considered is that the gaming situation does require a significant time commitment. The player must first become familiar with the rules of the game, then enter into several decision periods after each of which he receives feedback as to his progress. Finally, a debriefing session is desirable to summarize the learning both through the game and through individual interaction.

## A Gaming Format

A series of games are provided that present a broad perspective of business through studying some of the principal variables interacting in major functional areas. The participant thus takes an active part in the analysis and decision-making process required by the functional areas found in the business world. The games cover the fundamental areas of business and require quantitative, organizational, financial, human relations, as well as other business skills required to attain desired results. As has been mentioned, each game focuses on *relationships* among variables and it is this emphasis that proves to be the more valuable learning experience.

## MANAGEMENT DECISION SIMULATIONS

After playing some or all of the games provided in the text, participants should be encouraged to design their own simulation games, to test them, and to administer them for their peers. The educational sequence could be something like this:

1. A few minutes should be set aside at the beginning for further debriefing of the *previous game*. This can be based largely on responses of the designers to written critiques and suggestions that players submit after having played the game. These critiques should be reviewed by the game designers, commented on, evaluated, and summarized. Time should be allowed at the end of class for distribution of the next game along with any written briefing material or references to be studied so that strategies can be devised before play is begun.

2. The scheduled game is conducted. Experience has indicated that these functional simulations, like cases, require about 50 to 80 minutes. This allows for several periods of game play itself and any last minute oral briefing and clarification.

3. At the end of the game, 10 to 15 minutes should be allowed to permit the "losers" and "winners" to defend their strategies. Several minutes should be devoted for the participants to submit written critiques to the designers. The designers should incorporate valid suggestions and submit to the instructor a finished draft of the simulation, including briefing materials, game background, participant instructions, and referee instructions and scoring aids.

The simulation session moves rather swiftly, as one can imagine, Participants respond to this mode by stating that they gain a great deal of secondary benefit through:

1. A better understanding of the "other" functions in a business.
2. Increased involvement not only with the subject but also their peers.
3. An absolute awareness of the vital role of communication in professional life. The recognition of one's ability to transmit information and ideas.

4. A means of evaluating their own abilities to perceive problems and to devise strategies.
5. The opportunity of making new personal associations.

Mixing of the team constituents for each new game allows new interpersonal relationships. These by-products of the gaming experience could be regarded as equally important as the substantive contribution to functional knowledge. The games designed by teams force cooperative effort. After several games there may appear some consistent "winners" whose preparation, judgment, persuasiveness, and articulation would tend to indicate "business success."

The participants appear to learn the substantive material at a higher rate and in a more usable form. By trying to teach something through his game, the administrator-participant must have learned it himself. A participant who has briefed a class and has had them perform with a simulated experience in reliability, linear programming, pricing, inventory control, contract management, PERT, production scheduling, priority rules, and so on, has made a most significant contribution to his own knowledge and has contributed to the knowledge of others as well. Because of the severe time restrictions, the depth of any one concept or technique may not have been explored sufficiently by the players. However, they have achieved a perspective on the subject area that they could not have gained except in real-life, on-the-job experience.

The gaming mode also is an integrating or summarizing experience of the work a group may have had in the functional fields. The games designed and played could cover a gamut of interests—from an economic principle, to some quantitative phenomenon, to behavioral studies, even to mergers and acquisitions. This method of learning concepts, skills or techniques such as operations research is evolving rapidly as the growing libraries of games shows.

The participant may also adopt some possibly erroneous principles. For example: "Always allocate large resources early to research and then advertise heavily especially in areas of tough competition." Such implied concepts are a hazard but they can be neutralized by:

- Playing the game several times, changing the parameters significantly each time.
- Allow each team to describe their logic, their results, and lessons learned—probably the variety of approaches will negate any presumptuous strategy.
- What they can and should not do to fulfill the purpose of the game can be discussed before the actual play.
- Play several periods, initialize the game and start from that period.

### Computer Terminals in Gaming

Interactive terminals can be exceedingly helpful in processing data within the designer's model and, when appropriate, in performing data analysis with library programs of regression analysis, analysis of variance, etc. However, in some cases it is more economical to simulate the computer by employing desk calculators, nomographs, slide rules or extra referees rather than the "expense" of programming, testing, and running a computer-based game.

The trend to some form of computer scoring has been apparent. Many now have sufficient programming capability so that the challenge to create a computer-interactive simulation has begun to dominate game design.

Initial data for remote terminal or time-shared games can be entered via answering questions posed by the computer, such as the team number or the period number. From this point on, decisions are made by entering them as data or in response to specific questions. Certain options may be accepted (at a cost) such as information about a competitor or the market. Sometimes an amount of time may be specified within which answers must be provided or the team is "signed off."

With a computer-scored game, the administrator can easily change several environmental conditions or business parameters such as the growth of a demand, the price elasticity, and the resources available. Even the "winning" criterion may be changed depending on how innovative the designer-programmer chooses to be.

The time-share mode may be used not only to "score" the team but also to permit players to retrieve and analyze historical information developed in the game. The players may want to perform analysis of past sales, past production records, yield, inventory, etc. by utilizing the system's library routines.

If the game is conducted in a contemporary time reference, one can visualize certain data being available on the terminals such as "Survey of Current Business Statistics" and "Stock Market Indices," as if one is interacting with real-life information sources.

# Bibliography

1. Alberts, W. E.; "Testing Ground for Management Ideas—The Business Model"; *Proceedings of the Ninth Industrial Engineering Institute*, University of California; 1957.
2. Andrews, R. B., and Vollman, T. E.; "UNIPRODUCT: A Pedagogical Device"; *California Management Review*; Winter, 1967.
3. Bower, S., Nugent, C. E., and Stone, D. E.; "Time-Shared Computers in Business Education at Dartmouth"; *The Accounting Review*; July 1968.
4. Campbell, F., Pierce, D., and Torgersen, P. E.; "The Maintenance Game"; *The Journal of Industrial Engineering*; January–February 1964.
5. Carlson, Elliot; "Gamesmanship"; *Wall Street Journal*; July 8, 1966.
6. Cohen, K. J., and Rhenman, E.; "The Role of Management Games in Education and Research"; *Management Science*, Vol. 7, 1961.
7. Dearden, J., and McFarlan, F. W.; *Management Information Systems*; Irwin, Homewood, Illinois; 1966.
8. Dill, W. R., Jackson, J. R., and Sweeney, J. W. (Eds.); *Proceedings of the Conference on Business Games*; Tulane University, 1961.
9. Greene, J. R., and Sisson, R. L.; *Dynamic Management Decision Games*; J. Wiley and Sons, New York; 1959.
10. Greenlaw, P. S., Herron, L. W., and Rawdon, R. H.; *Business Simulation In Industrial and University Education*; Prentice-Hall, Inc., Englewood Cliffs, New Jersey; 1962.
11. Jackson, James R.; "Learning from Experience in Business Decision Games"; *California Management Review*; December 1959.

12. Jensen, B. T.; "Business Games for Executive Training"; *Advanced Management*; June 1963.
13. McKenney, J. L.; "An Evaluation of a Business Game in MBA Curriculum"; *Journal of Business*; July 1962.
14. Miller, J. J.; "The Game Is the Thing—Or Is It?" *Collegiate News and Views*; March 1969.
15. Nanus, B.; "Management Games: An Answer to Critics"; *The Journal of Industrial Engineering*; November–December 1962.
16. Rausch, E.; "Games Managers Play"; *Administrative Management*.
17. Shubik, M.; "Gaming: Costs and Facilities"; *Management Science*; October 1963.
18. Strother, G. B., Johnson, A. C., and Thompson, J. E.; *Educational Applications of Management Games*; Department of Health, Education and Welfare, Washington, D. C.; August 31, 1966.
19. Wilkinson, R. K., and Mills, G.; "The Use of a Business Game in Management Training"; *The Journal of Industrial Engineering*; July–August 1965.

# 2

# Concepts In Game Design

## GAME DESIGN

Designing a game requires careful, detailed research since it is to be played by others. It is similar to writing a case of an actual company where many, if not all, the strategies possible for arriving at a decision must be anticipated. In contrast to the qualified verbal responses of the case method, gaming almost always requires a quantifiable scoring of the responses.

Before areas of interest for gaming are selected or the design groups formed, several sample games should be played. These games provide some introduction as to what gaming is by experiencing the decision-making phenomena. To an ex-

tent, this is similar to learning to ride a bike, drive a car, or operate a remote computer terminal. No amount of checklists, written instructions, manuals, or even graphics can teach one how to operate within a man-machine system—it has to be experienced. Some games allow the player to compete against the designer's model and therefore attempt to synthesize this model. Others allow one to compete in a chance environment. Selected simulations may demonstrate some of the attributes to avoid in game design. For example, one might find scoring takes too long and detracts, if not distracts, from the game and the decision-making exercise.

The researching, studying, and analysis

in business simulations is to be encouraged. Doing as much research as one would ordinarily do for a term paper in addition to the ultimate requirement for display of this knowledge through the game presentation offers a high incentive to study, prepare, design, and "sell" a game. Not only is there motivation to research an area, but there is a necessity for effectively communicating this new-found knowledge to the participants. All manner of lessons in communication are learned or relearned in the design, presentation, and administration of the simulation.

Although designers may be more comfortable with games in their own discipline, the opportunity to probe more deeply into other disciplines should be encouraged. It is often desirable to form groups of mixed disciplines or groups of one discipline designing games in another. We share the common desire that our discipline be understood by those from other areas. A better understanding of the marketing function can be had by the finance group if they attempt to design a marketing game.

Based on the premise that the participants in gaming learn more through designing than through playing, this section is devoted to encouraging individuals and teams to develop their own simulations. Game designers become keenly aware of and develop an interest in management training and development as well as the functional area treated in the game. Building a management game utilizes a variety of skills in the areas of mathematics, communication, and education.

Some specialized knowledge in a field is also desirable in constructing the game. If it is a banking game, the members of the design team would be required to research banking operations in order to devise a suitable and challenging game in this field that could also be of benefit to bankers. A certain amount of mathematical manipulative skill is desirable for devising a good scoring model. The in-

valuable aid of nomographs, graphs, desk calculators, etc., can assist manual scoring. If it can be a computer-scored game, programming capability is desirable though programming in a time-shared mode with today's conversational languages is greatly simplified. The final design of a computer-based game is often facilitated by initially developing a manual scoring method. The advantage of computer scoring is the ability to work with more complex models or relationships and faster scoring.

There are at least three basic, yet perhaps contradictory, design requirements to be met by the designers. The game must:

· Have a purpose or objective.
· Be playable and simple.
· Be realistic and credible.

### Objective

A game is a representation, model, or abstraction of something that the designers and players experienced or may experience in real life. The purpose of the game should be that it fulfill some training goal. If the game is to teach linear programming, it may take one form in order to familiarize the participants with this mathematical optimization technique. To teach contract management, on the other hand, less mathematical modeling would be required with perhaps more risk evaluation.

The training objectives would dictate which variables are to be included or excluded. There is usually a continual compromising as to what is relevant to the concept to be taught and the contribution that a factor or variable makes to realism. If the objective of an inventory management game is to analyze the effect on operations of different valuation rules and to learn and understand these rules, then the details of these rules should be explored. (These valuation rules might be FIFO, LIFO, Average, etc.) If the objective is to look at the long-range financial considerations as a function of these rules and the rules do not have a critical effect on long-range financial planning, it may be desirable to allow the participant to choose an evaluation method or to choose one for him. (3)

There is usually some concern on the part of a designer as to whether everything in the game is to have a purpose. Should extraneous information or "noise" be introduced as in the real world, or should this be omitted? The very objective of a specific game could be to try to discover the effect of "noise" on the decisions. Noise is sometimes useful in the case approach to bring out the analytical and perceptive skills of participants. If done properly so that it does contribute to the realism and the decision makers do not feel deceived, some noise and internal contradiction can be tolerated.

Kibbee, Kraft, and Nanus (3) speak of what they call a "teeter-totter" principle. Each decision made by the participants should have compensating or balancing consequences. For example, if a team declared and distributed stock dividends, the model should reflect both the advantages and disadvantages of this decision. Distributing dividends may raise the stock price or increase a company's credit limit, but this might be counterbalanced by presenting a strain on its working capital with commensurate risks and problems. The net effect of their dividend policy remains for the team to discover. However, if the model provides that working capital is never endangered by the payment of dividends, then they should always be distributed. If the model does not provide a positive effect on stock price or other parameters, there would be no purpose in declaring a dividend. Similarly, in the case of inventory management, if there is no stockout cost, there is no purpose in carrying an extra quantity or safety stock to prevent a stockout, and no trade-off is experienced.

## Simplicity and Playability

The game itself should be designed as simply as possible consistent with achieving the desired objective. In contrast to the lengthy military war games and the large-scale management games that are designed to require and encourage extensive analysis, functional games are usually designed to teach one or two concepts.

A complex interfunctional game is often too difficult and unrewarding. The participant would like to change only one or two variables at a time, discover their effect, and use this information to move to better decisions. This demands that the rules for play be simple and that decisions be arrived at quite rapidly. This does not imply that the decisions are not complex, but instead that they do not require numerous computations, completing complicated transmittal and report forms, or continuous reference to arbitrary rules and statements in the background and instructional material. These games are to be designed to have several short periods (15 minutes or less) in which to make decisions and receive feedback. Clerical and arithmetic chores should be minimal because the participants should spend the majority of their time deciding, not computing.

Game mechanics can be simplified in a number of ways. When the time arrives for communicating the decision, the exception principle can be utilized whereby only that which is to be changed is submitted. The decision alternatives can sometimes be reduced to a prescribed group from which the participant makes his choice.

The value of the instant feedback phenomenon of learning is amply demonstrated through games. For this reason a computer should not be used for even scorekeeping unless it is at least figuratively at hand such as an interactive terminal for entering data. Turnaround

## MANAGEMENT DECISION SIMULATIONS

times in excess of five minutes for executing the program and distributing the results should be avoided. Instant measurement and feedback is the staff of success in the games. "How well am I doing?" is constantly asked in various ways by the players and they must receive either a partial or complete answer. This need for progress information, a basic educational tenet, is overwhelmingly apparent when observing any simulation. The player must perceive that he is making progress in his pursuits. A bench mark should be placed somewhere in the simulation and feedback sequence which gives him this sense of accomplishment. This is often achieved by posting some interim scores.

When there are some clerical computations to be made and submitted, it is desirable that the form be carefully laid out in a logical pattern of arithmetical steps. Sample calculations are desirable and it is wise to illustrate the whole decision sequence with an example of the zeroth (0th) period.

The clarity of the instructions, the briefing, and the debriefing at the conclusion govern the success of a game. The designers must give considerable attention to possible semantic or interpretive problems. The design team itself should run through the game several times in order to detect possible problem areas. Fellow workers, students, wives, and others can often contribute objective, helpful, and clarifying suggestions. These suggestions can affect the form, design, briefing material, and even the model itself.

### Realism and Credibility

To obtain and sustain interest and involvement in the game, the designers must give it the appearance of reality. This is known as verisimilitude. This illusion of reality can often be as convincing as reality itself as is witnessed when role playing is skillfully employed. Artificiality should be avoided, including the choice of name of

the game, names of people, and/or products, although existing names should be disguised.

If the player is to deduce a relationship from the feedback results as he changes variables, neither the exact relationship nor the precise real-life relationship are the important points. What is required is that the relationships make sense to the player. Thus, if a demand curve is to be deduced, the player may discover that if he increases price, the demand decreases, all other things remaining relatively constant. The game designers provide the verisimilitude by their choice of realistic amounts of elasticity, average values, and limiting values of the demand curve. However, the need for realism is often overemphasized. The more general the principles to be taught, the less the requirement for realism in the background material, the relationships, and the model.

*"When a game becomes realistic enough to accurately reflect the actual operations of the company, its use as a training tool becomes less important than its use as a research tool or its direct use as an aid to management decision making"* (3).

There is an opportunity of introducing real elements of a situation in a somewhat artificial manner. In inventory management games, costs for stockout are often used as penalties by subtracting an amount per unit or an amount per occasion during the play. In real life no such accounts appear in the accounting system and the costs of lost sales or other costs attributable to a stockout would be buried in the other operating costs or reduced sales orders and revenue. In a game it is possible to test the effect of decisions relating to preventing stockouts by allowing several different methods of incurring the penalty to be introduced, such as an immediate penalty, a penalty of reduced future sales, or both. Thus the introduction of a surrogate cost has permitted the testing of realistic inventory management decisions. Artificial variables may be introduced in other games to stimulate participant thinking about causes and effects. These variables may not show in the balance sheet of a real organization, but nonetheless they affect the conventional measures of success such as profits, share of the market, and so on.

Game designers realize very early the conflict between realism and simplicity of computation. Because the model or game is an abstraction or approximation of some real process, the problem is to determine the amount or degree of complexity required to provide the realism deemed necessary. A game model that is too complex does not permit identification of the underlying structural or causal relationships and the impact of the decisions cannot be determined. As a result, the learning experience is sublimated into trying to understand, play, and administer a complex game. Functional gaming experience indicates that simple game models are more effective than complex models in trying to serve the educational process. Given that there is no formula for trading off simplicity and realism, the designers should consider starting with the simplest model or game that develops the desired concept and then proceed to add complexity only as the need can be demonstrated by sample play and exchange.

The players desire to control the destiny of that which they are simulating *through their decisions.* They will tolerate the need for taking risks at times (known variability of a variable) and an amount of uncertainty such as occasional contingencies. However, if they are not making a choice among reasonable, rational alternatives—that is, *a decision*—and find themselves merely "grinding out" arithmetic answers or making "flip-of-the-coin" choices requiring no analysis, the game has become an exercise. The players must at least feel they are involved in a meaningful interaction with competitors or

there is a realistic yardstick against which they test their score, measure of success, or progress.

If the participants do not have reasonable control over their destiny through their decisions and are subject to imposed restrictions that take away the feeling of control, the game as a game is likely to be a failure. One could just as well have lectured or used a more efficient but less effective way of communicating an idea or information. The game and learning experience also suffer if the decision periods are independent and no progressive improvement is monitored. For example, if all new inputs were given each period without any relationship to prior periods or if the outputs are independent of prior analysis or decisions, then the simulation becomes a guessing game. Care must be exercised that the manual scoring in some games is not so time-consuming that the players lose interest. Often, because of cumbersome scoring, the game may even appear inconsequential.

The degree of realism is determined by the purpose of the game. If the purpose is to demonstrate competitive interaction, group interaction, demand curves, or any other particular or general phenomenon, then realism is of lesser importance. The participants then need only a rational background of facts, data, and reasonable response and feedback. If the game is to illustrate the dynamic interaction and behavior of a system such as a specific product in a particular environment which is subject to various states of nature, then the game model must be considerably more realistic and complex. All the possible interactions between the variables such as price, lead times, seasonality, and/or product quality must be carefully and accurately represented. (1)

There are several other factors that should influence a game's design, including stability and sensitivity. A game is stable if built-in restrictions prevent wide fluctuations in results due to a decision in a single period, as in the case of a team capturing the total market by offering the product at a very low price. Similarly, the design should prevent teams from early "bankruptcy," which would prevent their further participation. Sensitivity refers to the detection and evaluation of gross changes in team strategy. Drastic changes in policy may not be realistic and such phenomenon as "end-game" strategies should be discouraged by the design, built-in penalties, or game administration. Extreme and unrealistic policies must be prevented from being successful by careful design of rational penalties for irrational decisions and/or behavior.

### Criteria and Measures of Success

Gaming, simulation, and real life require a measurement of successful performance. In most functional games the possible success criteria are easy to identify. Almost everything can be reduced to a dollar basis with the objective of minimizing cost or maximizing profit. Some games, however, because of their very nature, may have criteria that are difficult to reduce to the common denominator of cost or profit, and success may be in terms of market share, arbitrary though rational administrator evaluation, or even nonquantifiable indicators.

There is much that one can research and learn from each gaming session. It is a true laboratory for studying the formation of organization structure; the formulation of goals; intragroup conflict; the identification that individual members make with the group; the types and the changes in leadership; the organizational processes of planning, implementation, and reassessment; and perhaps the effects of regrouping, adding new roles, new data, or externally imposed factors. The game designers are essentially designing a very sophisticated experiment. It is far more than, but no less than, a statistical experimental design. Because of the inadequate sample size, the results may not be statistically significant, but the process of formulating a hypothesis and attempting to test its validity is foremost in the objective of each game design and play. The game designers may hypothesize that a concept is to be learned or that certain group performance will result. Through the debriefing session, a discussion can then be directed toward an analysis as to how well the particular hypotheses were proven. It is these debriefing discussions that substitute for statistical experiments in examining the results of the gaming experience.

The players knowingly or otherwise also formulate hypotheses and perhaps superficially design experiments to test these hypotheses. For example, the players might hypothesize that within a reasonable range the concessionaire's price of food and beverages has no effect on the attendance at home games of a baseball team. Holding everything else constant, they could experiment with several price decisions to see if this affects attendance. The results they obtained would serve to confirm or deny the validity of their hypothesis concerning the relation between price and attendance.

# Bibliography

1. Meier, R. C., Newell, W. T., and Paser, H. L.; *Simulation in Business and Economics*; Prentice-Hall, New Jersey; 1969.
2. Naylor, T. H., Balintfy, J. L., Burdick, D. S., and Chu, K.; *Computer Simulation Techniques*; John Wiley & Sons, Inc., New York; 1966.
3. Kibbee, J., Kraft, C., and Nanus, B.; *Management Games*; Reinhold Publishing Company, New York; 1961.
4. Greene, J. R., and Sisson, R. L.; *Dynamic Management Decision Games*; John Wiley & Sons, Inc., New York; 1959.

# Designing a Business Game / *Theory and Application*

This chapter provides a framework or way of thinking about problem-solving situations. This framework should enable one to utilize information in a more meaningful way by assisting in recognizing relationships among variables. The framework consists of the development of a model that may be used by the reader in problem definition and design of additional business simulations. As was previously stated, simulation models represent abstractions of reality and are generally designed to provide understanding of key relationships among variables. One of the most effective methods of gaining this understanding is to actually evolve a model to describe or represent the relationship being considered. The philosophy

behind this approach lies in the fact that one develops a true understanding of some phenomenon while building a model to represent the relationships among its variables. The research and effort that goes into the model design aids the designer in clarifying his own thoughts and ideas about the relationships involved.

There are three basic phases to be discussed: (1) Information and Decisions, (2) the Model itself, and (3) Results and Feedback.

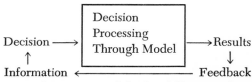

To design a model, the following five-

## MANAGEMENT DECISION SIMULATIONS

step process should be examined. The process is shown as a flow diagram, which itself is a type of model.

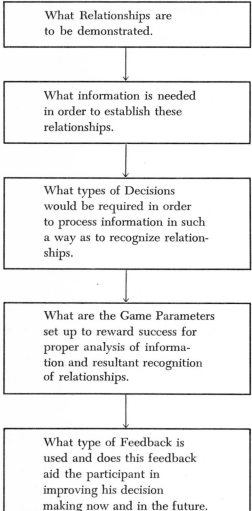

What Relationships are to be demonstrated.

What information is needed in order to establish these relationships.

What types of Decisions would be required in order to process information in such a way as to recognize relationships.

What are the Game Parameters set up to reward success for proper analysis of information and resultant recognition of relationships.

What type of Feedback is used and does this feedback aid the participant in improving his decision making now and in the future.

The above diagram attempts to represent the type of thought process that may be followed in the task of model design.

Each of the steps will now be discussed to provide a clearer understanding of model design and construction.

### The Relationships To Be Demonstrated

This must be the starting point in model design. It is at this point that the orientation is developed which will carry through the model design. The first problem that the game designer faces is an analysis of the trade-offs involved between designing a game that accurately represents reality and its complexities versus a game that is relatively easy to understand and requires a minimum of participant computation. The designer may consider all possibilities ranging from a general management simulation involving marketing, production, and financial decisions with possible analysis and scoring by a fairly intricate computer program to a relatively simple hand-scored simulation designed to demonstrate the relationship between such variables as the ordering costs and carrying costs in an inventory management environment.

Regarding the degree of sophistication to be built into the model, the designer should consider the capabilities of those to be participating in the game. Those with little business background or background in a very specialized area may have difficulty in recognizing complex or involved relationships, since they may not have been exposed to the principles that govern these relationships. For this category of participants less sophisticated models may provide a more useful learning experience. A second consideration lies in the amount of resources available to administer the simulation. These resources might include a computer, referees and, most importantly, the time available to play the game (one class or several class meetings).

These two considerations provide the input that the designer can evaluate in order to determine the type of model that best suits his purpose.

### Information Needed For Relationships

The next consideration for the model designer is to determine how to provide, through the use of the model, a vehicle for understanding the relationships. To achieve this result, the designer must decide what information is needed by the participant in order for him to make a proper decision.

Put another way, the game designer provides the necessary information which must then be *properly* processed or evaluated by the participant. The extent to which he successfully evaluates the information must be fed back to him in some form of output data (sales, profits, etc.). As the results improve through the decisions made, it can be implied that the participant has recognized a relationship among certain variables.

The information that the designer provides may be of various types. Typically, past sales, costs, financial or economic information is provided. Along with this information the decision system could include data that is really not necessary or at least not as important. This so-called "noise" provides an opportunity to gain invaluable experience in determining relevant versus unnecessary information—a problem most assuredly faced in the real-life business environment.

In determining the type of information to be provided, the designer should keep in mind how he anticipates the information will be utilized. Thus forecasting data may be incorporated and could be subjected to regression analysis in order to provide useful information. On the other hand, it may be desirable to set up the data in a probability distribution that would yield the required information to the player. Some data may be processed through quantitative models such as economic order formulae, linear programming, or waiting line equations to provide information.

## Types Of Decisions Required

First, the designer must select the principle or set of relationships he is trying to demonstrate through the model. Second, he provides the necessary information that would be appropriate for determining the particular relation.

Now the designer must consider the decisions required in the model that would allow or require the information to be processed by the decision maker in the desired manner. The desired manner in this case means the best way to demonstrate that a relationship does exist between a given set of variables.

The decisions required in most business simulation models concern themselves with financial expenditures (eg. advertising, new equipment), resource allocation (eg. inventory, personnel), or pricing decisions. To make these decisions in some optimum manner the game participant should have to organize the given information in such a way as to gain insight regarding the variables involved and their relationship.

## Game Parameters

The game parameters refer to those equations, graphs, or other techniques that are formulated by the game designer and are utilized by the game administrator to evaluate or score the decisions made by the participants. This segment of the model design is critical because these parameters are used to illustrate how variables relate to one another. Here we note why model design is such a valuable learning experience for the designer himself because he must have clear in his own mind how certain variables influence one another. He must then formulate an equation or graphical model to represent this relationship.

Criteria for the parameters include the following:

1. They must be realistic in their operation. That is, to as great an extent as possible, the parameters must conform to actual business practice or procedure.

2. They must be flexible enough so that as a participant changes his decision-making strategy, reflecting a new approach to the processing of information, the parameters will reflect this change and will provide feedback that will help the participant evaluate his approach.

3. The parameters need not be too complex in their operation. In some cases extreme complexity may lead the player to attempt to select a trial-and-error approach to decision making instead of thoroughly analyzing his information.

4. The parameters should be set up such that the better the participant analyzes his information and thus makes more appropriate decisions, the scoring or feedback from the parameters indicates to the participant his success in recognizing the relationship among the variables.

### Feedback

This final phase of the simulation design relates closely to the game parameters. The participant begins the game by interpreting the given information and makes his first set of decisions. At this time he may not comprehend relationships among the variables, but he may have made some preliminary assumptions that he is testing. His initial decisions are then scored, utilizing the game parameters, and the results are fed back to him. This information may be in the form of cost data, new sales data, or profit information, and it indicates to the participant the extent to which he was successful in his initial analysis of the situation. This feedback, in whatever form it may be, is useful in providing additional information to the participant, which he can then use to revise his assumptions on how certain variables interact or may be related. From the feedback, the participant, essentially, attempts to reconstruct the model that was used to describe the relationships.

In summary, the game or model can be utilized to illustrate concepts, principles, or relationships among variables not by simply stating the existence of such relationships but instead by providing an opportunity for the participant to determine these relationships for himself. This is done through analysis of the information, deciding among alternate courses of action, and the feedback of results regarding his success measured in relative or absolute terms. We are reminded again that the game designer himself has gained the most in that he has had to think through how and to what extent variables abstracted from the real world may be related and then to formulate some technique for describing this relationship.

### DESIGNING A BUSINESS GAME—AN ILLUSTRATIVE EXAMPLE

Utilizing the framework discussed, the evolution of a game will be traced. In this manner a step-by-step portrayal can be made of the concepts to be taught, the relationships (models) that could be utilized or developed by the participant, the feedback process and, finally, the criteria and evaluation of success. The complete game is reproduced at the end of this chapter and should be read in conjunction with the following sections.

### Relationships To Be Determined

The simulation to be developed concerns itself with inventory management and is designed to illustrate the operating use of economic order quantity models as well as statistically determined reorder points. The total model demonstrates the relationship between total costs versus order quantities and reorder points. There are trade-offs that must be made between stockout costs (those costs incurred when customer's orders cannot be met), inventory carrying costs (those costs incurred from having investments in inventory on hand at any given time), and ordering costs (the costs of the procurement and receiving function).

The dynamics of this stochastic process simulating real time and real data demonstrates that no perfect solution exists to the problem because of the variability of demand and lead time. However, by making an analysis of the various probabilities associated with the demand and lead time, in addition to appreciating the magnitude of the cost factors, strategies can be developed as to when and how much to order.

One model used to represent the relationship among some of the variables involved in inventory costs is shown below. It shows total cost ($T$) to be the sum of two basic operating costs: the carrying cost of the average inventory investment and the acquisition cost.

$$T = I \times C \times Q/2 + S \times A/Q$$

where:

I is the percentage of the period's investment carrying charge.
C is the purchase price/unit.
S is the acquisition cost/order.
A is the period's usage or requirements.
Q is the size of the lot procured.

Through differentiation, incremental analysis, or trial and error, the lowest operating cost is found at the point where carrying and acquisition costs are equal. If the cost of carrying inventory is equated to the cost of acquiring the inventory and the equation is solved for "Q," the economic reordering quantity is $\sqrt{2AS/CI}$. Ordering this amount on reaching the point of reordering will optimize (minimize) a portion of the total operating cost. The game could therefore be conducted in two ways: (1) As an aid to the participants in *discovering* the effect on cost as they decide or try several different reorder quantities or (2) the EOQ model can be given, Q computed, and the players left to prove its applicability. In the latter case, the player is then free to concentrate on the other decision aspects of the game—the most important of which is the decision about the inventory level at which this optimum quantity should be reordered, namely the reorder point.

Thus, the game designer has established one concept to be demonstrated— the relationship between size of the reorder quantity and predicting operating costs. There are other variables and relationships that influence cost (e.g., safety stock) and additional information must be given in order to illustrate and establish these relationships.

### Information Needed

In order for the participant to develop relationships between the variables, several bits of information should be provided.

First, background information concerning past demand should be given. This information might appear in the game as follows:

"Past history has shown that demands of the manufacturing department for this material have been random and have ranged from about 3 to 42 units per week, with occasional demand approaching 50 units. The demands are approximately normally distributed. There are no seasonal fluctuations, nor is there any upward or downward trend over the long run. Figure 1 shows the distribution of demand."

In addition to past demand information to be analyzed for determining the reorder quantity, the game could include information on the average and variability of lead time for deliveries of materials. (See Figure 2 of the game.)

A variable lead time is not necessary for a substantial simulation. Lead time may be held constant at 1 week for one iteration and then held constant at 2, 4, or longer on successive replications in order to observe planning phenomenon in action.

With these two distributions the interrelationships between order size, order point, and total operating costs begin to evolve. The objective is to determine how the reorder quantity impacts the reorder point and vice versa and how do both of these affect total cost. A large reorder quantity subjects the system to fewer opportunities or occasions for a stockout, thus saving stockout costs. A high reorder point suggests a high safety stock, which

# MANAGEMENT DECISION SIMULATIONS

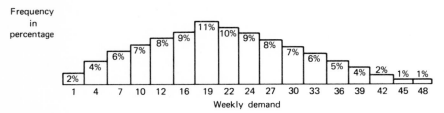

FIGURE 3.1

also reduces stockout occurrences. Both of these increase inventory carrying cost.

The safety stock and thus the reorder point is influenced by both the demand variability and the lead-time variability. The participant should either know or discover that these variabilities can conspire to cause a stockout, but that the extent and probability of this conspiracy can be deduced or computed. Thus, another relationship can be derived, namely the safety stock required to offer a chosen level of protection given a combined probable maximum demand during lead time. Here the additivity of variances of demand and lead time are demonstrated. (See Appendix).

Finally, the participant will require information concerning the costs resulting from the decisions. In the event of a stockout, a cost of $100 will be incurred for each *unit* not shipped. Depending on the intent of the designer, an alternate stockout penalty of $100 per *occasion* could be assessed. The difference between these two methods (or other methods) of incurring stockout costs is substantial, therefore the method to be used must be clearly stated.

Furthermore, the rules with respect to negative inventory balances or back orders must be provided and clearly stated. If back ordering is permitted, then back orders are to be filled from the next RECEIPT. If back ordering is not permitted, then the stockout costs are computed and the BALANCE forward is set to zero.

In order to utilize the EOQ model, additional information must be provided or generated. The item value, C, is needed and was given at $101 in this case. Making the item cost vary with quantity would introduce additional complexity, which could be a valuable variation of this game. Such phenomenon as quantity discounts and cost reduction curves have been explored in a game such as this and have significant effects on optimum order quantities. The reorder cost associated with placing an order was selected as $30. This also could be confounded by ordering more than one item from the same supplier on the same order. Multi-item orders and contractual arrangements offer interesting complexities to procurement decisions and could be included in other variations.

In addition to these costs, the cost of carrying an investment in the form of inventory is stated as approximately $.50/ week. This is the cost of carrying one unit valued at $101 for one week when the annual carrying cost is stated at 26%.

As was indicated before, past demand or expected annual demand is necessary information for the EOQ model. If some past demand is shown, it is desirable for the participant to analyze it to determine usages, trends for expected future demand, and seasonality indices if these can guide him toward more economical operations. In this example, 900 units per year is the estimated demand. Unless told otherwise, it is up to the participant to monitor the generated demand to verify this quantity. At the same time the participant may wish to or should be encouraged to test the sensitivity of EOQ to annual or quarterly demand variations. Another variation on this basic game would be to introduce seasonality and/or trends and note the effect this has on the player's analysis and decisions.

To summarize the information available and to simulate a real-life inventory record complete with examples of prior decisions, Figure 3 was designed. At this point the game designer has provided sufficient information necessary for the participant to apply existing models and to perceive and model other relationships that may exist among the variables associated with inventory management.

Figure 3 simulates the basic inventory card kept by many companies operating with a manual Kardex or Vis-a-Record system. The designer of this game also is attempting to get across an appreciation of the clerical function of inventory management performed by countless individuals in companies. There are several side aspects of involvement in a manual inventory system.

First, the clerical nature of the task is a reason for a declaration that such menial tasks should be borne by a computer system. After playing the game, it is extremely beneficial for the participants to attempt to flow chart the activities for computer processing. With the data base, the by-product information from computer processing such as computing usage rates, stock turnovers, and trends, can be discussed.

The designer also wishes the player to recognize the segregation of fixed, variable, and modifiable information. Perhaps the only fixed information would be the part name and number. However, the designer may wish to pursue or ask the participants to pursue concepts in part numbering and classification systems, including the importance of a company glossary of part names. This is always a controversial and stimulating discussion, especially when considering a consecutive, nonsignificant numbering scheme for computer-based systems with various retrieval requirements.

The values for the other variables in the heading section of the record are subject to updating. A periodic analysis of the demand (usage data) may reveal significant changes in the forecasted annual demand, and therefore the requirements should be updated. The reorder, stockout, and unit costs are also subject to change as new information is incorporated into these files.

The body of the inventory record contains the conventional columns of ORDER, RECEIPT, DEMAND, and BALANCE information. The DATE column might be unconventional. Here the designer was introducing the fiscal dating system, which identifies weeks in a year from 01 to 52. Generating usage data ($\Sigma$ demand/$\Delta$ weeks) and forecasting demand (usage during lead weeks in future periods) is easily performed with this system. The fiscal dating system employed utilizes the first digit to represent the year and the remaining two digits to represent the sequential weeks during the year. (To pursue this further, each day is 20 percent of a week. Therefore a decimal system is possible where 09.0 = Monday, of Week 09, 09.2 = Tuesday, and so on.)

The record format is very convenient for the game play; it even allows the participant to create a purchase order numbering scheme and to control his own purchase orders. Again the designer could

MANAGEMENT DECISION SIMULATIONS

have in mind to discuss several types of P/O numbering systems available in the briefing or debriefing session. For example, a unique and effective purchase order numbering scheme utilizes the buyer's number, the fiscal date, and a sequence number. Thus P/O #14115-23 was placed by Buyer #14 in 1971 during week 15 and it was the 23rd purchase order he had written that week. With this scheme, data processing or manual systems can easily compile who bought what, when, and the outstanding purchase commitments by several categories.

### Decisions Required

Given that most of the information has been provided for the player to devise strategies and speculate on relationships, the game designer must determine and specify what decisions are required.

The decisions required in this game can take the following form:

"After studying the distributions, costs, and data in Figure 3, and given the average DEMAND of 17 units per week, an average LEAD TIME of one week, and a BALANCE forward of 56 units, an initial decision must be made whether to enter an ORDER at the beginning of Week 09. If a recorder is considered necessary, the selected purchase order number and *selected* reorder *quantity* are entered on Week 09 line. Simultaneously the ordering costs are entered under the CHARGES column."

"At the beginning of each subsequent week's play, the participants again decide *if a reorder* is desirable, and if so for *what quantity*. The decision is based on the inventory balance from the previous week, the anticipated receipts, the anticipated demands over the anticipated lead time, and all other costs and/or factors deemed important."

For example, a decision maker may *think* 100 units should be ordered now though the EOQ may indicate a different amount. After this decision has been made, the participant enters the reordering cost (if any).

"Any RECEIPTS obtained for the week are added to the prior week's BALANCE forward. The DEMAND (generated by the referee) for that week is entered and subtracted leaving a new BALANCE forward. The carrying costs for this BALANCE are computed and entered in the CHARGES column. If a stockout occurred, the stockout costs are entered in the appropriate CHARGES column."

The criteria on which successful performance will be based should be clearly understood by the players. This information provides a guideline in directing the participant toward the appropriate analysis of the data. Thus, the instructions might provide the following information:

"Because the item is costly and strategic, your objective as Director of Materiel is to maintain an adequate inventory of the item, yet to keep inventory investment and ordering costs to a minimum. Thus those who operate the system 'best' should have the least cost for the periods played."

The player with the lowest total costs for the periods played is declared the "winner"—having managed the inventory system most assiduously. (There may be some doubt expressed by the "losers," which could be resolved, time permitting, by playing the game two or more times.

### Parameters

The participant should be given some insight into how the demand and lead time values will be determined. This information should be helpful to the player in performing the appropriate anaylsis of the data.

"At the beginning of each period or week, the referee will generate the LEAD TIME to be incurred by purchase orders placed on Monday of a given week (see Figure 2). The LEAD TIME is not *revealed* but is recorded on the referee's record sheet. (The 0, 1, or 2 lead weeks generated are added to this week's code and recorded identifying the specific week an order placed now will be received. The LEAD TIME is generated from a distribution allowing a 10 percent chance of an order placed now arriving in the same week (L = O), a 70 percent chance of it arriving during next week (L = 1), and a 20 percent chance of it arriving in two weeks (L = 2). The referee *then* announces the arrival or RECEIPT of orders that players may have placed previously whose arrival week, previously generated, has now been reached."

For example, if an order was placed by a player at the beginning of Week 12 and the lead time generated at that time is 1 week, its arrival week is recorded by the referee as Week 13. After the play of Week 12 and *after* the players have made their ordering decision for Week 13, the referee will announce the arrival or receipt of orders placed by participants during Week 12.

"After Purchase Orders (if any) have been placed and receipts of prior orders (if any) have been announced and entered, the referee generates and announces the week's DEMAND. The DEMAND is randomly generated from its frequency distribution. That is, DEMAND will be chosen according to its probability of occurring from the frequency distribution indicated in Figure 1. A demand of less than 3 units or more than 42 units will have little chance of occurring, but a demand of 12, 16, 19, 22, or 24 units would have a good chance of occurring."

"The DEMAND for any week is determined from the same random number table (see Appendix) and the frequency distribution shown in Figure 1. The random number assignments are shown above the respective values of the demand. The quantity of random numbers assigned to a cell is in the same proportion as the frequency distribution of demand. For example, if the next two digits in a sequence of random numbers are 21, this would represent a demand of 12 units from the frequency distribution of demand."

The demand for a week could also have been generated from a table of random normal deviates if the demand could be considered to have a normal distribution. For example, the next normal deviate in a sequence of random normal deviates (see Appendix) might be $+ .464$. Since the mean and standard deviation of this demand's distribution were given as 17 and 7 units, respectively, the generated demand would be $17 + .464 \times 7$ or 20 units.

## Feedback

The last area of the game design concerns itself with feedback to the participant. Through feedback the participant is able to update his information and gain additional insight into the relationships among the variables. For this illustrative game, the feedback information would be self-generated by the participant completing each line on the Inventory Record.

"At the end of each week the DEMAND generated is deducted from the stock available that week, yielding a new BALANCE forward. This information plus other information of past demands and lead times should assist the participant in determining whether to place a replenishment order the following Monday."

This feedback in the form of receipts and issues (demand) and the resulting stock balances allow the player to interact directly with each period's decisions. He may change strategies at any time, test the results of remaining with one strategy, and plan or set decision parameters. A test of the success of his decisions is made at the time the referee arbitrarily ends the simulation (to avoid "end gaming"). Adding the three CHARGES columns provides a measure of success and allows comparison with the other players on strategies, quantities, and decision rules.

Quite naturally, the simulation should be repeated with different demands being generated to establish whether the individual has made progress toward better inventory decisions. Also, with preestablished values for reorder points and reorder quantities, the game can be-

## MANAGEMENT DECISION SIMULATIONS

come a simulator model for repetitive computer runs testing these decision rules. Flow charting this game for open-loop or closed-loop computer simulation is a very educational experience. Establishing it as an interactive program on a time-share terminal leads to additional understanding of inventory behavior and decisions in the real world. As is apparent, any and all of the parameters can be changed individually or with a designed experiment to demonstrate their sensitivity and effect on operating costs. As was previously indicated, added complexity can be introduced through incorporation of seasonality, contract buys, quantity discounts, multi-item orders, and other phenomena.

Although the simulation previously traced was specifically designed to illustrate concepts or principles in inventory management, the process depicted would be similar in designing games to illustrate other principles or concepts.

In review, the game illustrates concepts and practice in inventory management decisions. Specifically, the following were included:

1. Simulation of a manual inventory system for recording orders, receipts, issues, and balances.

2. Developing and analyzing past data for incorporation in or designing models.

3. Structure and applicability of an economic order quantity.

4. Identity of factors determining re-order point.

5. Detecting interaction between order quantity, demand variability, and reorder points.

6. Evolving strategies and testing hypotheses with measurable results.

7. Appreciation for one subsystem in a Management Information System.

These objectives were accomplished in the game by focusing on the basic steps in game design.

1. Deciding on the relationship to be demonstrated.

2. Organizing, defining, and providing information needed to utilize or build the relationships.

3. Identifying and specifying the decisions required.

4. Defining game parameters that will be used.

5. Providing feedback for developing and testing relationships and thereby guiding the strategy revisions and decisions.

# IDS CORPORATION

## Introduction

There are many types of inventories and inventory problems, and there is generally no single approach to a particular problem. This simulation is concerned with order quantities and safety stocks. It has purposely been kept simple to demonstrate that an objective method leads to better results than those achieved using intuitive or subjective approaches.

## Background

Assume that your company, IDS, uses a number of raw material items in its manufacturing processes. This game is concerned with just one of these items.

Past history has shown that demands of the manufacturing department for this material have been random and have ranged from about 3 to 42 units per week, with occasional demand approaching 50 units. The demands are approximately normally distributed. There are no seasonal fluctuations, nor is there any upward or downward trend over the long run. Figure 1 shows the distribution of demand.

At the *end* of each week the number of units to be deducted from stock during that week is given. This information plus the other information of past demands should assist you in determining whether to place a replenishment order and what quantity to order. It is assumed that replenishment orders will be placed at the beginning of business on the next Monday. Lead time averages one week, therefore items ordered in a given week are not received until the following week and are not available to fill manufacturing requests the week they are ordered. Thus an order placed on Monday is usually delivered by the next Monday.

In the event of a stockout, it is estimated that your company will incur costs of $100 for each unit not issued to the requesting manufacturing departments. Furthermore, any negative balance is to be carried as a backorder, to be filled the following week.

Because the item is costly and strategic, your objective as Director of Material is to maintain an adequate inventory of the item, yet to keep inventory investment and ordering costs to a minimum. Thus those who operate the system "best" will have the least cost for the periods played.

## Participant Instructions

After studying the distributions, costs, and data in Figure 3, and given the average DEMAND of 17 units per week, an average LEAD TIME of one week, and a BALANCE forward of 56 units,

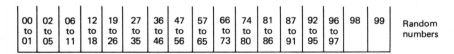

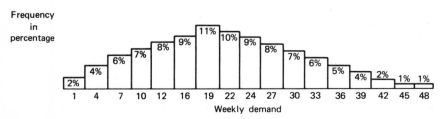

**FIGURE I.**

## MANAGEMENT DECISION SIMULATIONS

an initial decision must be made whether to enter an ORDER at the beginning of Week 09. If a reorder is considered necessary, the selected purchase order number and *selected* reorder *quantity* are entered on the Week 09 line. Simultaneously, the

ordering costs are entered under the CHARGES column.

At the beginning of each subsequent week's play, the participants again decide *if a reorder is desirable,* and if so for *what quantity.* The decision is based on the inventory balance from the previous week, the anticipated receipts, the anticipated demands over the anticipated lead time, and all other costs and/or factors deemed important.

At the beginning of each period or week, the referee will generate the LEAD TIME to be incurred by purchase orders placed on Monday of a given week (see Figure 2). The LEAD TIME is not *revealed* but is recorded on the referee's record sheet (the 0, 1, or 2 lead weeks generated are added to this week's code

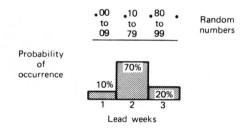

**FIGURE 2.**

### INVENTORY RECORD CARD

| Annual Reqmt | 900 units | Unit Cost | $101.00 | Part No. | C-310-418 |
|---|---|---|---|---|---|
| Reorder Costs | $30 | Carrying Cost | 26%/yr | Name | Bearing |
| Stockout Cost | $100.00/unit | | ($.50/wk.) | ROP | EOQ |

| Lead Time | M-Wk. | ORDER P/O No. | Qty. | RECEIPTS $ Value | Qty. | DEMAND Qty. | BALANCE Qty. | $ Value | CHARGES Ord'g | Stkout | Carry'g |
|---|---|---|---|---|---|---|---|---|---|---|---|
| 1 | 151 | #051 | 100 | | | 16 | 20 | $2,020 | 30 | | 10 |
| | 152 | | | $10,100 | 100 | 12 | 108 | | | | 54 |
| | 201 | | | | | 12 | 96 | | | | 48 |
| | 202 | | | | | 25 | 71 | | | | 36 |
| 1 | 203 | #103 | 50 | | | 29 | 42 | $4,242 | 30 | | 21 |
| | 204 | | | $ 5,050 | 50 | 14 | 78 | | | | 39 |
| | 205 | | | | | 9 | 69 | | | | 34 |
| 2 | 206 | #106 | 40 | | | 16 | 53 | | 30 | | 27 |
| | 207 | | | | | 27 | 26 | | | | 33 |
| | 208 | | | $ 4,040 | 40 | 10 | 56 | | | | 28 |
| | 209 | | | | | | | | | | |
| | 210 | | | | | | | | | | |
| | 211 | | | | | | | | | | |
| | 212 | | | | | | | | | | |
| | 213 | | | | | | | | | | |
| | 214 | | | | | | | | | | |
| | 215 | | | | | | | | | | |
| | 216 | | | | | | | | | | |
| | 217 | | | | | | | | | | |
| | 218 | | | | | | | | | | |

**FIGURE 3. Inventory Transaction Record**

and recorded identifying the specific week an order placed now will be received). The LEAD TIME is generated from a distribution allowing a 10% chance of an order placed now arriving early or this week ($L = 0$), a 70% chance of it arriving during next week ($L = 1$), and a 20% chance of it arriving in two weeks ($L = 2$). The referee *then* announces the arrival or RECEIPT of orders that players have placed whose arrival week, previously generated, has now been reached.

Any RECEIPT obtained for the week are added to the prior week's BALANCE forward. The DEMAND (generated by the referee) for that week is entered and subtracted leaving a new BALANCE forward. The carrying costs for this balance are computed and entered in the CHARGES column. If a stockout occurred, the stockout costs are entered in the appropriate CHARGES column.

### Referee's Instructions

The decision sequence is straightforward. The participant reviews the present and expected status of the item, places purchase orders, if necessary, receives material ordered previously, records the demand, computes the balance, and enters the appropriate charges. The referee, therefore, monitors this sequence for all players and generates two statistics—the LEAD TIME and the DEMAND.

With a copy of Figure 3 and reference to Figure 2 and the random number table, the referee chooses a random number each period, finds the corresponding LEAD TIME, and enters this to the left of the M-Wk. The P/O number assigned can then be recorded in the RECEIPTS value column opposite the expected arrival week. For example, if the lead time is 1 week for an order #111 placed in Week 11, then this P/O #111 can be entered in "Value" column opposite Week 12. When play of Week 12 is begun and after the players have decided about or-

dering, then receipt of all orders placed in Week 11 can be announced.

After Purchase Orders (if any) have been placed and RECEIPTS of prior orders (if any) have been announced and entered, the referee generates and announces the week's DEMAND. This DEMAND is randomly generated from its frequency distribution. That is, DEMAND will be chosen according to its probability of occurring from the frequency distribution indicated in Figure 1. A demand of less than 3 units or more than 42 units will have little chance of occurring, but a demand of 12, 16, 19, 22, or 24 units would have a good chance of occurring.

The DEMAND for any week is determined from the same random number table (see Appendix) and the frequency distribution shown in Figure 1. The random number assignments are shown above the respective values of the demand. The quantity of random numbers assigned to a cell is in the same proportion as the frequency distribution of demand. For example, if the next 2 digits in a sequence of random numbers are 21, this would represent a demand of 12 units from the frequency distribution of demand.

At the end of each week the DEMAND generated is deducted from the stock available that week, yielding a new BALANCE forward. This information plus other information of past demands and lead times should assist the participant in determining whether to place a replenishment order the following Monday.

The simulation will be terminated arbitrarily by the referee at any time. It will be done in a random manner so that the players are asked to provide operational accounting at any selected time without being able to bias the results. The CHARGES columns are totaled and the player with the lowest total costs may be declared the "winner" by virtue of having operated the inventory system most assiduously.

_____ **Bibliography**

1. Carlson, J. G., and Misshauk, M. J.; "A Model for Game Design"; *Journal of Training and Development;* December 1970.
2. Greene, J. R., and Sisson, R. L.; *Dynamic Management, Decision Games;* John Wiley & Sons, Inc.; New York; 1959.
3. Greenlaw, P. S., Herron, L. W., and Rawdon, R. H.; *Business Simulation in Industrial and University Education;* Prentice Hall, Inc., Englewood Cliffs, New Jersey; 1962.
4. Kibbee, J., Kraft, C., and Nanus, B.; *Management Games;* Reinhold Publishing Company, New York; 1961.

# Behavior in Gaming Situations

## WHY STUDY BEHAVIOR IN GAMES

Anyone who has made use of simulation and gaming techniques as a teaching or learning device has recognized that each session of a simulation will be different. The structure of the game may not have been modified, but each group of people involved in the gaming experience will approach it differently and will interact in a slightly different way. With this in mind, the game really has changed because in a very real sense one of the major variables in the game is different —namely, the participants with their unique goals and value systems.

The social scientists did not take long to realize the value of gaming and simulation as a tool for the study of human behavior.

"Management games seem to provide an excellent medium for focusing attention upon and helping develop insight into the dynamic interaction of human forces and non-human quantitative economic data. To a greater degree than in most training situations the participant in a business game can usually see clearly the effects of dissention, over-competitiveness or bitter antagonisms within the group upon team productivity and successful results" (8).

Within the game situation is an environment in which individuals communicate, interact, make decisions, develop organizations, and enter into conflict much as they do in the outside world. For this reason, any group that intends to make use of simulation would lose one of its major contributions if it did not devote at least some aspect of study and subsequent discussion to an analysis of the human behavior that took place within the groups during the simulation experience. This study could take the form of assigning certain individuals to act as "observers" during game play.

A major advantage of the game environment lies in the interaction situation it creates among the individuals participating in the game. A great percentage of the educational experience available in the classroom is based on one-way communication (instructor to student) and in some cases two-way communication (instructor to student, student to instructor). The learning is acquired by the student through the lecture and through the study of literature and text. There is no doubt that a large amount of knowledge or information can and ought to be transmitted in this way. There is, however, a great deal of learning, no less essential to the education of an individual, that is not effectively handled through lectures. This includes the ability of the individual to work with, understand, and communicate with other individuals within a group situation. This skill is essential, since the tools and techniques an individual acquires in the classroom or textbook will be of little value to him unless he can effectively implement them. In the business environment, effective implementation usually requires working with other people. Thus, the knowledge that an individual may have is practically useless unless it can be communicated to others. Finally, the action resulting from the communication of ideas must be coordinated in order to achieve a common goal.

There are courses in psychology that deal with the problems revolving around the group interaction. Unfortunately, there is little opportunity for the individual to enter into a group situation where specific attention will be directed toward the behavior observed within the group setting. The game situation serves as a type of behavioral laboratory in which all the processes inherent in group interaction come into play. In the game the participants bring to the situation certain needs, values, and attitudes. They are presented with a common problem or task and must communicate and coordinate activities in order to successfully complete the assignment. In this process an observer(s) can note the development of a leader or leaders within the group, possibly resulting in conflict or frustration among other members of the group. Certain individuals may develop roles that they play in the group process. As a result of the interaction of the group, certain norms of behavior may result, and the group may develop punitive actions against members who violate these norms. Thus, the game situation, if properly constructed, provides a valuable experience enabling the participants to gain greater insight into the process of group interaction and the impact of their own behavior on other members of the group. There appears to be no substitute for actual experience in conveying these concepts. It is particularly effective because it directly involves the individual in the world he is trying to understand (that of the group). This is difficult to achieve in either lecture or textbook presentations.

The remainder of this section deals with some of the principal behavioral concepts that may be studied in the game environment along with ways in which the game situation can be tailored to focus attention on some or all of these concepts. In addition, those games that lend themselves particularly well to behavioral study will be discussed.

At the conclusion of a game some period of time should be devoted to a discussion among the participants oriented toward an analysis of behavioral concepts.

The length of the discussion will be determined by the sophistication of the participants and the particular game that was played.

## Leadership

Recent writings in the area of leadership appear to be moving away from the concept of a single leader emerging within a group with all other members acting as followers.

In the management game reported by Huttle (11) in which a highly involved task situation was created, decision making could not be done by one person because of the complexity of the game. The team members sat around a large table with no formal structure imposed on them. Results indicated strong forces operating against a centralized leadership. Indications were that the general social atmosphere in which the project was conducted seemed to prevent the rise of strong decision leaders. According to Huttle,

"the theoretical importance of the project lies in the suggestion that the influence of the total informational environment on formal properties of the decision process in the teams was much stronger than was predicted and that the idiosyncracies of the teams and their component personalities were mainly apparent in the difference in economic performance, amount of factual information used and the number of evaluations made."

This suggests that within any group each member of that group contributes something to the direction the group takes. In this sense, each individual, to some degree, functions as a leader of the group. This is not to imply that the individuals share the leadership equally. In most cases, one individual exerts more control over group action than other members. But, there does seem to exist a continuum of leadership and control throughout the group.

As a guide to studying leadership development in the game situaion, four basic questions may be asked.

1. Is there more than one leader in the group?
2. What type of leadership styles are utilized?
3. From what source does the leader(s) derive his power?
4. What skills does the leader(s) exhibit?

In order to aid the observer(s) in answering these questions a three-part checklist is included which summarizes many areas of leadership within the group (See Exhibits I. II, III). Each observer may select one or more individuals within the group and utilize the checklist in order to determine the leader behavior exhibited by that member of the group. The observer(s) should note the significant statements or actions on the part of individuals within the group which led the observer(s) to his conclusions. These may be discussed at the conclusion of the game.

MANAGEMENT DECISION SIMULATIONS

EXHIBIT I(23)

| | *Notes* |
|---|---|
| *LEADER STYLE* (Style of leadership utilized by the group) | |

*Democratic*

Goals, objectives, and direction are derived through group participation.

Group members appear to feel free to discuss direction of group and make recommendations.

*Autocratic*

All decisions are made by one individual who assumes command, establishing direction, issuing orders, and making decisions.

*Laissez-Faire*

Group functions completely on its own with no apparent coordination or control being given by any one individual.

Each member goes in his own direction with little or no coordination between group members.

EXHIBIT II(7)

| SOURCES OF POWER (Base from which leader exerts influence | Notes |
|---|---|
| *Expert Power*<br><br>Leader exerts influence since he has knowledge or information other members of group do not possess. | |
| *Referent Power*<br><br>Based on followers' desire to identify with the leader because of charismatic quality inherent in personality. | |
| *Legitimate Power*<br><br>Derived from person's position within a group. Formally established by administrator. | |
| *Reward*<br><br>Leader has ability to reward in some way for compliance with his wishes. | |
| *Punishment*<br><br>Leader has ability to punish for not complying with his wishes. | |

MANAGEMENT DECISION SIMULATIONS

EXHIBIT III

*LEADER SKILLS* (Skills that individual can bring to bear in given situation)

*Technical Skill*

Ability of individual to solve task-related problems of the group based on some technical skill or ability (math, statistics, etc.)

*Administrative Skill*

Ability to plan, organize, and control activities of the group, essentially a coordination ability.

*Human Relations Skill*

Ability to work with others to get others to perform in a desired manner without feelings of suppression or frustration. Able to smooth over conflicts and keep group working together.

*Notes*

Within the game situation the administrator can structure the group in such a way as to facilitate the study of leader development in various situations. The group structure refers to the way in which the group organizes in order to perform its task. Various approaches to group structure will be discussed, citing their advantage in analyzing leader development.

### Structure Defined by Administrator

The administrator can impose a hierarchical structure on the group by assigning different individuals positions within the group, such as president, vice-president—finance, and vice-president—marketing. This type of structure provides an excellent opportunity to study the development of an informal organization, which may arise in addition to the formal structure imposed by the administrator. This may be especially true if persons selected to occupy power positions within the formal structure (president, etc.) are not the high-status members of the group. In this situation, other group members, possibly utilizing one or more sources of power (see Exhibit II) may attempt to gain control of the group. In order to study this process, it is advantageous to note how communication is flowing within the group (who is initiating communication, type of communication, who it is being directed toward) and where decisions are actually being made within the group. At the conclusion of the game, a comparison can be made between the formal structure, with its specific functions and responsibilities, and the actual structure as perceived by the administrator and/or observer(s) of the group process. If the two structures appear to be significantly different, an analysis of why the structure changed and why it ended up as it did is an extremely effective device for studying human behavior. Games that lend themselves to this type of study include *Taylor Manufacturing*, and *Parent Systems, Inc.*

### No Structure Imposed by Administrator

A second approach to leadership analysis through group structure or lack of structure appears in games such as *Ashton Mining* or *Cordell Manufacturing Company*. Since the games themselves require no fixed structure or roles, the administrator may simply apply a random process to group selection, imposing no structure on the group.[1] If the individuals are simply placed together, their first agenda item might be to develop some organized method of approaching the task. This organization process will usually evolve or cause the emergence of an initial leader. The process by which this leader emerges and is recognized by all or some members of the group should be of interest to observers. If several groups are going to be participating in the game, it is likely that each group will go about this organizational task in a slightly different manner. This provides the observer(s) with the opportunity to examine the various approaches taken by the groups, noting the different styles, skills, and power base of leaders in the different groups.

### Structure Determined by Test Results

A third alternative open to administrators would be to select teams based on

[1] A method of forming groups randomly is to have participants self-assign numbers by sounding off beginning with number 1 starting, say, at the right-hand corner of room. Depending on the number of teams required, they would be assigned as follows:

| Teams | I | II | III |
|---|---|---|---|
| Participant's number | 1 | 2 | 3 |
| | 4 | 5 | 6 |
| | 7 | 8 | 9 etc. |

Alternatively, members could sound off in groups of three.

## MANAGEMENT DECISION SIMULATIONS

results of psychological tests or sociometric choice. These tests might measure such factors as aggressiveness, achievement need, inner-directedness or authoritarianism, etc. Once the test results have been compiled, the groups might be selected such that highly authoritarian personalities are grouped together or participants having a high degree of inner-directedness would be grouped together.

This technique might be very effective in games such as *Aztec Trucking* or *Slade Beverage*. In the former, the conflict between working with the group to achieve a high level of team profit may conflict with an individual's desire to maximize his own revenue, perhaps at the expense of the group. This possibility provides an excellent opportunity to study the strength of individual needs and personal roles as opposed to group norms and goals. In the latter game (Slade) the game is such that one key bit of information (profit graph) is critical to group decision making. The extent to which this graph is controlled by one or more individuals within the group will have a great deal to do with leadership and conflict within the group. In these two games the personalities of the participants may significantly influence the way the group resolves problems inherent in the game situation.

After completion of the game, the group should discuss its operation and interaction with the observers and the administrator. At this time the administrator can reveal the basis on which the group members were selected and can compare notes of the observers with the profile measuring instrument. This procedure enables participants to become more aware of their own personality characteristics, since they have been working with individuals who by virtue of the tests exhibit similar personality traits.

On the other hand, the groups might be structured to include a mix of personality traits as revealed by the test results. The observers, with no prior knowledge of

the test results, could then note the different behavior patterns during the play. At the end of the game the observations may be revealed and then compared with the test results. Of considerable interest would be the validation of tests as to whether the instrument, if used in industry, could predict roles and behavior patterns.

### Communication and Organizational Behavior

The importance of communication is readily apparent since it is through this process that the group members interact with one another. It is through communication that values and attitudes are expressed and direction is given to individual group members. It is unfortunate that too many believe that if something has been said or written to another, communication has taken place. Because of the different values, goals, and previous experiences that each individual brings with him to the group, meaning can be misinterpreted or even distorted. For this reason, it is necessary for the sender to consider the person to whom he is sending a message, taking into account as much as possible the different values and background of both, and selecting a message that will most accurately convey his meaning.

With respect to communication in the gaming situation, Guetzkow and Bower (9) utilized a team of six members forming one company. The company was composed of three "salesmen" and three "producers." The salesmen received written orders from the "market" (administrator) and then made decisions as to which orders to relay and when and where to sell finished products. The producers received written orders, made decisions as to what, when, and where to produce, received completed orders from the "plants" (administrator), and relayed finished products to salesmen. In this way communication between "salesmen" and "producers" was structured. Guetzkow suggests that one can produce organizationlike behavior in groups of relatively few persons by imposing mediated (indirect) instead of face-to-face interactions. In the social world of our western culture, it is unusual to find small groups of persons with mediated rather than direct interrelations. Hence, it is customary to think of the differences between face-to-face groups and organizations as depending on the size of the groups. Guetzkow argues that increasing the size of the group is but one routine through which mediated interactions can be induced. He maintains that many of the so called "small-group" experiments, because of their use of nonsimultaneous relayed or mediated messages, actually are experiments in organizational behavior.

As one observes the group within the game situation, one should attempt to understand the difficulties that may develop with respect to communication. If the group appears to be experiencing difficulty communicating, the observer(s) should try to determine the exact nature of this difficulty. Once the cause of the problem has been recognized, future communication problems may be avoided.

As an aid to the observer(s) in cataloguing communication problems, Exhibit IV identifies some of the main causes of communication difficulties.

A second area of interest in studying communication in groups deals with the direction and frequency of interaction among members of the group. Observations should be made regarding where communication originates, the nature of the communication, and to whom it is directed. This information adds insight into the structure and nature of the group. An extremely useful technique for cataloguing this type of interaction is the *Bales Interaction Process Analysis*. In utilizing the interaction sheet (see Exhibit V), a tally mark is made each time a particular individual initiates communication of the type shown on the sheet.

If an interaction sheet is kept for each individual in the group, a communication profile can be developed which yields the communication pattern exhibited by each individual and, to a certain extent, defines the role that person played in the group process.

To provide a method in which differing approaches to communication may be studied, the administrator can modify the way in which information about the game operation is distributed within the group. Three basic options are available to the administrator.

### A. Complete Information to a Single Member of the Group

In this case the administrator will give all operating instructions and information to one member of the group. If the game being played utilizes a predetermined structure, the information would be given to the "president" of the company. If the group is unstructured, i.e., *Cordell Corporation,* or *Taylor Manufacturing Company*, then the group could be asked to elect a representative who would be given the game information. The purpose of this approach is to note how and if information is communicated from the person or persons receiving information to other members of the group.

The person originally receiving the game information has been placed in a very powerful position within the group (expert power). The observers might focus attention on the extent to which he is willing to share information, with whom he will share information, and how this eventually influences the structure of the group. The extent to which he must communicate information is a function of the game being played (too much information for one man to handle) and the capability of the individual.

This approach permits the observers to investigate factors that may cause companies to centralize or decentralize their operations. One theory holds that as the

MANAGEMENT DECISION SIMULATIONS

EXHIBIT IV(20)

*A Guide to Observing Communication*

## COMMUNICATION DIFFICULTIES (4)

*Difference of Opinion*

Difference that can be settled with reference to facts. One party is correct.

*Clash of Personalities*

Resulting from personality characteristics of individuals. Pride of party or self-concept may be threatened.

*Conflict in Social Roles*

Role of one individual brings him into conflict with another, particularly if a *role* change has taken place and other member of group may not act according to new role of member.

*Struggle for Power*

Attempts on part of one or more persons to change power structure within the group.

*Breakdown in Communication*

Interpretation of a statement or action on part of one member of group in a way that was not originally intended by another.

Notes

EXHIBIT V(2)

| | | *Notes* |
|---|---|---|
| Social emotional (positive) | (a) Shows solidarity (raises others' status, gives help, rewards). | ✓ ✓ ✓ ✓ |
| | (b) Shows tension release, jokes, laughs, shows satisfaction. | ✓ ✓ ✓ ✓ ✓ ✓ |
| | (c) Agrees—shows acceptance, understands, concurs. | ✓ ✓ ✓ |
| Task area | (d) Gives suggestion, direction. | ✓ ✓ |
| | (e) gives opinion, evaluation analysis, expresses feeling. | |
| | (f) Gives orientation, information, clarifies, confirms. | |
| | (g) Asks for orientation, information, repetition, conformation. | ✓ |
| | (h) Asks for opinion, evaluation analysis, expression of feeling. | ✓ ✓ |
| | (i) Asks for suggestion, direction, possible ways of action. | |
| Social emotional (negative) | (j) Disagrees, shows rejection, formality, withholds help. | ✓ |
| | (k) Shows tension, withdraws out of field. | ✓ |
| | (l) Shows antagonism, deflates others' status, defends or asserts self. | |

As a result of observing "John Smith" during the play of the game, the following profile may result. The checks (made by an observer) represent the number of times John Smith engaged in each of the activities. The profile indicates that John seems to have played a *positive social role* in the group's activities.

## MANAGEMENT DECISION SIMULATIONS

information that a single individual must process in a given time becomes too great, he must of necessity delegate information and decision-making responsibility to others in the organization (i.e., decentralize). Because of the amount of information and type of decisions required, certain games lend themselves to a more centralized approach than others. The *Slade Beverage* case is one example in which the profit graph plays a key part in decision making. Again, in the *Water Recreation Associates* game, a single member of the group can assume almost complete control through dominating the use of probabilty tables. On the other hand, games such as *Taylor Mfg., Cordell Company, Marstrat,* or *Ashton Mining Company,* because of the large amounts of data that must be analyzed and the variety of decisions that must be made, appear to require a more decentralized approach if they are to be completed within the allotted time.

### B. Complete Information to All Members of the Group

In most situations a complete copy of the game instructions is given to each member of the group; thus everyone has the same information to begin the task. This approach is particularly effective in games in which no clearly defined approach has been stated. In this situation the group must first determine how it will approach the problem and, since each individual has complete access to game information, each may feel qualified to develop an approach or establish an objective. In four- or five-man groups, it is likely that different individuals will approach the problem in different ways. This provides a setting in which conflict may develop among members of the group. Observers should note the extent to which individuals are willing to cooperate and exchange ideas in order to agree on a common goal or objective. In addition, it should be noted whether the

agreed-upon solution could be ascribed to a single individual or if it was a compromise among several individuals. Sample games that permit this type of analysis would be *Portfolio Management* or *Parent Systems, Inc.* In these games the objective can be reached utilizing several differing logics.

### C. Partial Information to Each Member of the Group

The administrator can divide the information given to the group so that each individual has only a part of the total amount needed to complete the task. In effect, the administrator has created a decentralized organization, at least with respect to information availability. Utilizing this approach, for example, inventory information and cost data could be given to one individual, market forecast information to another, and so on. Since all information should be utilized in order to make effective decisions in the game, this procedure provides an excellent method for developing an awareness of the need for coordinating and utilizing all members of the group. It also stresses information exchange between various members, since each must make others aware of what information he has to offer to the problem and its solution. Finally, it creates the need for someone to coordinate the exchange of information between members of the group and ultimately to make a decision.

Sample games included that lend themselves to this approach would be *Cordell Company, Marstrat,* and *Ashton Mining,* since these games contain a variety of information that can be separated into individual sections but must be integrated if effective decisions are to be made.

### Individual Needs and Roles

Maslow (16) and others have stated that each individual has basic needs that he seeks to satisfy. These needs and the methods used by individuals to satisfy them are considered the primary sources of motivation in determining individual behavior patterns. The needs that exist within each individual form a type of hierarchy with the more basic or lower level needs requiring satisfaction before higher level needs become active.

These needs influence behavior of individuals in a variety of ways. In a game utilized by Leavitt (14) results indicated that some participants may define a task differently than others. Some participants, given the task, proceeded to categorize targets and then went on to other parts of the program, while others treated the task from some social perspectives. Thus it must be recognized that an individual's needs at any given time will influence his behavior during game play.

According to Maslow, the hierarchy takes the following form with number 1 being the most basic need:

5. Self-actualization (becoming all that one is capable of being).
4. Esteem (self-respect and respect from others).
3. Affiliation (association with others).
2. Security (safety).
1. Physiological (hunger, thirst).

Once a need has reached a high degree of satisfaction it ceases to act as an effective motivator of behavior. In addition, different people will seek to satisfy their needs in different ways. The strength of a particular need and the way in which an individual seeks to satisfy his needs will be largely a function of the particular individual's personality and background.

A type of behavior that can be studied in the game situation is the reaction of an individual when he is blocked from satisfying a need. When the individual is prevented, either by another individual or the particular situation, from satisfying a need, he exhibits frustration. If, for example, a participant could not take part in a group discussion and decision re-

garding inventory levels because he did not understand a distribution demand and lead time, he would experience a certain amount of frustration. The extent to which he was emotionally involved in the game would govern the amount of frustration. The observer(s) should note and attempt to analyze the reaction of the participant to this frustration. A *positive response* might result in the participant seeking a quick explanation from a teammate, asking a few questions to gain understanding, or simply listening to the group discussion. On the other hand, a *negative response* might cause the individual to disrupt the activities of the group, to attempt to change the direction of the group away from this area, or to withdraw completely from the group discussion without any further concern for the group or the problem. This is by no means a complete list of manifestations, but is meant to illustrate what can be observed and discussed in studying small group behavior.

Within a group each individual plays a role. The role will define the type of behavior that an individual usually exhibits in given situations or when interacting with certain individuals. In the group situation it is of interest to observe the role that each individual plays within the group and the extent to which those roles help or hinder the group in the completion of its task.

Role behavior can be observed utilizing the Bales Interaction Analysis of Exhibit V. Exhibit VI may also aid the observer in analyzing the role each individual plays within the group process.

## Team Makeup

With respect to the influence that members may have on the group behavior McClintock, Nuttin, and McNeel (17) conclude "that prior experience with a group, whether successful or unsuccessful and occurring outside or within the laboratory context, leads to a higher level of

MANAGEMENT DECISION SIMULATIONS

EXHIBIT VI

*INDIVIDUAL ROLES* (This refers to the part each individual plays in the group process)

Notes

*Task Role*

Behavior or actions directed toward helping group achieve its goal or task.

*Maintenance Role*

Behavior directed toward helping the group overcome conflict and survive and maintain itself as a group.

*Personal Role*

Behavior by individual to satisfy his own personal needs without regard to goals of group.

cooperative behavior than no prior experience." An interesting extension of this
finding appears in a test of 93 graduate
business students at the University of
Pittsburgh assigned to play the Carnegie
Tech. Management Game (6). This game
is a major part of a 15-week course in
integrated decision making. The results
indicated an interesting conclusion that
cooperative behavior may not yield higher
group performance. In this study, men
were assigned to companies according to
whether they had been in the same or in
different quasi-training (T) groups. "Companies" reconstituted from two and three
subdivided quasi-T Groups performed significantly better in the game than companies comprised of wholly intact quasi-T
Groups. The latter reported less internal
conflicts, but appeared to be less effective
as companies because of over-confidence
in each other's dependability. Thus, co-
hesiveness, ease of communication, and
familiarity may hinder rather than help
generate adequate decisions, particularly
under the pressure of time found in most
gaming experiences.

Another area in which team makeup
influences the behavior of the group lies
in the rationality of decisions made by
the group. Lieberman (15) concluded
that individuals do not always behave as
the game model prescribes. His results
indicated that in certain game situations,
some intelligent individuals adopted a
mini-max strategy and others did not. To
account for this he indicated that people
will repeatedly make rational choices only
if they attempt to accumulate as much
"money" as possible and, given a rational
opponent, are willing to accept the con-
servative mini-max value of the game. If
participants are indifferent to the loss
of small amounts of money, there is little
to get them to act rationally.

The implications for game play are
apparent. In order to study realistically
the behavior of individuals, the manner
in which they behave in the gaming situation should be reasonably similar to their
behavior in the real world. If it is not,
that is, if participants do not take the
game seriously, then behavioral study
through gaming would be severely ham-
pered. In a simulation by Bass (4) this
problem is minimized. He utilized from
13 to 15 participants per team (company), whose job it was to produce end
items from sections of computer cards
assembled by stapling three sections to
form a single finished item. The participants in each company were structured
along differing organizational lines—line,
line-staff, operatives, etc. Raw materials
(cards) were sold for a period of time and
each group had to store inventory. The
assembled products were sold in periods
following raw material purchase. Staplers
and scissors were rented. Certain periods
were given to planning, retraining, etc. and
new product items were introduced. The
researchers found a positive association
between overall satisfaction and status.
Also, "management" of companies perceived greater task effectiveness, greater
maturity and stability, and ease of communication than did workers in the same
companies. Bass argues that since these
findings are similar to survey research,
simulation offers a useful approach to
studying organizations. In fact, the com-
pressed time dimension offered potential
overexcitation of behavior illustrative of
what might occur in less dramatic form or
actually only be felt, but not acted out in
real-life industry.

## The Debriefing Discussion

A discussion period should follow the
completion of each game. The purpose of
this discussion is not to criticize individuals for the way they behaved during a
given game (the administrator should
guard against this happening), but instead to give each team member timely,
candid, and semi-objective feedback regarding the way he was perceived by
other individuals. This information can

aid him in understanding the impact of his own behavior on other individuals with whom he is working.

Here again the game administrator must consider two basic areas of the feedback process. First, feedback among members of the same group and, second, feedback between groups. The within-group analysis involves each member of the group in a discussion of what he thought happened during the simulation situation. Each member can express his opinion, either orally or in writing, regarding the functioning of the group during the game. This discussion could focus first on the structure of the group and why the particular structure utilized was most beneficial toward completion of the task. Here an individual might express his ideas as to what he perceived his role to be as well as his perception of the role of each of the other members of the group. These perceptions could then be compared so as to note the extent to which there is agreement among various group members concerning the role structure within the group. The discussion should also treat the personal conflicts that may have developed within the group. Of interest would be the reason for these conflicts (personality clash, power struggle, role conflict, etc.) and how these conflicts may have been detrimental or helpful to the group process. The way in which the group dealt with the conflict situation might also be discussed. Thus, each group's discussion should focus on the interaction patterns that took place during the gaming session with an eye toward improving the understanding of behavior for each member of the group.

To provide feedback *between* various groups, it is often possible to let groups alternate on their game decision sessions. That is, one group may spend one or more decision periods observing another group making their decisions. They could then become involved in the game situation themselves, while another group has an opportunity to observe their interaction process. This process could be rotated several times, enabling each group to spend part of their time actually playing the game and another part observing other groups involved in the game situation. Both activities should enable each group member to gain knowledge and insight regarding individual behavior within groups. For purposes of this rotation process, it might be worthwhile to utilize different games from the text so that the observing group, while gaining knowledge regarding individual and group behavior, is not obtaining information specifically pertaining to the game operation. At the conclusion of this approach observers and participants could discuss the interaction within each group. In this way each group that had been involved in the game process would have an opportunity to obtain feedback as to how they were perceived by a group of their peers. This information would then be available for each group to use to improve their interaction process during future game situations.

The above procedures would enable each group to receive feedback in two essential areas. *First,* each member of the group would get feedback from other members of his group concerning their perception of his behavior within the group. *Second,* each group would receive feedback from other groups concerning behavior, both individual and group, that was perceived by the observing group during the gaming process.

# Bibliography

1.  Argyris, C.; *Personality and Organization*; Harper & Row; New York; 1957.
2.  Bales, R. F.; *Interaction Process Analysis*; Addison Wesley, Cambridge Mass.; 1950, p. 9.
3.  Bass, Bernard; *Organizational Psychology*; Allyn & Bacon; 1966.
4.  Cooper, W. W. (Ed.); "The Production Organization Exercise"; *New Perspectives in Organizational Research*; John Wiley, 1964.
5.  Dubin, R. et al.; *Leadership and Productivity*; Chandler Publishing Company, 1965.
6.  Dup, S. D., Bass, B. M., and Vaughn, J. A.; "Some Effects on Business Gaming of Previous Quasi T Group Affiliation"; *Journal of Applied Psychology*, Vol. 51, No. 5.
7.  French, John R. P., Jr., and Raven, Bertram; "Bases of Social Power"; *Group Dynamics*; D. Cartwright and A. Zander (Eds.); pp. 607–632.
8.  Greenlaw, Paul S., and Kight, S. S.; "The Human Factor in Business Games;" *Business Horizons*, Fall 1960, p. 59.
9.  Guetzkow, Harold, and Bowes, Ann; "The Development of Organizations in a Laboratory"; *Management Science*; Vol. 3, No. 4, July 1957.
10. Homans, G.; *The Human Group*; Harcourt, Brace and World; 1950.
11. Huttle, Herman; "Decision-Making in a Management Game"; *Human Relations*; Vol. 18, No. 1, 1965.
12. Kate, D., and Kahn, R.; *The Social Psychology of Organizations*; John Wiley & Sons, 1965.
13. Leavitt, Harold; "Frustration: The Roadblock"; *Managerial Psychology*; University of Chicago Press; 1964.

14. Leavitt, Harold; "Task Ordering and Organizational Development in the Common Target Game"; *Behavioral Science*; Vol. 5, No. 3, July 1960.

15. Lieberman B.; "Human Behavior in a Strictly Determined 3×3 Matrix Game"; *Behavioral Science*; Vol. 5, No. 4, October 1966.

16. Maslow, A. H.; "A Theory of Human Motivation"; *Psychological Review;* Vol. 50 (1943); pp. 370–396.

17. McClintock, J., Nuttin, J., and McNeel, S.; "Sociometric Choice, Visual Presence and Game Playing Behavior"; *Behavioral Science,* Vol. 15, No. 2, March 1970.

18. McGregor, Douglas; *The Human Side of Enterprise;* McGraw-Hill, Inc.; 1960.

19. Misshauk, M.; "Supervisory Skill Mix and Effect on Satisfaction and Productivity of Employees," unpublished document; Ohio State University; 1968.

20. Rothlishberger, F.; "Communication: The Administrator's Skill"; *Harvard Business Review.*

21. Sherif, M., and Sherif, C.; *Reference Groups;* Harper and Row; 1964.

22. Thibaut, John and Kelley, Harold; *The Social Psychology of Groups;* John Wiley; 1959.

23. White, R., and Lippitt, R.; *Leader Behavior and Member Reaction in Three Social Climates; Group Dynamics;* Cartwright, D. and Zander, A. (Eds.); Harper & Row, 1960.

# 5

# Management Decision Games

## Marketing

### (1) CLEAN AIR PETROLEUM PRODUCTS COMPANY

PRICING STRATEGY IN A BUSINESS
ENVIRONMENT

*Introduction* The Clean Air Petroleum Products game provides the participant with an opportunity to develop an awareness of the relationship between price elasticity and profit contribution within a constraint of limited resources.

The problem has been simplified by including only two products; however, the concepts also apply to companies producing a variety of products requiring many different raw materials.

*Background* Clean Air Petroleum Products Company was founded in 1962 and has been involved in the development of catalytic agents designed to reduce air pollution. Since its inception, the company has developed many additives that have subsequently been sold to gasoline companies for use in their products.

The company also manufactures two products that it sells to the general pub-

## MANAGEMENT DECISION SIMULATIONS

lic. Unlike the pricing of its industrial products, which are negotiated on individual bases, the two consumer products are sold at a price that is 200 percent of the standard variable manufacturing costs. The company developed this pricing policy at the time it introduced its first consumer product, Additive Z-8. However, since the introduction of its newest consumer product, F-9, six months ago, questions have been raised within the firm whether this policy reflects prudent business practices.

The manufacturing capacity during the period when the pricing decisions were made was 70,000 quarts per period. Since that time the capacity has been increased. (See Exhibit I)

*Products*    Z-8 is a common additive that the company has marketed since 1964. There are many comparable competitive products on the market, and Z-8 faces stiff competition. A market survey conducted by the firm has shown that Z-8 is quite sensitive to price changes. The survey further pointed out that if the firm were to raise the price of this product to approximately $5.00 per quart, the demand would be virtually zero. Z-8 presently sells for a price of $4.00 per quart, and the sales forecast is for 45,000 quarts for the current period. Sales history has shown that most back-ordered units of Z-8 were ultimately lost sales. Due to this, it cost the company 20 cents a quart in extra sales costs on back-ordered units.

F-9 is the new catalytic agent developed by Clean Air and has met with great market acceptance during the first six months of sales. The product is unique in its character and, at the present time, there are no comparable competitive products available. The initial market survey for this product has shown that a price between $8.50 and $8.60 per quart would result in virtually no demand. Consistent with current pricing policy, the price of

F-9 is $4.00 per quart, and a sales forecast, made prior to the introduction of F-9, indicates a demand of 32,000 quarts per period. Although the product has not been on the market for a great length of time, data has shown, with reasonable assurance, that a great majority of back-ordered units will ultimately result in sales. The company has determined that there is an extra sales cost of 10 cents per quart on all back-ordered units.

*Manufacturing    costs*    Manufacturing costs associated with the production of both Z-8 and F-9 are composed of a fixed production cost of $30,000 per period and a standard variable manufacturing costs of $2.00 per quart. The manufacturing capacity is such that any combination of Z-8 and F-9 must not exceed 130,000 quarts on the normal shift schedule. However, an additional shift may be scheduled to produce a total maximum of 162,500 quarts per period. The additional capacity results in an extra cost of 10 cents per quart for all production over 130,000 quarts. The shift premium cost is shared equally by the products. A graph of the total manufacturing capacity appears in Exhibit 3.

The firm's manufacturing lead times are such that all orders for the next period must be placed prior to the start of that period. Any orders made during the current production period will incur an additional $5000 late-order penalty.

Accounting has shown that the inventory carrying cost for both Z-8 and F-9 is 40 cents per quart per period.

*Objective*    The objective is to maximize profits from the sales of the two products, taking into consideration the effect of price changes and costs arising from the decisions made.

*Comments*

1. Each decision period is ten minutes long and at the end of the decision period all production orders must be placed. Any

EXHIBIT I

*DECISION FORM* (When Computer Scoring Need Submit Only P's & Q's)

TEAM _____

## Z-8

| Pe-riod | (P) Price | Beg. Inv. | (Q) Ordered | Avail. | (D) Demand | (I) End. Inv.[a] |
|---|---|---|---|---|---|---|
| 0 | $4.00 | 10,000 | 50,000 | 60,000 | 45,000 | 15,000 |
| 1 | $___ | 15,000 | ___ | ___ | ___ | ___ |
| 2 | $___ | ___ | ___ | ___ | ___ | ___ |
| 3 | $___ | ___ | ___ | ___ | ___ | ___ |
| 4 | $___ | ___ | ___ | ___ | ___ | ___ |
| 5 | $___ | ___ | ___ | ___ | ___ | ___ |
| 6 | $___ | ___ | ___ | ___ | ___ | ___ |

## F-9

| (P) Price | Beg. Inv. | (Q) Ordered | Avail. | (D) Demand | (I) End. Inv.[a] |
|---|---|---|---|---|---|
| $4.00 | 15,000 | 35,000 | 50,000 | 45,000 | 5,000 |
| $___ | 5,000 | ___ | ___ | ___ | ___ |
| $___ | ___ | ___ | ___ | ___ | ___ |
| $___ | ___ | ___ | ___ | ___ | ___ |
| $___ | ___ | ___ | ___ | ___ | ___ |
| $___ | ___ | ___ | ___ | ___ | ___ |
| $___ | ___ | ___ | ___ | ___ | ___ |

[a] Negative Ending Inventory equals backorder quantity.

# EXHIBIT II
## INCOME STATEMENT (Manual Scoring)

TEAM _____

### PRODUCT Z-8

| Period | 1 | 2 | 3 | 4 | 5 | 6 |
|---|---|---|---|---|---|---|
| (1) Sales D•P | $ | $ | $ | $ | $ | $ |
| (2) Var. Mfg. Cost $2 \cdot Q$ | | | | | | |
| (3) Inv. Carry'g. Cost $.4 \cdot I$ | | | | | | |
| (4) Shift Prem. Cost .05(G) | | | | | | |
| (5) Lost Sales Cost .2(-I) | | | | | | |
| (6) Total Cost $(2+3+4+5)$ | | | | | | |
| (7) Gross Profit (1–6) | | | | | | |
| (8) Fixed O'hd. $15,000 | | | | | | |
| (9) Net Profit (7–8) | | | | | | |
| (10) Prev. Profit | | | | | | |
| (11) Cum. Profit $(9+10)$ | | | | | | |

### PRODUCT F-9

| Period | 1 | 2 | 3 | 4 | 5 | 6 |
|---|---|---|---|---|---|---|
| (1) Sales D•P | $ | $ | $ | $ | $ | $ |
| (2) Var. Mfg. Cost $2 \cdot Q$ | | | | | | |
| (3) Inv. Carrying Cost $.4 \cdot I$ | | | | | | |
| (4) Shift Prem. Cost .05(G) | | | | | | |
| (5) Lost Sales Cost .1(-I) | | | | | | |
| (6) Total Cost $(2+3+4+5)$ | | | | | | |
| (7) Gross Profit (1–6) | | | | | | |
| (8) Fixed O'hd. $15,000 | | | | | | |
| (9) Net Profit (7–8) | | | | | | |
| (10) Prev. Profit | | | | | | |
| (11) Cum. Profit $(9+10)$ | | | | | | |

Total Cumulative Profit $ _____

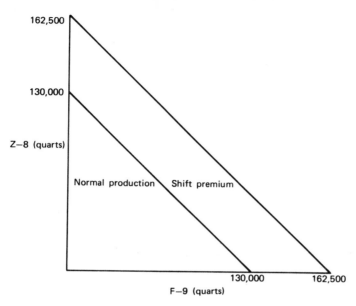

EXHIBIT III

order made after the decision period will be considered a late order and an additional $5000 charge will be made.

2. At the end of each decision period, the participants must provide the price for Z-8 and F-9, along with production orders for the two products.

3. At the end of the playing period, each group will be asked to generate its inventory status and income statement showing the results of their decisions for that period.

4. The demand created will be the normal demand for the next period plus any back-ordered units.

5. Period 0 will be considered a practice period and its results discarded. Official play begins with period 1.

## (2) SLADE BEVERAGE COMPANY

*Introduction* The Slade Beverage Company game essentially focuses on the interaction of pricing and advertising decisions relevant to varying production capacities. Thus, it represents to a large extent the complete decision-making complex that a company must consider in order to achieve its goals or objectives. This game provides the participant with the opportunity to integrate the decision of both marketing and production, recognizing the interrelationships that exist between the two areas. Changes in the environment provide an opportunity to study the flexibility of particular strategies and decision making.

Marketing decisions are often made on the basis of a guess or intuition instead of on a rational analysis of the measurable relationships among the principal variables involved.

It is intended, through the medium of this simulation, to show that it is possible to express some marketing relationships in quantitative form and, further, that it is possible to measure the outcome of alternative decisional strategies in terms of a predetermined optimization objective. In this manner, the decision maker learns that some decisions are better than others and that the differences in outcomes can be measured and expressed in quantitative terms.

*Background* The Slade Beverage Company (SBC) is a well-established

## MANAGEMENT DECISION SIMULATIONS

```
ENTER TEAM NO. AND PERIOD
T
?1,2
ENTER Z-8 PRICE & ORDER QTY
P1
?4.,30000
ENTER F-9 PRICE & ORDER QTY
P2
?5.,30000
```

```
                 TEAM #1          PERIOD #2

      PRODUCTS        Z-8               F-9

PRICES             $ 4.00           $ 5.00

DEMAND             42500 QTS        36280 QTS

QTY ORDERED        30000 QTS        30000 QTS
BEG'G INVENT       30361            21337
QTY AVAILABLE      60361            51337
END'G INVENT       17861            15056
B/O QTY                0                0


            I N C O M E   S T A T E M E N T

      PRODUCTS       Z8          F9          TOTAL

SALES REV.         170000      181405       351405

VAR.MFG.COST        60000       60000
INV.CARRY COST      12144        8535
SHIFT PREM.             0           0
LOST SALES COST         0           0
TOTAL MFG.COST      72144       68535       140679

GROSS PROFIT        97856      112870       210726

FIXED O'HEAD        15000       15000        30000

NET PROFIT          82856       97870       180726

CUM PROFIT          72851      159648       232499


TEAM 1   PERIOD 2   NET B/O'D  Z8        0   F9        0
```

local brewery in a large city in the Southwestern United States where, because of the climate, there is no seasonal effect on sales. Eastern breweries have recently moved into the area causing some concern to SBC's management. Plant expansion is out of the question for the next few years and, as a result,

the company is placed in the position of having to adjust its advertising and pricing decisions to conform to its production capacity in a given quarter.

Extensive market research has determined that there are three prices that can be charged for a six-pack of Slade's product: (1) $1.20, (2) $1.25, and (3)

$1.30. One of these prices will be optimal for a given level of advertising. Through certain ranges of advertising it has also been demonstrated that demand can be elastic or inelastic with respect to additional advertising dollars. In the aggregate, however, increased advertising will create increased demand at a given price. On the other hand, at a given level of advertising, demand may be increased by the lowering of price. The problem presented to you is to determine which of the three prices should be established and what level of advertising should be maintained in each period in order to maximize profits. Since the plant may be subject to some changes in production caused by breakdown, labor difficulties, material shortages, etc., proper consideration must be given to the probability that the demand created through advertising may not actually be met by the plant.

As a result of your request for further

**TABLE I.**

| Price | Advertising Expense (Dollars) | Demand Created (Units) |
|-------|-------------------------------|------------------------|
| 1 (1.20) | 0 | 700,000 |
| 2 (1.25) | 0 | 300,000 |
| 3 (1.30) | 0 | 100,000 |
| 1 | 220,000 | 1,500,000 |
| 2 | 25,000 | 700,000 |
| 3 | 140,000 | 600,000 |
| 1 | 110,000 | 1,100,000 |
| 2 | 140,000 | 900,000 |
| 3 | 220,000 | 900,000 |
| 1 | 230,000 | 2,100,000 |
| 2 | 200,000 | 1,000,000 |
| 3 | 250,000 | 1,500,000 |
| 1 | 520,000 | 3,600,000 |
| 2 | 235,000 | 1,500,000 |
| 3 | 410,000 | 1,900,000 |
| 1 | 580,000 | 3,900,000 |
| 2 | 350,000 | 1,900,000 |
| 3 | 530,000 | 2,200,000 |
| 1 | 900,000 | 4,000,000 |
| 2 | 380,000 | 2,600,000 |
| 3 | 580,000 | 3,500,000 |
| 2 | 480,000 | 3,200,000 |
| 3 | 900,000 | 3,600,000 |
| 2 | 565,000 | 3,700,000 |
| 2 | 910,000 | 3,800,000 |

## MANAGEMENT DECISION SIMULATIONS

information, arrangements have been made for you to receive a quarterly estimate of production capacity from the factory manager. Using this estimate, you are to determine the price and advertising level that will maximize expected profit.

*Preparation for the game*  Based on past history and current market research information, the relationship between advertising expense and the demand created for each of the three prices is shown in Table 1. Prior to game play, these relationships should have been plotted. The values shown represent exact relationships; that is, all points must fall on the curve. In addition, the participant should be prepared to employ some method of forecasting which will not consume too much time in calculation. Graphing, linear regression, or exponential smoothing are possible techniques to use. Empirical evidence has shown that three standard deviations for both production and demand are 100,000 units. Calculations to the nearest thousands are acceptable and slide rules may be useful.

*Rules of the game*

1. The game will be played for several three-month periods or quarters.

2. At the end of each quarter, the referee will tell you which memo from the factory manager you may read. This memo provides the production estimate for the next period. Do not read the other memos until notified.

3. You are to determine the price you will charge and the amount you wish to spend on advertising for the next period. This information will be submitted on the Marketing Decision Form.

4. The Marketing Decision Form will be returned to you at the end of the quarters showing the *actual production* that was realized and the *actual demand* that was created by your pricing and advertising decision.

### SLADE BEVERAGE COMPANY
### INCOME STATEMENT FOR PERIOD ___0___

| | | |
|---|---|---|
| 1. | Beginning inventory | 10,000 |
| 2. | Production | 1,100,000 |
| 3. | Goods available $[(1)+(2)]$ | 1,110,000 |
| 4. | Demand | 1,315,000 |
| 5. | Goods sold [Min. (3), (4)] | 1,110,000 |
| 6. | Ending inventory | 0 |
| | If $(3)>(4)$, $(6)=(3)-(4)$ | |
| | Otherwise $(6)=0$ | |
| 7. | Stockout quantity $= 0$ unless | 205,000 |
| | If $(4)>(3)$, $(7)=(4)-(3)$ | |
| 8. | Price per unit | $1.30 |
| 9. | Gross sales $[(5)\times(8)]$ | $1,443,000 |
| 10. | Fixed costs ($100,000) | $100,000 |
| 11. | Variable costs $[\$.80\times(5)]$ | $888,000 |
| 12. | Advertising costs | $250,000 |
| 13. | Total costs $[(10)+(11)+(12)]$ | $1,238,000 |
| 14. | Net profit $[(9)-(13)]$ | $205,000 |
| 15. | Storage costs $[\$.10\times(6)]$ | 0 |
| 16. | Stockout penalty $[\$1.00\times(7)]$ | $205,000 |
| 17. | Net profit (loss) after penalties $[(14)-(15)-(16)]$ | 0 |
| 18. | Cumulative profit (loss) from last period | 0 |
| 19. | Cumulative profit (loss) to date $[(17)+(18)]$ | 0 |
| | (Carry forward to next income statement) | |

5. With this information you are to complete an Income Statement for the period showing profit after penalties for storage or stockout conditions.

6. After completing your income statement, the period is over and a new production estimate will be given. Steps 2 to 5 will be repeated for successive periods.

## MARKETING DECISION FORMS
### Slade Beverage Company

PERIOD #___ MARKETING DECISION

Price _____

Adv. Exp. _____
(Transfer above data to Income Statement)

After above decisions have been turned in, the following will be supplied by the Referee.

Production _____

Demand _____


PERIOD #___ MARKETING DECISION

Price _____

Adv. Exp. _____
(Transfer above data to Income Statement)

After above decisions have been turned in, the following will be supplied by the Referee.

Production _____

Demand _____


PERIOD #___ MARKETING DECISION

Price _____

Adv. Exp. _____
(Transfer above data to Income Statement)

After above decisions have been turned in, the following will be supplied by the Referee.

Production _____

Demand _____


PERIOD #___ MARKETING DECISION

Price _____

Adv. Exp. _____
(Transfer above data to Income Statement)

After above decisions have been turned in, the following will be supplied by the Referee.

Production _____

Demand _____


PERIOD #___ MARKETING DECISION

Price _____

Adv. Exp. _____
(Transfer above data to Income Statement)

After above decisions have been turned in, the following will be supplied by the Referee.

Production _____

Demand _____


PERIOD #___ MARKETING DECISION

Price _____

Adv. Exp. _____
(Transfer above data to Income Statement)

After above decisions have been turned in, the following will be supplied by the Referee.

Production _____

Demand _____

MANAGEMENT DECISION SIMULATIONS

### PAST PRODUCTION RECORD

| Past Five Quarters | Production | Percentage of Capacity |
|---|---|---|
| 1 | 1,000,000 | 25 |
| 2 | 2,500,000 | 62 |
| 3 | 1,500,000 | 38 |
| 4 | 3,000,000 | 75 |
| Present | 1,100,000 | 28 |

### COST DATA

| | |
|---|---|
| Fixed costs | = $100,000 |
| Variable costs | = $.80/unit |
| Storage costs | = $.10/unit/period |
| Stockout costs | = $1.00/unit |

*Internal Letters*    In order to provide a more dynamic environment for the simulation, various internal letters have been included. The purpose of these letters is to change some aspect of the world in which the teams are functioning in order to test their ability to modify and adjust their decision making to the changing situation. The impact of the "letters" can range from competition or changes in production to new forms of legislation. The Administrator will select these letters in a prearranged sequence.

## (3) MARSTRAT

### A MARKETING STRATEGY GAME

*Introduction*    This game is designed to illustrate a marketing concept which says that "a firm should be customer-oriented instead of product-oriented." It views an industry as a customer-satisfying process and defines the difference between marketing and selling as a variance in approach. Marketing focuses on the needs of the buyer, while selling emphasizes the needs of the seller. Selling is preoccupied with the seller's need to convert his product into cash; whereas marketing promotes the idea of satisfying the needs of the customer by means of the product and a whole group of factors associated with creating, delivering, and consuming the product. A truly marketing-minded firm tries to create value-satisfying goods and services that consumers want to buy. Under the marketing concept, the firm must think of itself not as producing goods or services, but as doing the things that will make customers want to do business with it. It is a philosophy of business operation and not merely a function of business.

Marketing planning, when properly done, reduces the number of crisis-type business decisions with resulting actions that lack sound and careful consideration. Marketing planning prevents false starts and wasted effort. The marketing concept demands integration of effort in order to maximize profits.

Assuming that management wishes to adopt the marketing concept in the running of their business, what steps do they follow? How do they proceed?

The best way the entire company can strive toward achieving its marketing objectives is to formalize a marketing plan. In this way, company personnel are made fully aware of the marketing strategies and programs that have been designed to achieve the marketing objectives. Hence, the first step is to know where the company is going. Thereafter, all policies and tactics, whether short or long range, can be fitted into the overall plan. To determine where a company should be going, the following points need to be considered:

1. An appraisal of the company's resources—finances, personnel, equipment, etc.

2. An analysis of its history—how it got where it is, what it is known for, what it is least respected for or actually criticized for.

3. A study and appraisal of its competition—who are the competitors and what are they doing, etc.

4. An analysis of the customer—what are his needs, problems, tastes, changing wants, preferences, and expectations.

Finally, it should be noted that short-run goals cannot be separated from long-run goals. Everything a company does today in some way locks it into some inflexible future posture and commits it to some irrevocable course of action.

*Background*    The game you are about to play centers around an unusual product—A FOOTBALL TEAM! But don't be misled. Marketing principles are just as applicable to a sports organization in its business management as to a firm in the consumer goods industry.

You and your associates have acquired control of the Center City "Tigers," one of the football teams that make up the Associated Football League. Your group is knowledgeable in the ways of sound management practice. Your objective is to apply this knowledge so as to maximize the financial position of the "Tigers."

The Tigers have not done well for the past several years, but you feel that the potential to reverse this situation is very good. The Center City Jets, a baseball team, and the Center City Marvels, a basketball team, have been very successful to date. The Jets play in their own baseball stadium which was built just a few years ago. The Marvels currently play their home games at the Center City Sports Arena. Both the Jets and the Marvels have achieved increased attendance at home games for the past several years, but the Tigers' attendance trend has been downward.

The Tigers' stadium was built in 1948 and was last renovated in 1957. The seating capacity is 85,000. Center City is the center of a fast growing metropolis. In 1950 the area population (Center City and the surrounding towns) was 985,000, in 1960 it was 1,690,000, and by 1970 it had grown to 2,410,000.

*Survey*    In order to gain some insight into those factors which influence attendance, management conducted an extensive public opinion survey. The results of the survey have been summarized into 15 representative statements as follows:

"The Tigers? Aren't they a baseball team? No, that's the Jets, let me see . . . , the Tigers—hmmm . . . !

"The Tigers play more like pussycats!"

"What we need is a winning team."

"You know, I've never been able to find a water fountain in that stadium!"

"Boy, parking is difficult!"

"For what they offer, they charge too much."

"Hey man, that team just don't send me; you know what I mean?"

"The restrooms are dirty."

"I don't like stale peanuts!"

"Yeah, I used to go to see them play, but it just got to be too much trouble."

"Man, that team is bad—they are lucky to win them three games last season."

"The Tigers got no oomph anymore!"

"I used to take my wife, but she didn't like it, so I quit taking her. Now I don't go so often anymore."

"Who are the Tigers?"

"See the Tigers play, what for?"

"The Tigers don't have the appeal they once had."

In addition to the above survey, a review of the players and the coaching staff disclosed the following:

1. The coaching staff is considered to be very competent.

2. The team, in general, is better than its past year's record indicates. However, the average age of the players is 29.5. Several of the players are beginning their tenth season in the league.

A business, to be successful, must offer a combination or sequence of goods and services that customers demand and in a form that they desire. That's your objective—to satisfy your customers.

Based on the above information, each team should now prepare a list of those marketing factors that they feel are significant in influencing attendance at future football games.

## MANAGEMENT DECISION SIMULATIONS

*Player Introduction* The marketing concept is broad enough in theory that it can be adopted as a major guiding force in the marketing of a football team —the Center City Tigers.

Utilizing the background information and the data that follow, each team will be required to make a number of decisions that are similar to those required in the operation of any business. Decisions will be made for the following dynamic factors:

| | |
|---|---|
| *Pricing strategy* | Ticket price |
| | Parking fee |
| | Food and drink prices |
| *Advertising strategy* | General advertising |
| | Special sales promotion |
| *Product improvement strategy* | Player and coach improvement |
| | Facilities |

Although a team's decisions appear to involve only the allocation of funds on the aforementioned factors, they have in actuality a direct relationship to attendance and, therefore, the revenue that will be achieved.

Strategically allocating the funds available in each playing period to the decision factors is important since the factors are dynamic and interactive. Even though the long-term goals may be in conflict with short-term goals, the decisions should reflect long-term objectives since this is a multiyear game.

Each group may ask itself "Where do we start and how should the funds be allocated to produce the highest return?" It is suggested that all data concerning the variables be analyzed in relation to the environmental conditions presented in the background material. The economy is dynamic and volatile; the importance associated with the factors are *subject to change* as a result of shifting market forces.

Decisions made on one period may have a direct effect on the type of decisions to be made in the next. It is very important that the efforts (decisions) made supplement rather than nullify each other.

As in any dynamic situation, the combination of factors producing the highest return are subject to change. In each period an optimum point can be achieved by applying sound strategy.

*Game Data*

> *Potential attendance (10 home games: 7 conference and 3 exhibition):*

Per game: 85,000    Per year: 850,000

> *Average ticket price*

$2.00 $2.50 $3.00 $3.50 $4.00 or $4.50

Only one price may be chosen each year. Price is relatively elastic and a price line should be adopted which produces the greatest revenue. Pricing decisions are important in that they should "fit" a team's long-term marketing strategy.

> *Parking fee:*
>
> $.50   $1.00   $1.50   or   $2.00

Only one of the above parking fees may be chosen *each* year.

*Food and drink prices:* The following food and drink packages are available:

| | Package | | |
|---|---|---|---|
| | A | B | C |
| Hot Dogs | .25 | .50 | .60 |
| Cold Drinks | .15 | .25 | .35 |
| Beer | .40 | .60 | .80 |
| | $.80 | $1.35 | $1.75 |

Only package prices A, B, or C may be chosen *each* year.

*Total budget available for each year:* Total expenditures in the first year are limited to $2,000,000 ($800,000 are fixed expenses). The budget for each succeeding year is $2,000,000 less the *loss,* if any, from the prior year. That is, if

$200,000 is a net *loss* in the first year, only $1,800,000 is available in the second year.

Any profits earned, however, will be utilized by management to pay outstanding debts and provide earnings to the owners. Outstanding debts are those incurred by the prior management team.

NOTE: All spending must be in $100,000 increments.

*General advertising:* General advertising consists of radio, TV, newspaper, and other ads in accepted media.

*Special sales promotion:* This includes any special promotion designed to increase total attendance. For example, ladies night, group discounts, and fan appreciation gifts.

*Improvements in coaching and playing personnel:* Improvements can be accomplished through the investment of funds in *$100,000 increments.* These funds are used to sign new players and/or coaches.

*Facilities:* This includes expenditures to improve parking conditions, the stadium, seats, grounds, etc.

*Decision forms* Decision forms have been provided for recording your price decisions and for allocating your budget funds. The forms are self-explanatory. The result of your decisions for each of the four years is to be entered in the appropriate spaces in *decimal millions.* It should be noted that the total budget available on line 7 is limited to $2,000,000 in each period *less the loss, if any, from the prior period.*

*Market Research Information* Each management team has the opportunity to invest a certain amount of their available budget in order to obtain information

that may be beneficial in their decision-making process. If market research information is desired, the cost is to be deducted from the team's budget for that year.

The type of information available and the cost to the firm is as follows:

*Ticket price* ($15,000/yr)—% of people expressing dissatisfaction with ticket price.

*Advertising* ($15,000/yr)—% of people in community who are not familiar with the team.

*Sales promotion* ($15,000/yr)—% of people who would like to see more promotional activities.

*Product improvement* ($20,000/yr)—% of people in community who stay away from games because of poor team.

*Facilities* ($20,000/yr)—% of people who expressed dissatisfaction with facilities.

*Food and drink* ($20,000/yr)—% of people who complain about prices.

*Parking* ($10,000/yr)—% of people who complain about parking problems.

*Feedback of Results* At the end of each year (4 in total), the decision form will be turned into the referees and scored. The profit or loss, win-loss record, and attendance achieved will be entered on the Decision-Making Form and returned to your team. The team that earns the greatest amount of revenue after expenses for the four years wins. The performance (only the win-loss record and the number of tickets sold) for all the teams will be posted on the board at the beginning of each period.

In addition to the above data, the team management must contend with factors beyond its control that will have an impact on profits (i.e., weather, injuries, etc.).

MANAGEMENT DECISION SIMULATIONS

## EXHIBIT I. PAST HISTORY DATA

| | PRODUCT | | | PRICING | | | ADVERTISING AND SALES PROMOTION | |
|---|---|---|---|---|---|---|---|---|
| Year | Attendance | Record (%) | Facilities Expend. ($) (000) | Food & Drink (pkg) | Ticket | Parking | Adver- tising (000) | Sales Prom. (000) |
| 1960 | 680,000 | .700 | $200 | $1.75 | $3.00 | $1.00 | $300 | $300 |
| 1961 | 700,000 | .800 | 150 | 1.35 | 3.00 | 1.00 | 400 | 400 |
| 1962 | 630,000 | .690 | 200 | 1.35 | 3.00 | 1.00 | 300 | 400 |
| 1963 | 610,000 | .700 | 100 | .80 | 3.00 | 2.00 | 300 | 300 |
| 1964 | 580,000 | .550 | 325 | 1.75 | 3.50 | 1.50 | 200 | 400 |
| 1965 | 540,000 | .550 | 100 | 1.35 | 3.50 | 1.00 | 300 | 300 |
| 1966 | 490,000 | .500 | 100 | 1.35 | 4.00 | 1.50 | 100 | 200 |
| 1967 | 510,000 | .400 | 200 | 1.75 | 4.50 | 1.00 | 200 | 300 |
| 1968 | 480,000 | .450 | 100 | 1.75 | 4.00 | 1.50 | 200 | 300 |
| 1969 | 450,000 | .450 | 200 | 1.35 | 3.50 | 1.00 | 200 | 300 |

## EXHIBIT II.  MARKETING DECISIONS                    Team No. _____

| PRICING DECISIONS | YEAR 1 | YEAR 2 | YEAR 3 | YEAR 4 |
|---|---|---|---|---|
| 1. Average Price of a Ticket | $ | $ | $ | $ |
| Market Res. Inf. ($15,000/yr)[a] | %☐ | %☐ | %☐ | |
| 2. Price for Parking Car | $ | $ | $ | $ |
| Market Res. Inf. ($15,000/yr)[a] | %☐ | %☐ | %☐ | |
| 3. Food and Drink Prices (Specify A, B or C) | $ | $ | $ | $ |
| Market Res. Inf. ($15,000/yr)[a] | %☐ | %☐ | %☐ | |

### BUDGET ALLOCATION DECISIONS
#### ($100,000 Increments)

| | YEAR 1 | YEAR 2 | YEAR 3 | YEAR 4 |
|---|---|---|---|---|
| 1. General Advertising | $ | $ | $ | $ |
| Market Res. Inf. ($20,000/yr)[a] | %☐ | %☐ | %☐ | |
| 2. Special Sales Promotion | $ | $ | $ | $ |
| Market Res. Inf. ($20,000/yr)[a] | %☐ | %☐ | %☐ | |
| 3. Improvement of Players and Coaches | $ | $ | $ | $ |
| Market Res. Inf. ($20,000/yr)[a] | %☐ | %☐ | %☐ | |
| 4. Improvement of Facilities | $ | $ | $ | $ |
| Market Res. Inf. ($10,000/yr)[a] | %☐ | %☐ | %☐ | |

[a] If marketing research is desired, please check appropriate box and charge yourself accordingly.

*Last Year's Budget and Profit Picture*

## BUDGET EXPENDITURES

| | |
|---|---:|
| General Advertising | $ 200,000 |
| Special Sales Promotion | 300,000 |
| Improvement of Players and Coaches | 200,000 |
| Improvement of Facilities | 200,000 |
| Fixed Expenses | 800,000 |
| Total Expenditures | $1,700,000 |

### OPERATING DATA

| | |
|---|---|
| Ticket Price Charged | $3.50 |
| Price for Parking a Car | $1.00 |
| Food and Drink Prices (Package B) | $1.35 |
| Attendance | 450,000 |

### Profit and/or Loss

1. *Net Revenue Ticket Sales*
   Attendance × Ticket Price
   450,000 × $3.50           = $1,575,000

2. *Net Revenue Parking*
   (Assume that 1 out of 3 people bring their own car)
   ⅓ Attendance × Parking Fee
   ⅓ 450,000 × $1.00        =    150,000

3. *Net Revenue Food and Drink*
   (Assume half of all people attending have refreshments, only 20% of revenue goes to management, remaining 80% goes to concessionaire.)
   ½ × Attendance × ⅕ × Food & Drink Pkg.
   ½ × 450,000 × ⅕ × $1.35    =    60,750

   | | | |
   |---|---|---:|
   | *Total Net Revenue* | = | $1,785,000 |
   | *Less Total Expenditures* | = | 1,700,000 |
   | *Net Profit* | = | 85,000 |

# Production

## (4) ASHTON MINING COMPANY

*Introduction*   In the Ashton Mining Company game variables relating to scheduling, producing, and transporting a product to a given market must be ascertained and controlled. Although the environment deals with mining operations, this game can easily be applied to other areas of production and distribution. The participant plans production in order to maximize profits from the total operations. In meeting this objective, the costs of production, transporting the output, and the relative value of the output from each operation must be considered.

*Background*   Your management team has just taken over the supervision of Ashton Mining Company which produces a complex ore containing silver, lead, and zinc.

There are four separate mining opera-

tions in production, and mine No. 5 is ready to begin production at Period 11. The mines are located at varying distances from the concentrating mill and are subject to certain production limitations and costs. Transportation of the ore from each mine to the mill requires a different transportation system, which is also subject to certain limitations.

Ore value per ton varies from mine to mine and within each mine. This is because ore from each mine is a composite of ores from a number of locations in the mine. These ores must be mined in the sequence in which they are found and developed. Ore values per ton are also influenced by the prevailing metal prices, which vary from period to period. You will receive the market value per ton for each mine that the mill (Administrator) has computed for you. The market value is based on the grade of ore received at the mill and the prevailing metal prices.

*The problem*   You are concerned with obtaining the optimum profit for each mine consistent with production costs,

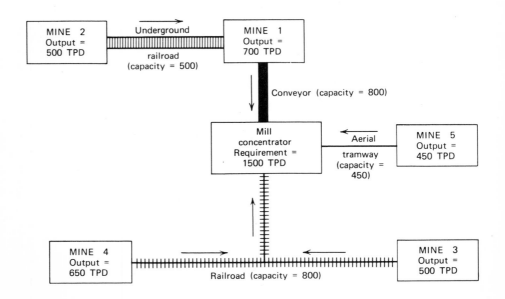

transportation costs, development costs, and ore values per ton. Therefore, you are to maximize net profit considering the ore values, costs, and the following restrictions:

1. You must deliver to the mill a constant 1500 tons of ore per day or 135,000 tons per 90-day working quarter.
2. For each ton of ore removed from any mine, work is necessary to make an additional ton ready for mining. This work is known as development costs and can be found in the Mine Cost and Production Data Sheet.
3. Production can be varied between mines as you see fit. However, the rated capacity of any mine cannot be exceeded and also at least 20% of rated production must be maintained at each mine.

*Mine Reports*

*Mine No. 1*    This is the oldest mine of the company and has been a consistent producer. The Concentrating Mill was built adjacent to this mine and has been expanded a number of times as other mines have been brought into production. Diamond drilling work done recently indicates that the ore value per ton will remain steady over the next couple of years with the same variation it has been experiencing in the recent past.

NOTE: Production output from Mines Nos. 1 and 2 combined cannot exceed 800 tons per day—refer to Transportation System Map.

*Mine No. 2*    Originally developed as a separate mining operation some time ago, extensive mining of the ore reserves has shown that this mine produces from an extension of the ore reserves from Mine No. 1. The two mines are now connected by an underground trolley rail system, which transports the ore from Mine No. 2 to Mine No. 1 where they share the same facilities for delivering ore to the mill. The plant geologist is of the opinion that the ore value per ton can be expected to remain stable with normal fluctuations.

NOTE: Production output from Mines Nos. 1 and 2 combined cannot exceed 800 tons per day—refer to Transportation System Map.

*Mine No. 3*    This mine resulted from attempts to explore the surrounding area for profitable reserves that could be used as a basis for expanding the concentrating mill. A small railroad was built to the mine site to bring the ore to the mill. The plant geologist feels there is some possibility that the ore values per ton might increase slightly in the near future.

NOTE: Production output from Mines Nos. 3 and 4 combined cannot exceed 800 tons per day—refer to Transportation System Map.

*Mine No. 4*    The same exploration that developed the ore reserves in Mine No. 3 also developed a promising area in the vicinity of Mine No. 4. This was put into operation about five years ago. The same railroad that was built for Mine No. 3 was extended to Mine No. 4. As yet, this mine has not completely lived up to its potential. However, the plant geologist states that newer areas being developed could have a significant beneficial effect on the average ore value per ton.

NOTE: Production output from Mines Nos. 3 and 4 combined cannot exceed 800 tons per day—refer to Transportation System Map.

*Mine No. 5*    This mine is being opened in a completely new area that was discovered two years ago and has considerable potential. It is presently under construction and will be ready to start production at the beginning of Period 11. An aerial tramway with a capacity of 450 tons per day will carry the ore from this mine to the mill. Initially, the

MANAGEMENT DECISION SIMULATIONS

EXHIBIT II. MINE COST AND PRODUCTION DATA SHEET

|  | Mine No. 1 | Mine No. 2 | Mine No. 3 | Mine No. 4 | Mine No. 5 |
|---|---|---|---|---|---|
| Capacity (tons per day) | 700 | 500 | 500 | 650 | 450 |
| Production costs/ton |  |  |  |  |  |
| 0–200 tons per day | $16 | $17 | $18 | $15 | $17 |
| 201–400 " " " | 14 | 16 | 17 | 13 | 15 |
| 401–700 " " " | 12 | 15 | 16 | 11 | 14 |
| Transportation costs |  |  |  |  |  |
| 0–200 tons per day | $ 8 | $ 9 | $12 | $11 | $ 5 |
| 201–400 " " " | 7 | 8 | 11 | 10 | 5 |
| 401–700 " " " | 5 | 6 | 9 | 9 | 5 |
| Development costs |  |  |  |  |  |
| 0–200 tons per day | $ 9 | $ 9 | $ 8 | $11 | $13 |
| 201–400 " " " | 8 | 7 | 7 | 10 | 12 |
| 401–700 " " " | 8 | 7 | 5 | 9 | 9 |
| Concentrator cost |  |  |  |  |  |
| (Allocated equally) | $ 8 | $ 8 | $ 8 | $ 8 | $ 8 |

EXHIBIT III. DOLLAR VALUE PER TON (past eight periods)

| Period | Mine No. 1 | | Mine No. 2 | | Mine No. 3 | | Mine No. 4 | |
|---|---|---|---|---|---|---|---|---|
|  | $\mu$ | $\sigma$ | $\mu$ | $\sigma$ | $\mu$ | $\sigma$ | $\mu$ | $\sigma$ |
| 1 | 59 | 15 | 51 | 6 | 47 | 12 | 70 | 18 |
| 2 | 57 | 13 | 54 | 7 | 49 | 12 | 61 | 18 |
| 3 | 62 | 11 | 61 | 6 | 54 | 13 | 64 | 15 |
| 4 | 45 | 12 | 65 | 8 | 63 | 14 | 72 | 14 |
| 5 | 67 | 12 | 52 | 7 | 60 | 14 | 63 | 15 |
| 6 | 66 | 14 | 54 | 6 | 46 | 13 | 61 | 10 |
| 7 | 53 | 10 | 55 | 6 | 45 | 13 | 73 | 12 |
| 8 | 50 | 13 | 60 | 8 | 56 | 13 | 72 | 11 |

Mine No. 5 yet to begin operations.

EXHIBIT IV. RELATIVE METAL PRICE INDEX (past two years)

Present = 1.00

| PERIOD | RELATIVE PRICE INDEX |
|---|---|
| 1 | 82 |
| 2 | .84 |
| 3 | .87 |
| 4 | .89 |
| 5 | .91 |
| 6 | .94 |
| 7 | .97 |
| 8 (Present) | 1.00 |

ore value per ton is expected to be quite variable because little of the mine will have been developed and there will not be an opportunity to blend the ore from a number of working areas. This problem is expected to diminish in time and the

ore values per ton should stabilize at a relatively high value.

*Play of the game*

1. Review the historical ore values for each mine, the costs of production that can be expected at various production levels, and the historical metal price trend.

2. Plan your production level for each mine during the quarter taking into account the restrictions previously outlined.

3. Remember that Mine No. 5 will begin operation at the beginning of Period 11 and it is required to produce the minimum of 20% of its rated production capacity.

4. Calculate the total costs per ton for each mine at the specific production level you have selected by consulting the cost table.

5. You have been given a past history of the value per ton of ore at each mine (Exhibit III). Future ore values will be generated by the Administrator during the game based on probability distribution in the past and the mine geologist's reports.

EXHIBIT V. DISTRIBUTIONS OF $ VALUE PER TON

| Mine | Periods | $30 | $40 | $50 | $60 | $70 | $80 | Standard Deviation | Mean |
|---|---|---|---|---|---|---|---|---|---|
| 1 | all | 5% | 10% | 30% | 30% | 20% | 5% | 12.1 | 57 |
| 2 | all | 0 | 10 | 20 | 45 | 25 | 0 | 6.8 | 59 |
| 3 | 1–8 | 5 | 15 | 35 | 20 | 15 | 10 | 12.0 | 56 |
|  | 9–12 | 0 | 10 | 30 | 25 | 20 | 15 |  |  |
|  | 13–16 | 0 | 5 | 20 | 30 | 25 | 20 | 9.4 | 64 |
| 4 | 1–2 | 30 | 25 | 20 | 15 | 10 | 0 | 22.6 | 56 |
|  | 3–4 | 25 | 20 | 20 | 15 | 15 | 5 |  |  |
|  | 5–6 | 20 | 20 | 20 | 25 | 15 | 5 |  |  |
|  | 7–8 | 15 | 15 | 15 | 25 | 25 | 10 |  |  |
|  | 9–10 | 10 | 15 | 15 | 25 | 25 | 15 |  |  |
|  | 11–12 | 5 | 10 | 15 | 25 | 25 | 20 |  |  |
|  | 13–14 | 0 | 5 | 10 | 35 | 35 | 25 |  |  |
|  | 15–16 | 0 | 0 | 10 | 30 | 30 | 30 | 9.8 | 68 |
| 5 | 11–12 | 20 | 20 | 0 | 0 | 30 | 30 | 20.2 | 59 |
|  | 13–14 | 15 | 15 | 5 | 5 | 35 | 25 |  |  |
|  | 15–16 | 0 | 0 | 20 | 30 | 30 | 20 | 10.0 | 65 |

COST CALCULATIONS

| Period | Mine | Production Tons/Day | Production Cost ($) | Transportation Cost ($) | Development Cost ($) | Concentrator Cost | Cost Per Ton ($) |
|--------|------|---------------------|---------------------|-------------------------|----------------------|-------------------|------------------|
| 9 | 1 | | | | | | |
|   | 2 | | | | | | |
|   | 3 | | | | | | |
|   | 4 | | | | | | |
|   | 5 | | | | | | |
| 10 | 1 | | | | | | |
|    | 2 | | | | | | |
|    | 3 | | | | | | |
|    | 4 | | | | | | |
|    | 5 | | | | | | |
| 11 | 1 | | | | | | |
|    | 2 | | | | | | |
|    | 3 | | | | | | |
|    | 4 | | | | | | |
|    | 5 | | | | | | |

## PROFIT DETERMINATIONS

| Period | Mine | Maximum Production | Production Tons/Day A | Cost Per Ton B | (From Administrator) Value/Ton C | Index D | Market $/Ton E=C×D | Profit $/Day A×E−B | Profit $/Qtr. |
|---|---|---|---|---|---|---|---|---|---|
| 9 | 1 | 700 | | | | | | | |
| | 2 | 500 | | | | | | | |
| | 3 | 500 | | | | | | | |
| | 4 | 650 | | | | | | | |
| | 5 | 0 | | | | | | | = |
| 10 | 1 | 700 | | | | | | | |
| | 2 | 500 | | | | | | × 90 | |
| | 3 | 500 | | | | | | | |
| | 4 | 650 | | | | | | | |
| | 5 | 0 | | | | | | | = |
| 11 | 1 | 700 | | | | | | × 90 | |
| | 2 | 500 | | | | | | | |
| | 3 | 500 | | | | | | | |
| | 4 | 650 | | | | | | × 90 | |
| | 5 | 450 | | | | | | | = |

6. In order to obtain the market price or revenue per ton of ore, the ore value/ton is multiplied by the relative price index (Exhibit IV) for the given period. This index reflects the inflationary rise in value of ore in the marketplace.

7. The gross profit per mine per day would then equal the revenue/ton minus the costs/ton (from Exhibit II). Profit = (ore value × price index − cost). In order to obtain a quarterly profit, the above profit figure would be multiplied by 90 days.

## (5) TAYLOR MANUFACTURING COMPANY

*Introduction*    The Taylor Manufacturing Company, founded in 1837, manufactures a line of toy wagons and cars. Through enlightened design, effective selling, and modern methods in its manufacturing process, the company has continued to prosper.

Mr. Nicholas, manager of production control and inventory management, left the company on August 30th. Management will have difficulty replacing him because he knew this task down to its most minute detail and rarely ran short of an item.

The general economic conditions appear good, but competition is increasing and Taylor's share of the market will decrease if they disappoint their customers. It is important that sufficient stocks of finished goods be maintained in this seasonal business.

Two models of a toy wagon, Model A and Model B, are manufactured. Model A is a deluxe model retailing for over $18.00. Model B is the company's standard, high-volume model and retails usually for about $13.00. Management believes that if proper control is maintained on Model A, this will be the company's most profitable year.

Mr. Nicholas kept a lot of information in his head. In assuming his duties you (your team) should attempt a more formal approach by:

1. Developing a sales forecast for the next few months—October, November, and December.

2. Determining the production and purchasing requirements for these months.

3. Costing out each month's activities.

The actual demand for each month will be generated close to the end of each month by the administrator. This actual demand can be used to revise the forecast for the next period's decisions. A profit and loss statement is to be computed and submitted to the administrator at the end of each period. The team with the most profits at the conclusion of the game will be considered the winner.

Exhibit I shows the wagon itself and the explosion of the parts. Sales for the last year are given in Exhibit II with space for entering the forecast for the next fiscal year.

The sales manager suggested that the apparent sinusoidal pattern can be described by a general equation such as:
$$\hat{S} = A + B * M + C \text{ Sine } (30 * M)$$
where $\hat{S}$ = estimate of sales.

  $M$ = fiscal month beginning Sept. 1.

  $A$ = the average demand and corresponds to a deseasonalized rate of sales.

  $B$ = the rate at which the deseasonalized sales rate is changing (the trend).

  $C$ = a constant derived from the data indicating the extent of seasonal variation.

| | | |
|---|---|---|
| Sine | 0° | = 0.00 |
| Sine | 30° | = 0.50 |
| Sine | 60° | = 0.87 |
| Sine | 90° | = 1.00 |
| Sine | 120° | = 0.87 |
| Sine | 150° | = 0.50 |
| Sine | 180° | = 0.00 |
| Sine | 210° | = 0.50 |
| | etc. | |

EXHIBIT I   TOY WAGON   MODEL "A"

(P/N 13102)

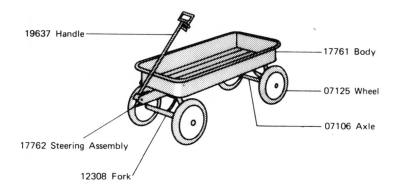

19637 Handle

17761 Body

07125 Wheel

07106 Axle

17762 Steering Assembly

12308 Fork

Model "A" Wagon comes knocked down (KD)
in Carton # 15821

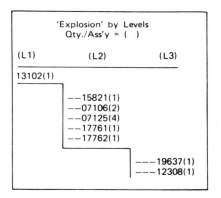

'Explosion' by Levels
Qty./Ass'y = (  )

(L1)        (L2)          (L3)

13102(1)

──15821(1)
──07106(2)
──07125(4)
──17761(1)
──17762(1)

───19637(1)
───12308(1)

Thus last year's sales can be approximated by the equation:

$$\hat{S} = 4000 + 150 * M \\ + 1500 * \text{Sine } (30 * M)°$$

Before he left on August 30, Mr. Nich-

olas helped place purchase orders, Nos. 901 and 902, for 6000 wheels and 3000 handles, respectively. As time went on during September, there was increasing concern about the planning activity. In order to assist getting visibility on the

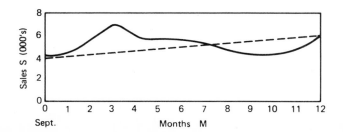

MANAGEMENT DECISION SIMULATIONS

EXHIBIT II. TAYLOR MANUFACTURING COMPANY

| | PAST YEAR'S SALES | | THIS YEAR'S SALES | | |
| Month | Formula Forecast | Actual | Formula Forecast | Actual | Revised Forecast |
|---|---|---|---|---|---|
| September | 4000 | 4000 | 5800 | 5900 | _____ |
| October | 4900 | 4750 | _____ | _____ | _____ |
| November | 5500 | 5500 | _____ | _____ | _____ |
| December | 5950 | 7000 | _____ | _____ | _____ |
| January | 5900 | 4500 | _____ | _____ | _____ |
| February | 5500 | 5000 | _____ | _____ | _____ |
| March | 4900 | 5000 | _____ | _____ | _____ |
| April | 4300 | 4500 | _____ | _____ | _____ |
| May | 3900 | 4000 | _____ | _____ | _____ |
| June | 3850 | 3900 | _____ | _____ | _____ |
| July | 4200 | 4100 | _____ | _____ | _____ |
| August | 4900 | 5100 | _____ | _____ | _____ |

outstanding and required orders, a form was devised (Exhibit III) that would depict the manufacturing plan month by month. The above open purchase orders should be posted to this form as well as to the perpetual inventory records as will be discussed next.

A physical inventory was ordered for the end of September in order to initiate a perpetual inventory system. The results of the physical count and other information are shown in Exhibit IV and should be transferred to the inventory records, Form 1. A stockout is noted for the packing cartons.

Another worksheet, which was developed to help determine net requirements for the successive periods, is shown in Exhibit V. Here the forecasted gross requirements are shown for each item. The balance on hand is entered for the beginning of each month and the subtraction leads to the net requirements to fulfill the forecast. The month of September is entered.

Exhibit VI is a recap of what is believed to have happened during the turmoil of September. Actually only one

adjusting entry had to be made (see P/N 12308).

*Participant's instructions*

1. The perpetual inventory system is to be initiated as of October 1. Enter the data from Exhibit IV on each inventory card (Form 1). The calculations for EOQ and ROP are done but should be checked.

2. A forecast should be made of October, November, and December shipments on Exhibit II.

3. October's forecast should be posted to Exhibit V and the net requirements computed.

4. With these net requirements, lot sizes, and forecasts, work orders and purchase orders should be released for the desired quantities and recorded on Exhibit III. The man-hour requirements should be computed and posted. All hours beyond 8 hours/day will be paid a premium of 50%.

5. These work and purchase orders should be posted to the perpetual inventory records as well. Exhibit VII shows the effect on the inventory balance of each type of transaction.

6. The time will now be shifted to the end of the month. The quantity to be shipped in October will be generated by the

EXHIBIT III. ORDER RELEASE WORK SHEET

DATE _____

## MANUFACTURING

| P/N | NAME | October 1 W/O Release | | | | November 1 W/O Release | | | | December 1 W/O Release | | | |
|---|---|---|---|---|---|---|---|---|---|---|---|---|---|
| | | W/O No. | Quantity | Total Hrs.* | O'T Hrs. | W/O No. | Quantity | Total Hrs. | O'T Hrs. | W/O No. | Quantity | Total Hrs. | O'T Hrs. |
| 07106 | Axle | M1001 | | | | M1113 | | | | M1221 | | | |
| 12308 | Fork | M1002 | | | | M1114 | | | | M1222 | | | |
| 17761 | Body, wagon | M1003 | | | | M1115 | | | | M1223 | | | |
| 17762 | Strg, assemby. | M1004 | | | | M1116 | | | | M1224 | | | |
| 13102 | Wagon, KD | M1005 | | | | M1117 | | | | M1225 | | | |

## PURCHASING

| P/N | NAME | Sept. 1 P/O Release Sched. | | | | Oct. 1 P/O Release Sched. | | | | Nov. 1 P/O Release Sched. | | | |
|---|---|---|---|---|---|---|---|---|---|---|---|---|---|
| | | P/O No. | Quantity | Lead Wks. | Rcvd. Dlvy. | P/O No. | Quantity | Lead Wks. | Rcvd. Dlvy. | P/O No. | Quantity | Lead Wks. | Rcvd. Dlvy. |
| 07125 | Wheel | P0901 | | | | P1016 | | | | P1112 | | | |
| 19637 | Handle | P0902 | | | | P1017 | | | | P1113 | | | |
| 15821 | Carton | P0904 | | | | P1018 | | | | P1114 | | | |

\* 4 men are fabricators ∴ over 640 hrs./mo. = overtime hours.
\* 1 man is an assembler ∴ over 160 hrs./mo. = overtime hours.
\* 1 man is a packer ∴ over 160 hrs./mo. = overtime hours.

EXHIBIT IV. RESULTS OF SEPT. 30 PHYSICAL INVENTORY AND OTHER ANALYTICAL INFORMATION (enter on new perpetual inventory records system)

| P/N | NAME | Make/Buy | EOQ* | Lead Weeks | ROP | Std. Cost/Unit | Std. Hrs./100 | On Order | Prod. or Rcvd. | On Hand |
|---|---|---|---|---|---|---|---|---|---|---|
| 13102 | Wagon, KD | M | — | 0 | 500 | 8.50 | 3.0 | W/O | 6,000 | 200 |
| 07125 | Wheel | B | 10,000 | 6 | 6,000 | .50 | — | 6,000 | 24,000 | 2,500 |
| 07106 | Axle | M | 7,000 | 1 | 3,000 | .35 | 2.0 | W/O | 10,260 | 10 |
| 17762 | Strg. Assy. | M | 3,000 | 0 | 500 | 1.20 | 3.0 | W/O | 6,300 | 400 |
| 12308 | Fork | M | 5,000 | 1 | 2,000 | .35 | 3.0 | W/O | 5,950 | 5 |
| 19637 | Handle | B | 5,000 | 4 | 7,500 | .40 | — | 3,000 | 8,000 | 2,010 |
| 17761 | Wagon Body | M | 10,000 | 1 | | 3.00 | 4.0 | W/O | 5,020 | 550 |
| 15821 | Carton | B | 10,000 | 2 | 4,000 | .50 | — | 0 | 0 | 0 |
| | | | | | | | 15.0 hrs/100 | | | |

$$EOQ = 3500 \sqrt{\frac{\text{Qty per one end-item}}{\text{Cost/Pc.}}}$$ (Assumes order cost $25.00 and carrying cost @ 2%/month.)

W/O = Work order releases

ROP assumed @ 1-1/2 usage during lead time.

Materials burden applied = .40 × Invoice Cost.

Factory burden applied = Included in man-machine hour rate.

Normal production capacity = 250/day × 20 days/mo. = 5,000/month.

Man hours/day Reqd. per 250 = Packers = 250/.75 × 3 = 10 hours
(Performance = 75%) = Assemblers = 250/.75 × 3 = 10 hours
= Fabricators = 250/.75 × 9 = 30 hours

At 250 equivalent units/day, the packer and assembler must work 2 hours overtime. The fabricators can produce 32/30 × 250 or about 270 units in an 8 hour day. The jobs are not interchangeable and pay $2.00, $3.00, and $4.00 per hour, respectively. Overtime is at 1-1/2 base rate.

## EXHIBIT V. FORECAST AND NET REQUIREMENTS WORKSHEET (Model A)

| P/N | Part Name | | September | October | November | December |
|-----|-----------|------|-----------|---------|----------|----------|
| 13102 | Wagon, KD | Fcs. | 5,800 | | | |
| | | Bal. | 100 | 200 | | |
| | | Net | 5,700 | | | |
| 07125 | Wheel | Fcs. | 23,200 | | | |
| | | Bal. | 2,500 | 2,500 | | |
| | | Net | 20,700 | | | |
| 07106 | Axle | Fcs. | 11,600 | | | |
| | | Bal. | 1,750 | 10 | | |
| | | Net | 9,850 | | | |
| 17762 | Strg. Assy. | Fcs. | 5,800 | | | |
| | | Bal. | 100 | 400 | | |
| | | Net | 5,700 | | | |
| 12308 | Fork | Fcs. | 5,800 | | | |
| | | Bal. | 400 | 5 | | |
| | | Net | 5,400 | | | |
| 19637 | Handle | Fcs. | 5,800 | | | |
| | | Bal. | 310 | 2,010 | | |
| | | Net | 5,490 | | | |
| 17761 | Wagon body | Fcs. | 5,800 | | | |
| | | Bal. | 1,530 | 550 | | |
| | | Net | 4,270 | | | |
| 15821 | Carton | Fcs. | 5,800 | | | |
| | | Bal. | 6,000 | 0 | | |
| | | Net | 0 | | | |

This worksheet is only a guide for planning net requirements of receipts during the next month. Thus, the forecast would be entered, the balance on hand subtracted, and the net requirements derived. The actual orders placed would probably be above these net requirements to allow for safety stock and economical order quantities.

## EXHIBIT VI. RECAP OF SEPTEMBER TRANSACTIONS

| P/N | Part Name | Sept. 1 Bal. In | Recvd. | Issued | Adj. | Oct. 1 On Hand |
|-----|-----------|---------|--------|--------|------|---------|
| 13102 | Wagon, KDA | 100 | 6,000 | 5,900 | | 200 |
| 07125 | Wheels | 2,500 | 24,000 | 24,000 | | 2,500 |
| 07106 | Axles | 1,750 | 10,260 | 12,000 | | 10 |
| 17762 | Strg. Assy. | 100 | 6,300 | 6,000 | | 400 |
| 12308 | Fork | 400 | 5,950 | 6,300 | −45 | 5 |
| 19637 | Handle | 310 | 8,000 | 6,300 | | 2,010 |
| 17761 | Wagon body | 1,530 | 5,020 | 6,000 | | 550 |
| 15821 | Carton | 6,000 | 0 | 6,000 | | 0 |

MANAGEMENT DECISION SIMULATIONS

## EXHIBIT VII. THE EFFECT OF A TRANSACTION FOR Q UNITS ON PERPETUAL INVENTORY RECORD

| Type of transaction | Ordered | Balance on order | Received | Issued | Balance on hand | Quantity reserved for issue | Balance available |
|---|---|---|---|---|---|---|---|
| Open a purchase or work order | Q | +Q | | | | | |
| Receipt of goods | | −Q | Q | | +Q | | +Q |
| Reserve, apportion, or allocate | | | | | | Q | −Q |
| Issue goods | | | | Q | −Q | | |
| Issue without prior reservation | | | | Q | −Q | | −Q |

administrator and posted on Exhibit II and the inventory card for P/N 13102, the top assembly. Can all these be shipped in October? This is partially answered by assuming that the parts ordered during the month were received except P/O No. 901 for wheels, which have a six-week lead time. However, a next assembly sequence (gozinto) must be followed in order to have sufficient quantities at all levels. (See Exhibit I for the explosion.) This means the most 17762's that can be assembled depends on the availability of Level 3 parts, namely P/N's 19636 or 12308. Similarly, the number of wagons that can be packed depends on the minimum equivalent quantity of each of the parts at Level 2 (L2). Therefore, if 6000 complete wagons are to be shipped, 6000 equivalent quantities must have become available (on hand and receipts) at level 2. These became available if 6000 equivalent quantities were available of level 3 items.

7. Post the quantities ordered, received, and issued to the next assembly or final package for each item and compute the balance on hand as of the end of the month. Post these balances to Exhibit V, the Net Requirements Worksheet.

8. Compute the profit or loss for the month on Exhibit VIII.

    (a) Multiply the quantity actually shipped by $12.00 to determine revenue. (This is Taylor's price to distributors.)

    (b) The cost of sales is $8.00 multiplied by the number of units shipped.

    (c) Premium labor is added at $2.00, $1.50, and $1.00 per fabrication, assembly, or packing overtime hour, respectively. Inventory carrying charges are computed at 2% multiplied by the standard cost of each item carried.

TEAM

EXHIBIT VIII.  PROFIT AND LOSS STATEMENT  (Model A)

| | September | October | November | December |
|---|---|---|---|---|
| SHIPMENTS × $12.00 | 5,900 | | | |
| REVENUE | $ 70,800 | $ | $ | $ |
| Std. cost of sales shipments × $8.00 | $ 47,200 | $ | $ | $ |
| Premium labor | | | | |
|   Fab.   OT × $2.00 = | $ 0 | | | |
|   Assy.  OT × $1.50 = | 26 | | | |
|   Pkg.   OT × $1.00 = | 17 | | | |
| | $ 43 | $ | $ | $ |
| Inventory carrying/100 | | | | |
|   Wagon  @ $16.00 = | $ 32 | | | |
|   Wheel   @   1.00 = | 25 | | | |
|   Axle     @    .70 = | 0 | | | |
|   Stg. Assy. @  2.40 = | 12 | | | |
|   Fork     @    .70 = | 0 | | | |
|   Handle  @    .80 = | 20 | | | |
|   Body     @   6.00 = | 33 | | | |
|   Carton  @   1.00 = | 0 | | | |
| | $ 122 | $ | $ | $ |
| TOTAL COST | $ 47,365 | $ | $ | $ |
| NET CONTRIBUTION | $ 23,435 | $ | $ | $ |

**Form 1**

Part Name _____  ROP _____  Part No. _____

Hrs, $ Per 100 _____  EOQ _____  Lead Weeks _____

| DATE | NO. | ORDERED | REC'D | DEMAND | ON HAND | APPOR-TIONED | AVAIL-ABLE |
|---|---|---|---|---|---|---|---|
| | | | | | | | |

Form 1

---

**Form 1**

Part Name _____  ROP _____  Part No. _____

Hrs, $ Per 100 _____  EOQ _____  Lead Weeks _____

| DATE | NO. | ORDERED | REC'D | DEMAND | ON HAND | APPOR-TIONED | AVAIL-ABLE |
|---|---|---|---|---|---|---|---|
| | | | | | | | |

Form 1

---

**Form 1**

Part Name _____  ROP _____  Part No. _____

Hrs, $ Per 100 _____  EOQ _____  Lead Weeks _____

| DATE | NO. | ORDERED | REC'D | DEMAND | ON HAND | APPOR-TIONED | AVAIL-ABLE |
|---|---|---|---|---|---|---|---|
| | | | | | | | |

Form 1

---

**Form 1**

Part Name _____  ROP _____  Part No. _____

Hrs, $ Per 100 _____  EOQ _____  Lead Weeks _____

| DATE | NO. | ORDERED | REC'D | DEMAND | ON HAND | APPOR-TIONED | AVAIL-ABLE |
|---|---|---|---|---|---|---|---|
| | | | | | | | |

Form 1

**Form 1**

Part Name _____  ROP _____  Part No. _____

Hrs, $ Per 100 _____  EOQ _____  Lead Weeks _____

| DATE | NO. | ORDERED | REC'D | DEMAND | ON HAND | APPOR-TIONED | AVAIL-ABLE |
|------|-----|---------|-------|--------|---------|--------------|------------|
|      |     |         |       |        |         |              |            |
|      |     |         |       |        |         |              |            |
|      |     |         |       |        |         |              |            |
|      |     |         |       |        |         |              |            |

Form 1

---

**Form 1**

Part Name _____  ROP _____  Part No. _____

Hrs, $ Per 100 _____  EOQ _____  Lead Weeks _____

| DATE | NO. | ORDERED | REC'D | DEMAND | ON HAND | APPOR-TIONED | AVAIL-ABLE |
|------|-----|---------|-------|--------|---------|--------------|------------|
|      |     |         |       |        |         |              |            |
|      |     |         |       |        |         |              |            |
|      |     |         |       |        |         |              |            |
|      |     |         |       |        |         |              |            |

Form 1

---

**Form 1**

Part Name _____  ROP _____  Part No. _____

Hrs, $ Per 100 _____  EOQ _____  Lead Weeks _____

| DATE | NO. | ORDERED | REC'D | DEMAND | ON HAND | APPOR-TIONED | AVAIL-ABLE |
|------|-----|---------|-------|--------|---------|--------------|------------|
|      |     |         |       |        |         |              |            |
|      |     |         |       |        |         |              |            |
|      |     |         |       |        |         |              |            |
|      |     |         |       |        |         |              |            |

Form 1

---

**Form 1**

Part Name _____  ROP _____  Part No. _____

Hrs, $ Per 100 _____  EOQ _____  Lead Weeks _____

| DATE | NO. | ORDERED | REC'D | DEMAND | ON HAND | APPOR-TIONED | AVAIL-ABLE |
|------|-----|---------|-------|--------|---------|--------------|------------|
|      |     |         |       |        |         |              |            |
|      |     |         |       |        |         |              |            |
|      |     |         |       |        |         |              |            |
|      |     |         |       |        |         |              |            |

Form 1

MANAGEMENT DECISION SIMULATIONS

## (6) WATER RECREATION ASSOCIATES

*Introduction*  This is a classical exercise in making fundamental capacity decisions, realigning strategies resulting from Monte Carlo generated demands and realistic contingencies introduced on a random basis. The game is pleasurable, educational, and realistic and does not require a computer, even for scorekeeping. On the other hand, it could also serve as a good illustration for flow charting and programming for interactive computer play.

The optimum strategy could be simulated from a large number of computer trials.

It is expandable by designing-in queueing or waiting lines. For example, the idea of a long waiting line causing defections could be tested. Different arrival rates occurring during the day could be simulated. It is possible to test various ill-will costs and to balance them against the number of operators or other ways of temporarily increasing capacity.

This is a situation similar to a great many service activities that could be simulated such as bank tellers, toll booth operators, tool crib attendants, checkout stands, receiving docks, and construction site activities.

*Background*  Water Recreation Associates is currently expanding its sport fishing operation and facilities. Past operations have consisted of operating various bait and tackle stores, one harbor cruise boat, and three sport fishing boats.

Coincident with the expansion of the Molina Beach breakwater and development of the resulting harbor area into the King Harbor Small Boat Marina, Water Recreation Associates negotiated with the city of Molina Beach for approximately two and one-half acres of land to be developed into a small-boat launching facility.

You have been hired to start in on the ground floor of this operation. It is now your responsibility to turn the two and one-half acres of black top into a profit-making small-boat launching facility.

*Discussion*  Through discussions with other managers of launching facilities you have learned that the utilization of concrete launching ramps does not create enough revenue to pay for the expense of installation, high accident insurance premiums, high maintenance, and moss removal costs. You have determined that overhead sling-type boat hoists offer greater profit potential by providing faster service and lower total cost.

Through preliminary investigation of numerous manufacturers offering overhead, movable sling-type hoists, you have narrowed your selection down to hoists from two manufacturers, hereafter to be known as "Hoist A" and "Hoist B." Although both hoists appear to be of equal quality and workmanship, there is a significant difference in the initial cost of each hoist and also in the speed of operation of each hoist.

Although the initial cost differential of each hoist appears to be significant, you feel the difference in operating speeds might more than offset this cost differential. The cost of Hoist A was computed to be $150.00 per day of operation and includes maintenance and spare parts on a regularly scheduled basis. The $150.00 per day also includes the total yearly amortized costs of the hoist spread over the 140 days of annual operation of the active boating season. The similar costs of Hoist B were computed at $200.00 per day of operation including maintenance, spare parts, and amortization.

The difference in the speed of operation of the two types of hoists was found to be because of motor size, gear ratios, and types of hoist slings. The difference in number of boats processed is computed to be one boat per hour greater for Hoist B than for Hoist A (a processed boat includes one that is both put into and taken out of the water). Both manufacturers were in agreement that no matter which hoist or combination of hoists were chosen, no more than four hoists could be operationally effective on the allotted two and one-half acres.

The most profitable means of meeting demand must now be determined. This will involve three basic decisions. You must decide how many hoists, of which type, will be manned by how many operators. The number of operators is important to the speed of operation.

Table I indicates the number of boats per day that any particular combination of type of hoist and number of operators can handle:

## TABLE I

| Type of Hoist | Number of Operators/Hoist | | | |
|---|---|---|---|---|
| | 1 | 2 | 3 | |
| A | 90 | 105 | 120 | Boats/ |
| B | 105 | 120 | 135 | Day |

If during the game you wish to change from one type of hoist to another, a $200.00 fee/hoist is required to cover the cost of changeover.

If you change the total number of operators, an added cost of $50.00 per operator is charged whether an operator is added or deleted.

Both manufacturers are ready to install their hoists on receipt of your order. You must now attempt to determine the demand. The original premise that a launching facility would be profitable was based on a marketing survey completed at the request of Water Recreation Associates. The firm doing the survey felt that the results would be more meaningful if they were broken down into two categories based on weather conditions. Subsequently, the final results were divided into two probability distributions. The first probability distribution was con-

cerned with the number of boats that could be expected on a bright, sunshiny day. The second probability distribution was for the number of boats to be expected on a foggy, windy, or overcast day.

From local weather bureau statistics, it was determined that there was an 80% probability for good weather during the boating season. Similarly, the probability for bad weather was 20%. The distribution and expected values are as follows:

### GOOD WEATHER

| Boats Handled | Probability | Expected No. of Boats |
|---|---|---|
| $x$ | $G(x)$ | $xG(x)$ |
| 275 | .11 | 30.25 |
| 325 | .15 | 48.75 |
| 375 | .19 | 71.25 |
| 425 | .21 | 89.25 |
| 475 | .15 | 71.25 |
| 525 | .12 | 63.00 |
| 575 | .07 | 40.25 |
| | 1.00 | 414.00 |

### BAD WEATHER

| Boats Handled | Probability | Expected No. of Boats |
|---|---|---|
| $x$ | $B(x)$ | $xB(x)$ |
| 75 | .10 | 7.50 |
| 125 | .15 | 18.75 |
| 175 | .21 | 36.75 |
| 225 | .19 | 42.75 |
| 275 | .15 | 41.25 |
| 325 | .11 | 35.75 |
| 375 | .09 | 33.75 |
| | 1.00 | 216.50 |

*Further significant data*

1. Length of operating Day: 15 hours
2. Labor rate per manhour: $2.00

## MANAGEMENT DECISION SIMULATIONS

3. Revenue per boat handled: $4.00
4. Demand:
   (a) Demand will be generated from a Monte Carlo sampling of the good (80%) and bad (20%) weather probability distributions.
   (b) For each *day*, a weather forecast will be made. After the forecast is determined and before the actual demand is generated for that day, you will have the opportunity to change the number of operators at stated cost.
5. Capacity per day:
   (a) Number of boats that could be handled per day by Type A hoists and "X" number of operators (from Table I) multiplied by number of Type A hoists; plus
   (b) Number of boats that could be handled per day by Type B hoists and "X" number of operators (from Table I) multiplied by number of Type B hoists.
6. Ill-will cost incurred because of insufficient capacity to service a boat in a day's operations: =$1.00.∴. Ill will = (Demand − Capacity) ⚬ $1.00.
7. The game should run for five periods of ten days each. Between each *period*, there is the opportunity to change the type or number of hoists at the following price schedule:

   Installation or removal of hoist    $200.00

8. Contingencies will be introduced via Monte Carlo sampling from a binomial distribution. A contingency situation is generated 40% of the time. Given that a contingency has occurred, the specific contingency is randomly selected from the list given.

The game will be run over several periods between which you will have a *limited* time to modify your decisions.

### Contingencies

1. Operators demand and get a pay raise of $.50 per hour for each employee. Condition to exist for rest of game or until rescinded.
2. Two operators call in sick. Labor expenses stay the same (sick pay)—capacity drops appropriately for this day.

3. Motor on one Type B hoist burns out. Operators change motor to save downtime—subtract 70 boats from this day's capacity.
4. Boat fire disrupts service—subtract 15 boats from this day's capacity.
5. One operator calls in sick. Labor expense stays the same (sick pay)—capacity drops appropriately for this day.
6. Great catch on bass increases next day's demand by 20%.
7. Tanker springs oil leak offshore—drop demand 30% for next two days because of oil slick.
8. One operator comes to work with sprained wrist—decrease capacity 10% on one hoist for this day.
9. Strap breaks on one Type B hoist. Court costs to fight claims of injured customer = $200.00 subtracted from revenue.
10. In-law from Oklahoma arrives. Wants to work at hoist for free just to be near the water—increases capacity 2% for rest of period.
11. Union attempts to organize operators. Fifty percent of operators picket all day today—drop capacity accordingly.
12. Junior Chamber of Commerce attempts to stimulate tourism to Molina Beach. Asks all prices be decreased 10% for rest of period. You agree to this.
13. End of period increased property tax assessment—subtract $50.00 per hoist from revenue for this period only.
14. Improvements in reliability on Type B hoists reduce total cost by $10.00 per day for Type B hoist only. Condition to exist for rest of game or until rescinded.
15. Love-in held in neighboring park distracts operators—subtract 2% from this day's capacity for each operator employed.
16. Operators demand, and get, bonus for extra effort required on Fourth of July—subtract $20.00 per operator from revenue.
17. Rescind Contingency No. 1 if it has previously been enacted.
18. Increased cost of materials raises prices for Type A hoists $15.00 per day and $10.00 per day for Type B hoists for rest of game.
19. Reports indicate poor fishing in area for next day—drop demand by 20%.
20. World record bass caught previous day—demand increases by 10%.

SCORE SHEET–WATER RECREATION ASSOCIATES

Period _____    Team # _____

Contingency Notes

## HOIST EXPENSE

| Types of hoists used | Hoist expense per day | × | Number of hoists used | = | Cost per day | × | 10 days | = | Total period cost |
|---|---|---|---|---|---|---|---|---|---|
| Type A | $150.00 | × | | = | | × | 10 | = | |
| Type B | $200.00 | × | | = | 10 | × | | = | |

Total hoist cost

## LABOR EXPENSE

| Days | Number of operators used | × | 15 hours per day | = | Labor hours used |
|---|---|---|---|---|---|
| 1st | | × | | = | |
| 2nd | | × | | = | |
| 3rd | | × | | = | |
| 4th | | × | | = | |
| 5th | | × | | = | |

Total labor hours used

| Days | Number of operators used | × | 15 hours per day | = | Labor hours used |
|---|---|---|---|---|---|
| 6th | | × | | = | |
| 7th | | × | | = | |
| 8th | | × | | = | |
| 9th | | × | | = | |
| 10th | | × | | = | |

$\times$ $2.00 = Labor expense

## REVENUE & PENALTIES

| Days | Demand | Capacity | Number serviced | Number turned away | Days | Demand | Capacity | Number serviced | Number turned away |
|------|--------|----------|-----------------|--------------------|------|--------|----------|-----------------|--------------------|
| 1st  |        |          |                 |                    | 6th  |        |          |                 |                    |
| 2nd  |        |          |                 |                    | 7th  |        |          |                 |                    |
| 3rd  |        |          |                 |                    | 8th  |        |          |                 |                    |
| 4th  |        |          |                 |                    | 9th  |        |          |                 |                    |
| 5th  |        |          |                 |                    | 10th |        |          |                 |                    |

Total serviced _____ × \$4.00 = _____ Revenue

Total turned away _____ × \$1.00 = _____ Penalties

## RESULTS

_____ − ( _____ + _____ + _____ + _____ ) = _____
(Revenue)   (Penalties   Hoist expense   Labor expense   Hoist change fees)   Profit

# Finance

## (7) PARENT SYSTEMS, INC.

*Introduction*    The Parent Systems, Inc. merger game provides an opportunity to analyze decision patterns necessary within a company when it is considering the acquisition of another corporation. The participants consider acquisition candidates and then make a series of decisions concerning the new acquisition at the conclusion of the game. Each team should defend its decisions, making it necessary for each individual or team to have solid reasons behind their selection.

Acquisition of another company is a means for achieving growth. Many business goals can be achieved through acquisition, such as:

  · Broadening the product line.
  · Strengthening the company's financial position.
  · Acquiring key personnel.
  · Obtaining land, buildings, and equipment needed for expansion.
  · Stabilizing cyclical or seasonal trends in the business.


Other reasons for acquiring another company are for investment, to serve a market need, to achieve product diversification, to achieve vertical integration, to increase borrowing capacity, to increase the company's earnings per share, and to assure a source of supply of a critical item.

Locating companies to acquire can be accomplished through studies by staff groups, working with investment bankers, through leads provided by commercial banks, by utilizing consultants, and through business brokers. Once a company has been selected as a possible acquisition, a strategy of how to approach the company must be developed. If the approach is successful and the company is acquired, this company must then be successfully integrated into the parent company.

*Objective*    The purpose of this simulation is to demonstrate the management problems that arise from the time a company decides to acquire another to the end result of integrating the two companies. These problems include the selection of a merger candidate, developing strategies of initial approach and continuing negotiation, evaluating the significant financial elements in a proposed acquisition, and successfully integrating the newly acquired organization into the operations of the acquirer. No attempt will be made in this game to investigate the technical, legal, or taxation aspects of reorganization, the application of antitrust laws, or the many different financial arrangements (except very generally) that can be negotiated. The game is, instead, an effort to acquaint the student with some of the internal management problems that arise in mergers, not only for the acquiring company, but also for the company that is acquired.

The object of the game is to successfully acquire one of two prospects that other companies (teams) are also trying to acquire.

*Background*    Each team will consider itself to be the Acquisition Development Staff of Parent Systems, Inc. The president of your company has assigned you the task of acquiring either one of two companies that he considers to be good prospects and that he has preselected from a list of candidates which you previously prepared for him. Your job is to select the *one* company that you feel best fits with P.S.I., devise a strategy of approach, initiate negotiations, successfully

## MANAGEMENT DECISION SIMULATIONS

acquire the company for a reasonable price, and integrate it into P.S.I. with a minimum of disruption. However, since it is known to you that other companies are also wooing your two prospects, the time you have to gather additional data before making your decision is limited. From the information at your disposal you must formulate an acquisition strategy that not only embodies sound business practice but that also considers the perceived distinct "personality" of the company to be acquired.

*Game sequence*

1. The descriptive data of your company (Parent Systems, Inc.) is to be studied by each team.

2. Similarly, descriptions of the two acquisition candidates should be studied.

3. There will be available five handouts for each of the two companies (ten total), which contain additional information about the companies. However, the press of time, limited investigatory funds, and rival conglomerates will be simulated by making only five of the ten studies available to any one team. Each team may request any combination of five supplemental handouts (i.e., all five about one company, three about one and two about the other, etc.), and may request them either all at once or in any sequence. The requests are made by checking off the appropriate "Information Supplements" and submitting them to the administrator who will complete the information and return the forms.

4. Each team must then decide which company it will attempt to acquire. Keep in mind that the object is to acquire only one of the companies. It may be more advantageous to pursue that company which you believe none of the other teams are attempting to acquire. You may or may not reveal to the other teams the firms for which you are negotiating, depending on the strategy you choose.

5. After the decision is made as to which company to acquire, Questionnaire 1 is to be completed according to your chosen strategy and submitted to the administrators

for evaluation. Consider each question as being asked by your prospect's management. Each answer will receive up to 10 points as determined from the administrator's suggested score for the company selected. The evaluation will be totaled and returned to your team to provide some feedback regarding the success of your acquisition strategy. Questionnaire 2 will then be completed, submitted, evaluated, and returned. Although the other questions are worth up to 10 points, question 1 regarding offering price will be given up to 20 points.

6. On the basis of cumulative questionnaire points, two teams will "succeed" in acquiring the companies (one, if all teams pursued the same company). The overall "winner" is determined by the highest point total.

*Parent Systems, Inc. (P.S.I.)*  P.S.I. is a highly diversified conglomerate engaged in the automotive, metals, information-processing, electronics, and aerospace industries. The company has grown rapidly by pursuing a strategy of acquiring other companies and successfully integrating the acquisitions into P.S.I.'s operations.

As shown below, the financial condition of the company is good and a strong growth trend is evident.

The company is organized in a diverse fashion as depicted in the following description.

P.S.I. has plants and offices located throughout the United States, but has no international operations to date. The corporate office and staff are located in New York City in the heart of the financial district.

The Automotive Group is located in Detroit; the Information Processing Group is headquartered in Los Angeles, but has offices in Chicago and New York; the Electronics Group is located in Los Angeles; and the Metals Group is located in the Pittsburgh area. Consolidated Finance Company is located in New York, and Aerolabs, Inc. is in Washington, D.C.

The management of P.S.I. is energetic,

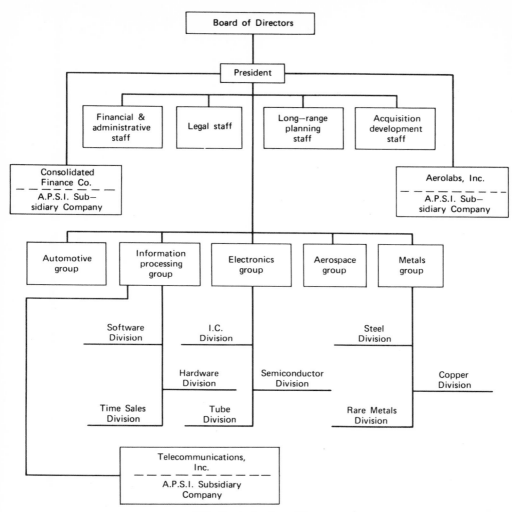

PSI Organization Chart

intelligent, and wholly devoted toward the goal of increasing P.S.I.'s size and wealth. Briefly, the key men can be characterized as follows:

President—no college, professional manager, down-to-earth, honest, hard driving—salary $250,000.

Financial & Administrative V.P.—Yale, liberal arts, expert in acquisition finance, temperamental, dedicated—salary $125,000.

Acquisition V.P.—M.I.T., E.E.; USC, MBA; young, pleasant, sharp, previously employed with IBM—salary $60,000.

Automotive Group V.P.—no college, up-thru-the-ranks, natural leader of men—salary $125,000.

*Acquisition Candidates*
*Computer Software Development Company (C.S.D.)* Computer Software Development is a publicly owned company engaged in the development of computer programs and operating systems for sale to computer users. The firm was started in 1966 by three former employees of IBM who still retain the major portion of the stock. The company has experi-

MANAGEMENT DECISION SIMULATIONS

## PSI FINANCIAL DATA

| Year | Sales ($Millions) | Net Earnings ($Millions) | EPS ($) | Stock Price ($) |
|------|-------------------|--------------------------|---------|-----------------|
| 1963 | 104 | 10.4 | 1.25 | 25–70 |
| 1964 | 130 | 14.3 | 1.45 | 20–40 |
| 1965 | 196 | 17.0 | 1.75 | 30–50 |
| 1966 | 260 | 19.5 | 2.05 | 30–50 |
| 1967 | 325 | 28.5 | 2.85 | 45–80 |
| 1968 | 520 | 39.0 | 3.55 | 60–150 |
| 1969(E) | 650 | 52.0 | 4.05 | 70–100 |

| Year | Net Worth ($Millions) | Cash ($Millions) | Total Debt ($Millions) |
|------|-----------------------|------------------|------------------------|
| 1963 | 26 | 5 | 13 |
| 1964 | 45 | 9 | 26 |
| 1965 | 78 | 8 | 52 |
| 1966 | 110 | 13 | 130 |
| 1967 | 136 | 19 | 116 |
| 1968 | 156 | 26 | 180 |
| 1969(E) | 195 | 33 | 240 |

## C.S.D. FINANCIAL DATA

| Year | Sales ($Millions) | Net Earnings ($Millions) | EPS ($) | Stock Price ($) |
|------|-------------------|--------------------------|---------|-----------------|
| 1966 | .1 | .15 | — | |
| 1967 | .5 | .15 | — | |
| 1968 | 1.9 | .45 | .40 | 10–35 |
| 1969(E) | 5.8 | .90 | .85 | 25–50[a] |

[a] Recent stock price $40.

| Year | Net Worth ($Millions) | Cash ($Millions) | Total Debt ($Millions) |
|------|-----------------------|------------------|------------------------|
| 1966 | .10 | .02 | .10 |
| 1967 | .25 | .07 | .15 |
| 1967 | 2.65 | .50 | 1.10 |
| 1969(E) | 3.60 | .30 | 4.00 |

enced good growth and the propects for the future appear favorable.

Selected financial data for Computer Software Development Company is presented on prior page.

The offices of C.S.D. are located in Denver, Colorado, but sales are made to customers throughout the United States.

*Georgetown Metals Company*    Georgetown Metals Company is a publicly owned corporation engaged primarily in making ferrous castings for the metals industry. The firm was established in 1925 and has experienced slow but steady growth. Although the stock is traded publicly, the majority of the stock is owned by the founding family, which is still actively engaged in the management of the company.

Below is selected financial data for Georgetown Metals Company for recent years.

The plant and offices of Georgetown Metals Company are in Western Pennsylvania.

### GMC FINANCIAL DATA

| Year | Sales ($Millions) | Net Earnings ($Millions) | Stock Price ($) | Net Worth ($Millions) | Cash ($Millions) | Total Debt ($Millions) |
|------|------|------|------|------|------|------|
| 1964 | 51 | 1.6 | 20–28 | 20 | 4 | 8 |
| 1965 | 54 | 1.6 | 22–27 | 21 | 4 | 9 |
| 1966 | 57 | 1.7 | 24–37 | 22 | 5 | 8 |
| 1967 | 65 | 2.4 | 31–51 | 23 | 3 | 11 |
| 1968 | 61 | 2.0 | 36–45 | 24 | 4 | 9 |
| 1969 | 62 | 2.0 | 37–42 | 25 | 5 | 8 |

NOTE: 500,000 common shares outstanding, no preferred. Recent stock price $40.

MANAGEMENT DECISION SIMULATIONS

## ORGANIZATION CHARTS

1. _____ Computer Software Development Company

2. _____ Georgetown Metals Company

Location:
Facilities:
No. of Employees:

Location:
Facilities:
No. of Employees:

## BIOGRAPHIES OF KEY PERSONNEL

3. _____ Computer Software Development Co.

4. _____ Georgetown Metals Company

President:

President:

Vice President—Marketing:

Vice President—Finance:

Information Supplements 5 and 6

## COMPANY PHILOSOPHY AND FRINGE BENEFITS

| | |
|---|---|
| 5. _____ Computer Software Development Company | 6. _____ Georgetown Metals Company |
| Philosophy Toward Employees: | Philosophy Toward Employees: |
| Salaries: | Salaries: |
| Fringe Benefits: | Fringe Benefits: |
| 1. | 1. |
| 2. | 2. |
| 3. | 3. |
| 4. | 4. |
| 5. | 5. |

Information Supplements 7 and 8

## PROJECTED FINANCIAL DATA

7. _____ Data Provided by Computer Software Development Co. to P.S.I.

| Year | Sales | Net Earnings | E/S | Net Worth | Cash | Total Debt |
|------|-------|--------------|-----|-----------|------|------------|
| 197_ | | | | | | |
| 197_ | | | | | | |
| 197_ | | | | | | |

-------------------------------------------------------------------

8. _____ Data Provided by Georgetown Metals Company to P.S.I.

| Year | Sales | Net Earnings | E/S | Net Worth | Cash | Total Debt |
|------|-------|--------------|-----|-----------|------|------------|
| 197_ | | | | | | |
| 197_ | | | | | | |
| 197_ | | | | | | |

MANAGEMENT DECISION SIMULATIONS

## BUSINESS OUTLOOK

9. _____ Outlook for Computer Software Development Company

---

10. _____ Outlook for Georgetown Metals Company

## (8) PORTFOLIO MANAGEMENT COMPANY

*Introduction* The Portfolio Management Company game is designed as a financial exercise to provide students with the opportunity to gain insight into the area of real estate value estimation (comparison, reproduction costs, capitalization, etc.). The game focuses on the capitalization method of evaluation and places primary emphasis on effective financial decision making. The ability to forecast and to appreciate the value of money in relation to time is significant. In the actual playing of the game, effective use can be made of leverage and present value methods in order to maximize profits.

The game is one of the few available that provides insight into the rather so-phisticated art of real estate investment decision making.

*Background*
Real estate investment is a sophisticated art for the professional and anyone working in this field should have a background commensurate with the responsibilities.

*Value estimation* There are three ways to approach a value estimate:

1. *Comparison*: A comparison is made regarding price, value, utility, and location in relation to other comparable property in the same or similar type of neighborhood.

2. *Reproduction costs*: This approach computes the current cost of reproducing the improvements with an added value for the land which is arrived at by comparison with other lands (deductions are made for depreciation).

3. *Capitalization*: Value is established

by consideration of the present and prospective future income of the property as well as a recapture of investment in buildings and equipment as they depreciate.

An appraiser may use all three methods in appraising certain properties. No single approach by itself can always be counted on to produce reliable estimates of value. Each parcel of real estate differs in some respect from other properties. Various appraisals are made for different purposes, and the use to which the property is put will add greater weight to a specific approach. The most popular and most relied on method for valuing income property (residential, commercial, or industrial), however, is the capitalization method, which is also known as the "capitalization of net income" and the "present value of an income stream."

## The Capitalization Method

Assume the annual gross income from a property to be $12,000, taxes $1200, insurance $250, maintenance and repairs $600, utilities $150, building manager $450, reserves for replacement $350, and building depreciation allowance of $1300. Also, assume a vacancy allowance of 5% and a capitalization rate of 8% (return on investment for all cash purchase). The net income would be computed as follows:

| Gross Income | | $12,000 |
|---|---|---|
| Fixed Expenses | $3,250 | |
| Reserves-Replacements | 350 | |
| Vacancy (5% of $12,000) | 600 | |
| Depreciation (2% per yr.) | 1,300 | |
| | | 5,500 |
| Net Income | | $ 6,500 |

*The value of the property* would be $6500 divided by .08 or *$81,250.*

Several assumptions have been made here for purposes of brevity and illustration. The gross income was assumed not to vary over time. Normally, the income would drop as the building aged. Fixed expenses were assumed constant, although maintenance usually increases with age and our history of taxes is ever increasing.

Vacancy varies with supply and demand—5% was assumed to be an average in the above example. Depreciation was computed on the basis that the building had an approximate value of $65,000 from the comparison or cost of reproduction method, and that its remaining useful life was 50 years. To completely write-off the value of the building in 50 years would require a 2% expense allowance per year. The 2% depreciation or $1300 per year is further assumed to be stored in a safety deposit box rather than being reinvested. We are also assuming this income into perpetuity. Many other refinements are possible. However, as in many other fields, it is easy to lose sight of a good practical approach by becoming too involved in the theoretical aspects of the problem.

## Leverage

*Definition* Finance books define leverage as "prior claim financing" or "trading on the equity." Real estate investors define it as "using other people's money to make money."

*Example* Let us assume that an individual has $100,000 to invest (scale it up or down if you wish). Properties are available at all price levels for a return 10% net (this is a reasonable assumption), and the following financing is available:

1. Seventy percent first mortgage loans at 7% from lending institutions.
2. Twenty percent second mortgage loans at 8% from property owner.

## MANAGEMENT DECISION SIMULATIONS

Consider two possibilities:

1. *A $100,000 all cash purchase*, which returns $10,000 per year net or 10%; and
2. *$100,000 cash down on a million dollar property*, which would earn 10% or $10,000 on the $100,000 invested, 3% (dif-

ference between 10% income and 7% interest charge) on $700,000, or $21,000 annual return, and 2% on $200,000 or $4000 annual return. Thus, the return on this second financing method would be $35,000 ($10,000 + $21,000 + $4000) or 35% plus the fact that you now control a $1,000,000 property.

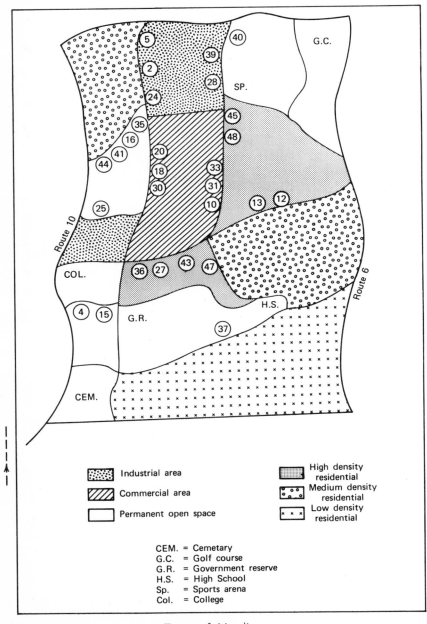

Town of Harding

*Environment*

*The company* The TransNational Corporation is located in the City of Harding in Parker County (see maps) where the construction and real estate industry is normally booming. Presently, however, the real estate market is rather poor. Vacancy factors are dropping rap-

idly because of a halt in construction and an increase in the population growth rate. Demand for property, rents, and values *should* increase in the near future.

*Business conditions* Possibly a careful review of general business conditions might be helpful. Kiplinger states that we are going to have a leveling off

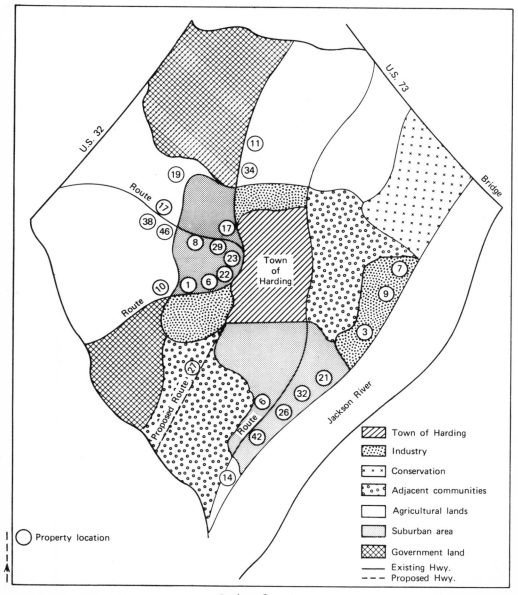

Parker County

MANAGEMENT DECISION SIMULATIONS

period for the next six months to a year, and then the country is going to experience the biggest boom it has ever known for the next two decades. Writers for the *Wall Street Journal* seem to have mixed emotions about the future, and in general their consensus would indicate that the business cycle could go either way. Then there are those authorities who seem somewhat pessimistic about the future. Many of them think that we are headed for real trouble. This might seem like a confusing picture to the average individual, but with our knowledge of forecasting and statistics, coupled with such tools as present value formulas and tables, we should be able to proceed with vigor and confidence.

## TRANSNATIONAL CORPORATION
### Interoffice Memo

From:   The President
To:     The Manager of Finance

Date: May, 1967

Subject: PORTFOLIO "99"

A decision has been made to expand the sphere of corporate holdings to include real estate investment. These new acquisitions will include income properties of several types and will be known as Portfolio "99".

Competitive financial institutions have been growing at a pace that we have been unable to match. It is the opinion of our Executive Committee, however, that carefully selected real estate investments will improve our profit picture.

A copy of the plan is attached for your review.

John Wexler
President

### GAME STRUCTURE

*Objective:* The objective is to maximize profit. The team with the highest net worth at the end of the game is the winner.

*Lessons to be learned:* Effective decision making coupled with proper timing is the key to success. The ability to forecast and to appreciate the value of money in relation to time is significant. The tools of leverage and present value methods can be utilized to advantage.

*Teams:* Each team will consist of three or four players representing members of the finance department. The finance manager will have final authority, as it is assumed that each of his decisions has the approval of the vice president of finance and, in turn, the president.

*General information:* The elapsed time from the start of the game to the end of play will consist of 20 years (the 20-year period will be broken down into *four decision-making periods* of five years each). Participants will make decisions regarding the purchase and/or sale of property at the beginning of each period. Each team will begin play with $100,000 in cash (credit with the central agency), and an additional $50,000 will be credited to their account in each of the remaining three periods.

The *sale of property* will be on a *closed-bid basis* with the sale being made to the highest bidder. Information available to the teams concerning each property will be similar to that shown in Exhibit I.

It will be up to each team to determine the *rate of return* that they expect to realize on their investment. With information

EXHIBIT I. PROPERTY INFORMATION FORM

All income is based on 100% occupancy.

G. I.   = Gross income
N. I    = Net income
Ins.    = Insurance
O. Exp. = All other expenses including depreciation.
V. F.   = Estimated vacancy factor
(All figures are yearly values)

| PROPERTY I | | |
|---|---|---|
| G. I. | | $10,000 |
| Taxes | $1300 | |
| Ins. | 700 | |
| O. Exp. | 3000 | 5,000 |
| N.I. before V.F. | | $ 5,000 |
| V.F. (10%) | | 500 |
| True N.I. | | $ 4,500 |

similar to that shown in Exhibit I, it will then be the responsibility of each team to determine the value of each property to enable them to make realistic bids.

*Outlook:* Land values in Parker County have increased on the average of about 5% per year over the past decade. A general consensus of the economic forecast for the next twenty years is presented in Exhibit II.

*Rules:*

1. *Financial obligations.* All financial obligations must be kept current. Inability to pay will result in a penalty of $10,000.

2. *Purchase and sale.* Purchase and sale of property will be handled *only* through the administering central agency. No sales or purchases between teams are possible. The central agency will post at the end of each period the *fair market value* at which

EXHIBIT II. ECONOMIC FORECAST

A.   CHANGE IN G.N.P. (base 1967)

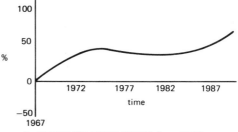

B. CONSUMER PRICE INDEX (base 1967)

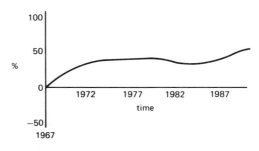

it will purchase outstanding properties. A team may not own more than two properties at any one time. A team, if it desires, may carry a maximum of one property from period to period. Teams without a property will be assigned a property for purchase at a price determined by the central agency.

3. *Limitations on bidding.*
(a) Bids are to be made in units of $1000 only for ease of computation.
(b) In addition, a team may only bid up to its maximum capitalization amount.
(c) A team may not bid an amount that would return greater than 20% on its money, i.e., 20% return is the maximum amount a team may bid on a property.

4. *Purchase plans.* Two purchase plans are available: (a) all cash or (b) one-third down with a mortgage. Only a 20-year, 6% mortgage will be available, with balance due and payable in full at time of sale or end-of-game. Annual payments at 6% in-

# MANAGEMENT DECISION SIMULATIONS

## EXHIBIT III. BID AND SALE SHEETS

Team

| BID SHEET |
|---|
| Team No. _____ Period _____ |
| Property _____ |
| Bid _____ |
| Financing Plan: |
| Cash _____ |
| Mortgage _____ |

| BID SHEET |
|---|
| Team No. _____ Period _____ |
| Property _____ |
| Bid _____ |
| Financing Plan: |
| Cash _____ |
| Mortgage _____ |

| NOTICE OF SALE |
|---|
| Team No. _____ Period _____ |
| Property _____ |
| Current Market Value _____ |

| NOTICE OF SALE |
|---|
| Team No. _____ Period _____ |
| Property _____ |
| Current Market Value _____ |

terest amortized over 20 years amounts to $87 per year per $1000 borrowed. Funds not invested will earn 5% interest compounded annually.

5. *Property.* All property is assumed to be new and rented at the beginning of play. Buildings have an average useful life of about 50 years, and the beginning land value amounts to about 25% of the property value.

6. *Bidding forms.* Bidding forms for the purchase of property, shown in Exhibit III, are to be turned in at the beginning of each period. *Sales forms,* also shown in Exhibit III, are to be turned in where applicable at the end of each period.

7. *Master form.* A master form showing the running current status of each team is shown in Exhibit IV. Each team will be responsible for keeping this master form up to date, although a similar record will also be kept by the central agency so that no misunderstandings will develop. These forms

will be used to tally the final scores at the game's end.

*Tables:* Present value tables for several interest rates are given at the end of this paper and may prove useful during the game. A 5% *compound interest table* and a 6% *mortgage table* are also given.

*Note of caution:* Conditions may very well change during the course of the game, but no more so than you might expect in real life. Don't get in over your head. Taxes do rise. Maintenance will increase. Uncollectable rents can be a problem. Percentage of vacancies do vary.

The game is not intended to be wild. Rather, it is intended to be meaningful. Unlike what many people think, professionally approached real estate investment is complicated yet fascinating, and extremely rewarding.

EXHIBIT IV. COMBINED INCOME AND CONTROL FORM

|  | Period I | Period II | Period III |
|---|---|---|---|
| 1. Beginning cash | $_____ | $_____ | $_____ |
| 2. Properties purchased<br>#_____ #_____ | $____ $____ | $____ $____ | $____ $____ |
| 3. Down payment—(2) or<br>1/3 of (2) if mortgaged | ____ ____ | ____ ____ | ____ ____ |
| 4. Mortgages (if any)<br>(2) − (3) | ____ ____ | ____ ____ | ____ ____ |
| 5. Cash balance—(1) − sum of<br>prop. just purchased—<br>line (3) | ____ | ____ | ____ |
| 6. Cash + interest (5 years)<br>(5) × 1.28 | ____ | ____ | ____ |
| 7. Gross income less V.F.<br>(from Exhibit I) | ____ ____ | ____ ____ | ____ ____ |
| 8. Mortgage payments—<br>$87/$1000 | ____ ____ | ____ ____ | ____ ____ |
| 9. All other expenses<br>(from Exhibit I) | ____ ____ | ____ ____ | ____ ____ |
| 10. Net income<br>(7) − (8) + (9) | ____ ____ | ____ ____ | ____ ____ |
| 11. Penalty ($10,000 for<br>insufficient cash) | ____ | ____ | ____ |
| 12. Mortgage balance<br>    Time held for:<br>    (.845) Per. I<br>(4) × (.640) Per. II<br>    (.366) Per. III<br>    (0.00) Per. IV | ____ ____ | ____ ____ | ____ ____ |
| 13. Cash received on sale<br>Sale price − (12) | ____ ____ | ____ ____ | ____ ____ |
| 14. Total cash<br>(6) + (10) + (13) − (11) | ____ | ____ | ____ |
| 15. Equity in property<br>(2) − (12) if unsold | ____ | ____ | ____ |
| 16. Net worth—(14) + (15) | ____ | ____ | ____ |

Transfer (14) to (1) and for property unsold; (12) to (4), (8) to (8), (7) to (7), and (9) to (9).

MANAGEMENT DECISION SIMULATIONS

PROPERTY LIST                                                    Schedule **E**

*Period 1*

NOTE: Referee's copy for property inventory and disposition.

| PROPERTY 17 | | DISPOSITION | PROPERTY 21 | | DISPOSITION |
|---|---|---|---|---|---|
| G.I. | $37,440 | I _____ | G.I. | $17,600 | I _____ |
| OP. EXP. | 14,976 | II _____ | OP. EXP. | 7,040 | II _____ |
| N.I. before V.F. | $22,464 | III _____ | N.I. before V.F. | $10,560 | III _____ |
| V.F. _____% | _____ | IV _____ | V.F. _____% | _____ | IV _____ |
| True N.I. | _____ | | True N.I. | _____ | |

| PROPERTY 29 | | DISPOSITION | PROPERTY 47 | | DISPOSITION |
|---|---|---|---|---|---|
| G.I. | $ 3,360 | I _____ | G.I. | $ 5,280 | I _____ |
| OP. EXP. | 1,344 | II _____ | OP. EXP. | 2,112 | II _____ |
| N.I. before V.F. | $ 2,016 | III _____ | N.I. before V.F. | $ 3,168 | III _____ |
| V.F. _____% | _____ | IV _____ | V.F. _____% | _____ | IV _____ |
| True N.I. | _____ | | True N.I. | _____ | |

| PROPERTY 6 | | DISPOSITION | PROPERTY 31 | | DISPOSITION |
|---|---|---|---|---|---|
| G.I. | $ 3,840 | I _____ | G.I. | $ 4,960 | I _____ |
| OP. EXP. | 1,536 | II _____ | OP. EXP. | 1,984 | II _____ |
| N.I. before V.F. | $ 2,304 | III _____ | N.I. before V.F. | $ 2,976 | III _____ |
| V.F. _____% | _____ | IV _____ | V.F. _____% | _____ | IV _____ |
| True N.I. | _____ | | True N.I. | _____ | |

| PROPERTY 39 | | DISPOSITION | PROPERTY 16 | | DISPOSITION |
|---|---|---|---|---|---|
| G.I. | $21,440 | I _____ | G.I. | $ 4,160 | I _____ |
| OP. EXP. | 8,576 | II _____ | OP. EXP. | 1,664 | II _____ |
| N.I. before V.F. | $12,864 | III _____ | N.I. before V.F. | $ 2,496 | III _____ |
| V.F. _____% | _____ | IV _____ | V.F. _____% | _____ | IV _____ |
| True N.I. | _____ | | True N.I. | _____ | |

| PROPERTY 1 | | DISPOSITION | PROPERTY 4 | | DISPOSITION |
|---|---|---|---|---|---|
| G.I. | $13,600 | I _____ | G.I. | $ 7,680 | I _____ |
| OP. EXP. | 5,440 | II _____ | OP. EXP. | 3,072 | II _____ |
| N.I. before V.F. | $ 8,160 | III _____ | N.I. before V.F. | $ 4,608 | III _____ |
| V.F. _____% | _____ | IV _____ | V.F. _____% | _____ | IV _____ |
| True N.I. | _____ | | True N.I. | _____ | |

| PROPERTY 23 | | DISPOSITION | PROPERTY 37 | | DISPOSITION |
|---|---|---|---|---|---|
| G.I. | $22,400 | I _____ | G.I. | $ 8,320 | I _____ |
| OP. EXP. | 8,960 | II _____ | OP. EXP. | 3,328 | II _____ |
| N.I. before V.F. | $13,440 | III _____ | N.I. before V.F. | $ 4,992 | III _____ |
| V.F. _____% | _____ | IV _____ | V.F. _____% | _____ | IV _____ |
| True N.I. | _____ | | True N.I. | _____ | |

PROPERTY LIST                                                      Schedule F

*Period II*

NOTE:  Referee's copy for property inventory and disposition.

| PROPERTY 5 | | DISPOSITION | | PROPERTY 48 | | DISPOSITION | |
|---|---|---|---|---|---|---|---|
| G.I. | $28,960 | I | | G.I. | $11,680 | I | |
| OP. EXP. | 11,584 | II | | OP. EXP. | 4,672 | II | |
| N.I. before V.F. | $17,376 | III | | N.I. before V.F. | $ 7,008 | III | |
| V.F. _____% | | IV | | V.F. _____% | | IV | |
| True N.I. | | | | True N.I. | | | |

| PROPERTY 9 | | DISPOSITION | | PROPERTY 24 | | DISPOSITION | |
|---|---|---|---|---|---|---|---|
| G.I. | $19,680 | I | | G.I. | $33,600 | I | |
| OP. EXP. | 7,872 | II | | OP. EXP. | 13,440 | II | |
| N.I. before V.F. | $11,808 | III | | N.I. before V.F. | $20,160 | III | |
| V.F. _____% | | IV | | V.F. _____% | | IV | |
| True N.I. | | | | True N.I. | | | |

| PROPERTY 45 | | DISPOSITION | | PROPERTY 33 | | DISPOSITION | |
|---|---|---|---|---|---|---|---|
| G.I. | $34,880 | I | | G.I. | $ 6,400 | I | |
| OP. EXP. | 13,952 | II | | OP. EXP. | 2,560 | II | |
| N.I. before V.F. | $20,928 | III | | N.I. before V.F. | $ 3,840 | III | |
| V.F. _____% | | IV | | V.F. _____% | | IV | |
| True N.I. | | | | True N.I. | | | |

| PROPERTY 43 | | DISPOSITION | | PROPERTY 40 | | DISPOSITION | |
|---|---|---|---|---|---|---|---|
| G.I. | $14,480 | I | | G.I. | $19,200 | I | |
| OP. EXP. | 5,792 | II | | OP. EXP. | 7,680 | II | |
| N.I. before V.F. | $ 8,688 | III | | N.I. before V.F. | $11,520 | III | |
| V.F. _____% | | IV | | V.F. _____% | | IV | |
| True N.I. | | | | True N.I. | | | |

| PROPERTY 41 | | DISPOSITION | | PROPERTY 27 | | DISPOSITION | |
|---|---|---|---|---|---|---|---|
| G.I. | $18,240 | I | | G.I. | $ 5,920 | I | |
| OP. EXP. | 7,296 | II | | OP. EXP. | 2,368 | II | |
| N.I. before V.F. | $10,944 | III | | N.I. before V.F. | $ 3,552 | III | |
| V.F. _____% | | IV | | V.F. _____% | | IV | |
| True N.I. | | | | True N.I. | | | |

| PROPERTY 2 | | DISPOSITION | | PROPERTY 25 | | DISPOSITION | |
|---|---|---|---|---|---|---|---|
| G.I. | $16,640 | I | | G.I. | $20,640 | I | |
| OP. EXP. | 6,656 | II | | OP. EXP. | 8,256 | II | |
| N.I. before V.F. | $ 9,984 | III | | N.I. before V.F. | $12,384 | III | |
| V.F. _____% | | IV | | V.F. _____% | | IV | |
| True N.I. | | | | True N.I. | | | |

MANAGEMENT DECISION SIMULATIONS

**PROPERTY LIST**                                                    Schedule G

*Period III*

NOTE:   Referee's copy for property inventory and disposition.

| PROPERTY 7 | | DISPOSITION | | PROPERTY 12 | | DISPOSITION |
|---|---|---|---|---|---|---|
| G.I. | $15,200 | I | | G.I. | $32,000 | I |
| OP. EXP. | 6,080 | II | | OP. EXP. | 12,800 | II |
| N.I. before V.F. | $ 9,120 | III | | N.I. before V.F. | $19,200 | III |
| V.F. _____% | | IV | | V.F. _____% | | IV |
| True N.I. | | | | True N.I. | | |

| PROPERTY 32 | | DISPOSITION | | PROPERTY 8 | | DISPOSITION |
|---|---|---|---|---|---|---|
| G.I. | $12,480 | I | | G.I. | $26,560 | I |
| OP. EXP. | 4,992 | II | | OP. EXP. | 10,624 | II |
| N.I. before V.F. | $ 7,488 | III | | N.I. before V.F. | $15,936 | III |
| V.F. _____% | | IV | | V.F. _____% | | IV |
| True N.I. | | | | True N.I. | | |

| PROPERTY 42 | | DISPOSITION | | PROPERTY 36 | | DISPOSITION |
|---|---|---|---|---|---|---|
| G.I. | $14,880 | I | | G.I. | $27,200 | I |
| OP. EXP. | 5,952 | II | | OP. EXP. | 10,880 | II |
| N.I. before V.F. | $ 8,928 | III | | N.I. before V.F. | $16,320 | III |
| V.F. _____% | | IV | | V.F. _____% | | IV |
| True N.I. | | | | True N.I. | | |

| PROPERTY 30 | | DISPOSITION | | PROPERTY 14 | | DISPOSITION |
|---|---|---|---|---|---|---|
| G.I. | $ 9,600 | I | | G.I. | $29,920 | I |
| OP. EXP. | 3,840 | II | | OP. EXP. | 11,968 | II |
| N.I. before V.F. | $ 5,760 | III | | N.I. before V.F. | $17,952 | III |
| V.F. _____% | | IV | | V.F. _____% | | IV |
| True N.I. | | | | True N.I. | | |

| PROPERTY 10 | | DISPOSITION | | PROPERTY 15 | | DISPOSITION |
|---|---|---|---|---|---|---|
| G.I. | $23,680 | I | | G.I. | $13,120 | I |
| OP. EXP. | 9,472 | II | | OP. EXP. | 5,248 | II |
| N.I. before V.F. | $14,208 | III | | N.I. before V.F. | $ 7,872 | III |
| V.F. _____% | | IV | | V.F. _____% | | IV |
| True N.I. | | | | True N.I. | | |

| PROPERTY 13 | | DISPOSITION | | PROPERTY 26 | | DISPOSITION |
|---|---|---|---|---|---|---|
| G.I. | $23,200 | I | | G.I. | $11,200 | I |
| OP. EXP. | 9,280 | II | | OP. EXP. | 4,480 | II |
| N.I. before V.F. | $13,920 | III | | N.I. before V.F. | $ 6,720 | III |
| V.F. _____% | | IV | | V.F. _____% | | IV |
| True N.I. | | | | True N.I. | | |

PROPERTY LIST                                    Schedule H

*Period IV*

NOTE:   Referee's copy for property inventory and disposition.

| PROPERTY 19 | | DISPOSITION | PROPERTY 11 | | DISPOSITION |
|---|---|---|---|---|---|
| G.I. | $16,000 | I _____ | G.I. | $ 8,800 | I _____ |
| OP. EXP. | 6,400 | II _____ | OP. EXP. | 3,520 | II _____ |
| N.I. before V.F. | $ 9,600 | III _____ | N.I. before V.F. | $ 5,280 | III _____ |
| V.F. _____% | _____ | IV _____ | V.F. _____% | _____ | IV _____ |
| True N.I. | _____ | | True N.I. | _____ | |

| PROPERTY 18 | | DISPOSITION | PROPERTY 28 | | DISPOSITION |
|---|---|---|---|---|---|
| G.I. | $ 9,120 | I _____ | G.I. | $10,040 | I _____ |
| OP. EXP. | 3,648 | II _____ | OP. EXP. | 4,016 | II _____ |
| N.I. before V.F. | $ 5,472 | III _____ | N.I. before V.F. | $ 6,024 | III _____ |
| V.F. _____% | _____ | IV _____ | V.F. _____% | _____ | IV _____ |
| True N.I. | _____ | | True N.I. | _____ | |

| PROPERTY 46 | | DISPOSITION | PROPERTY 35 | | DISPOSITION |
|---|---|---|---|---|---|
| G.I. | $30,880 | I _____ | G.I. | $ 2,880 | I _____ |
| OP. EXP. | 12,352 | II _____ | OP. EXP. | 1,152 | II _____ |
| N.I. before V.F. | $18,528 | III _____ | N.I. before V.F. | $ 1,728 | III _____ |
| V.F. _____% | _____ | IV _____ | V.F. _____% | _____ | IV _____ |
| True N.I. | _____ | | True N.I. | _____ | |

| PROPERTY 34 | | DISPOSITION | PROPERTY 38 | | DISPOSITION |
|---|---|---|---|---|---|
| G.I. | $ 6,720 | I _____ | G.I. | $27,840 | I _____ |
| OP. EXP. | 2,688 | II _____ | OP. EXP. | 11,136 | II _____ |
| N.I. before V.F. | $ 4,032 | III _____ | N.I. before V.F. | $16,704 | III _____ |
| V.F. _____% | _____ | IV _____ | V.F. _____% | _____ | IV _____ |
| True N.I. | _____ | | True N.I. | _____ | |

| PROPERTY 3 | | DISPOSITION | PROPERTY 22 | | DISPOSITION |
|---|---|---|---|---|---|
| G.I. | $24,640 | I _____ | G.I. | $ 7,200 | I _____ |
| OP. EXP. | 9,856 | II _____ | OP. EXP. | 2,880 | II _____ |
| N.I. before V.F. | $14,784 | III _____ | N.I. before V.F. | $ 4,320 | III _____ |
| V.F. _____% | _____ | IV _____ | V.F. _____% | _____ | IV _____ |
| True N.I. | _____ | | True N.I. | _____ | |

| PROPERTY 44 | | DISPOSITION | PROPERTY 20 | | DISPOSITION |
|---|---|---|---|---|---|
| G.I. | $10,560 | I _____ | G.I. | $25,600 | I _____ |
| OP. EXP. | 4,224 | II _____ | OP. EXP. | 10,240 | II _____ |
| N.I. before V.F. | $ 6,336 | III _____ | N.I. before V.F. | $15,360 | III _____ |
| V.F. _____% | _____ | IV _____ | V.F. _____% | _____ | IV _____ |
| True N.I. | _____ | | True N.I. | _____ | |

MANAGEMENT DECISION SIMULATIONS

# Logistics

## (9) AZTEC TRUCKING COMPANY

*Introduction*    The Aztec Trucking Company game is designed to familiarize the participant with some aspects of marketing logistics. The simulation requires the participants to coordinate a fleet of trucks, competitively selling and delivering a product in various cities within a time constraint. The objective is to maximize profits by employing strategies and tactics that minimize transportation costs yet obtain maximum product price. The game requires the participant to relate such variables as market potential, selling price, time, distance, and cost and to formulate a distribution strategy based on the above variables. One aspect of the game that adds to its realism lies in the fact that the success or failure of a team's strategy will depend on the strategy selected by the competing teams. In addition, the selling price within a given market will vary depending on supply to that market, which is also a function of the various team strategies.

Specifically, the purpose of the game is to distribute the team's truckload of avocados in any of eleven cited cities across the continental United States trying to obtain the best possible price for each case of avocados sold.

EXHIBIT 1.  PRELIMINARY BRIEFING

"RECORD AVOCADO CROP COMING TO MARKET"

A record crop of avocados—the exotic fruit of the Aztecs—is now coming on the market with fruit of high quality at very reasonable prices, according to the California Dept. of Agriculture's Crop and Livestock Reporting Service.

More than 92% of the nation's avocados are grown in seven Southern California coastal counties with most of the acreage in San Diego County, followed by Ventura, Santa Barbara, Orange, Los Angeles, Riverside and San Bernardino counties.

This year's production is estimated at 165,-000,000 pounds, more than twice last year's light crop.

*History*

One of the most romantic of all fruits, the avocado, or "ahuacatl" as it was called by the Aztecs, is often considered the New World's greatest gift to gastronomy, a service spokesman said. It is distinctive for its buttery texture and nutlike flavor which resemble those of no other fruit or vegetable.

Believed to have originated in Mexico, the

SOURCE: *Los Angeles Times*, December, 1968.

avocado spread to Peru and to the West Indies. When the Spanish explorer Hernando Cortez reached Mexico City in 1519, Montezuma II, Aztec emperor of the city, served him avocado and word of this unusual fruit spread to Europe.

As an early English admirer of the avocado expressed it in 1672, "It nourisheth and strengtheneth the body, corroborating the vital spirits, and procuring lust exceedingly."

Sailors of the old windjammer ships nicknamed the avocado "midshipmen's butter" when they ran across it in tropical ports.

The young George Washington, visiting the Barbados Islands in 1751, wrote that "agovago pears" were abundant and popular there.

One of the early American admirers of the avocado was the journalist Richard Harding Davis, who discovered it in Venezuela in the 1890s. Davis gave some of the fruit to his New York restaurateur friend Charles Delmonico, who ordered a regular supply and included them on his expensive menus.

The first known successful planting of avocados in California was by R. B. Ord at Santa Barbara, in 1871.

In 1911, Carl Schmidt, a nurseryman from

Altadena, was sent to Mexico to find outstanding avocados and track them down to the trees from which they came.

### Growing Seasons

He found a promising one in Atlixco, and the budwood sent to California adapted itself so well that it survived the severe freeze of 1913. As a tribute to its hardiness, it was given the Spanish name Fuerte, meaning vigorous or strong.

Today, the Fuerte is the leading winter variety of California avocados, with its smooth, light green skin and large size, while the Hass with a darker pebbled skin is the leading summer variety.

Avocados are marketed the year around in California. They are not fattening, according to nutritionists. One half of a four-inch avocado contains only 139 calories. It contains no starch, very little sugar, is low in carbohydrates and high in protein, and contains 14 essential minerals and nine vitamins.

### Value

Best known as a salad fruit, the avocado can be served as Guacomole dip. It also may be served in sandwiches, soups, in ice cream and in beverages.

Today avocados are one of California's major specialty crops with an annual value to growers of $16,000,000. There are some 5000 avocado growers in the state, and the average size grove is approximately four acres. To bring customers a high quality product, growers continue to experiment with new varieties and with improved cultural techniques.

This year's crop is of high quality and the retail price is attractively low just now, dept. marketing experts said. Now during the holidays is a good time to try new uses for this versatile fruit. An avocado margarita, anyone?

*Background* (A briefing on the avocado market is given in Exhibit I.) Since an avocado has approximately one week

## EXHIBIT II

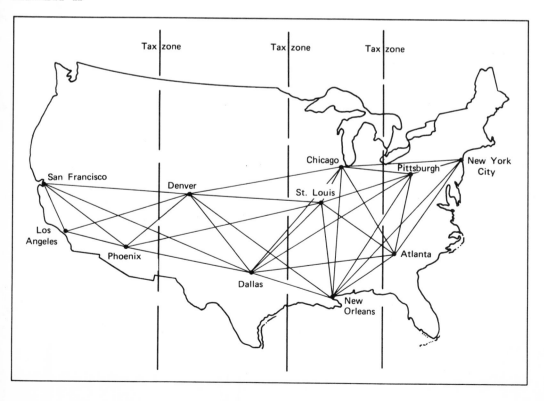

## MANAGEMENT DECISION SIMULATIONS

in which to ripen, each truck will be loaded with freshly picked avocados and your team will market these avocados on any day of six possible trading intervals. Each team will start in Los Angeles with an equal number of cases of avocados to be sold in whichever market (city) they choose out of the possible eleven selected markets. However, *on* and *only on* the sixth day (period of play) *each team must deliver sixty (60) cases of avocados in New York City* to meet a contract obligation for international shipment by air. *All trucks must be in New York City on the sixth day* to pick up cargo for shipment west.

The selling price is a function of the total avocados offered for sale in a city and the market potential in that city. The market potential is also governed by prior sales in the city.

### Objective

1. To achieve the highest net profit after six periods (days) of play.
2. To make teams aware of coordina-

tion needed for effective distribution of product.

3. To provide a dynamic environment in which a team must maintain a flexible decision-making policy due to impact of competition on demand and price.

### PLAYER'S INSTRUCTIONS

1. A team should consist of from 2 to 4 members. Each team will start in Los Angeles with trucks loaded with avocados. Each truck contains 120 cases and there is one truck for each team member. Each member should, therefore, also consider himself a driver. The Los Angeles market is to be excluded.

2. Each driver, on arriving at a city (<1250 miles from last stop), offers for sale some portion of his truck's cargo from 0 to 120 cases in multiples of ten cases. These are sold that night and the driver is free to travel to the next city or layover to sell more the next day.

3. Each team can only go to the 11 given cities and only on the preset routes. All other markets and routes are off limits.

4. Each truck may travel a maximum of 1250 miles per day to get to a city (one

### EXHIBIT III. MILEAGE CHART

| From | To L.A. | San Fran. | Phoenix | Denver | Dallas | Chi. | St. Lou. | New Orl. | Pitts. | Atla. | NYC |
|---|---|---|---|---|---|---|---|---|---|---|---|
| Los Angeles | ... | 400 | 400 | 1200 | 1400 | 2200 | 2050 | 1900 | ... | ... | ... |
| San Francisco | ... | ... | 800 | 1250 | 1750 | ... | ... | ... | ... | ... | ... |
| Phoenix | ... | 800 | ... | 800 | 1000 | ... | 1500 | ... | ... | ... | ... |
| Denver | ... | 1250 | 800 | ... | 800 | 1000 | 850 | 1250 | ... | ... | ... |
| Dallas | ... | 1750 | 1000 | 800 | ... | 950 | 650 | 500 | 1200 | 800 | ... |
| Chicago | ... | ... | ... | 1000 | 950 | ... | 300 | 950 | 450 | 700 | 850 |
| St. Louis | ... | ... | 1500 | 850 | 650 | 300 | ... | 700 | 600 | 550 | 950 |
| New Orleans | ... | ... | ... | 1250 | 500 | 950 | 700 | ... | 1100 | 500 | 1350 |
| Pittsburgh | ... | ... | ... | ... | 1200 | 450 | 600 | 1100 | ... | 700 | 400 |
| Atlanta | ... | ... | ... | ... | 800 | 700 | 550 | 500 | 700 | ... | 850 |
| New York City | ... | ... | ... | ... | ... | ... | ... | ... | ... | ... | ... |

REMINDER: Trucks can travel only 1250 miles a day (one play). In going to any city above that limit more than one day is required.
Truck travel from any city is restricted to only those cities for which mileage is given.

play). Once a truck is enroute to a city which is more than one day away (> 1250 miles) it must continue the following day to the same scheduled city. It is also possible to travel through cities without stopping if the distance is less than 1250 miles. For example, one may drive from St. Louis to New York City in one play even though you go right through Pittsburgh. *The deciding factor for traveling within one period of play is mileage.*

5. There is a fixed contract price to each team of $50/case for exactly *60 cases* in New York City. If a team arrives in New York with less than 60 cases, they default on the contract and must "dump" the cases at $10 per case. *Each team must have all its trucks in* New York on the sixth day even if the contract is defaulted. A fine of $500 will be charged for each absent truck.

6. If total sales in a given city are greater than its market potential, or if calculated price is less than $10, all cases will sell for $10 each.

7. Transportation Expenses are:
$0.20 per mile plus
$2.00 per case whenever a tax zone is crossed.

8. There is an additional charge (Layover Charge) of $75 per day, to be assessed each truck staying in the same city (including NYC) for more than one play.

9. Each driver is on an incentive that gives him a bonus of 10% of the net profit his truck earns. This is computed when he reaches New York City. Thus there is a winning team and a winning driver.

*Initial Market Potential*   The initial Market Potential is a function of a demand factor and the number of trucks utilized in a game. Thus, the demand factor can be assumed to be based on history, population, climate and ecological data. Thus, if the class is divided into *five* teams, each team having *three* trucks, the total market potential for each city would be determined by multiplying the demand factor by *fifteen*. A sample calculation of the Initial Market Potential for Dallas would be 80 × 15 = 1200 cases and for Chicago 60 × 15 = 900 cases.

The total trucks for this play is _____ teams × _____ trucks/team = _____ trucks ($T$).

| City | Demand Factor | × | Trucks ($T$) | = | Initial Market Potential ($M_b$) |
|---|---|---|---|---|---|
| San Francisco | 100 | × | _____ | = | _____ |
| Phoenix | 90 | × | _____ | = | _____ |
| Dallas | 80 | × | _____ | = | _____ |
| New Orleans | 85 | × | _____ | = | _____ |
| St. Louis | 60 | × | _____ | = | _____ |
| Denver | 70 | × | _____ | = | _____ |
| Chicago | 60 | × | _____ | = | _____ |
| Atlanta | 90 | × | _____ | = | _____ |
| Pittsburgh | 80 | × | _____ | = | _____ |
| New York City | 20 | × | _____ | = | _____ |

*Current market price*   The current market price in a city is a function of the initial period's price ($P_0 = \$50.00$) and the current market potential index. The model used is as follows:

$$P_i = P_o \left(1 - \left(\frac{S + C_i}{.5 M_o}\right)\right)$$ where $P_i$ is a city's market price today, $M_o$ is its original market potential, $S$ is cumulative sales to date, and $C_i$ is the quantity of cases sold that day (night). Enter the current price in Exhibit V. (The administrator is free to use any other pricing model such as simple $P_i = P_o - .10(S + C_i)$ etc.)

EXHIBIT IV.  ROUTE AND REVENUE RECORD

**Day 1**

Cases Carried _____

Route
Fr _____
To _____ (Offered for sale)

| | | | | |
|---|---|---|---|---|
| Operating Cost | = | $ .20/mile * _____ miles | = | $_____ |
| Toll Tax | = | $ 2.00/case * _____ cases | = | $_____ |
| Layover | = | $75.00/day * _____ days | = | $_____ |

_____ cases * _____ $/case ∴ $_____ = $_____
(Offered for sale) * (Selling price)   (Revenue)   (Total Exp.)

$_____
(Net Profit)

---

**Day 2**

Cases Carried _____

Route
Fr _____
To _____ (Offered for sale)

| | | | | |
|---|---|---|---|---|
| Operating Cost | = | $ .20/mile * _____ miles | = | $_____ |
| Toll Tax | = | $ 2.00/case * _____ cases | = | $_____ |
| Layover | = | $75.00/day * _____ days | = | $_____ |

_____ cases * _____ $/case ∴ $_____ = $_____
(Offered for sale) * (Selling price)   (Revenue)   (Total Exp.)

$_____
(Net Profit)

---

**Day 3**

Cases Carried _____

Route
Fr _____
To _____ (Offered for sale)

| | | | | |
|---|---|---|---|---|
| Operating Cost | = | $ .20/mile * _____ miles | = | $_____ |
| Toll Tax | = | $ 2.00/case * _____ cases | = | $_____ |
| Layover | = | $75.00/day * _____ days | = | $_____ |

_____ cases * _____ $/case ∴ $_____ = $_____
(Offered for sale) * (Selling price)   (Revenue)   (Total Exp.)

$_____
(Net Profit)

**Day 4**

Cases Carried ___

Route
Fr ___
To ___

___ cases
(Offered for sale)

Operating Cost = ___ miles * $ .20/mile = $ ___
Toll Tax = ___ cases * $ 2.00/case = $ ___
Layover = ___ days * $75.00/day = $ ___

___ $/case
* (Selling price)

∴ $ ___ − ___ = $ ___
(Revenue) (Total Exp.)

= $ ___
(Net Profit)

- - - - - - - - - - - - - - - - - - - - - - - - - - - - - - - - - -

**Day 5**

Cases Carried ___

Route
Fr ___
To ___

___ cases
(Offered for sale)

Operating Cost = ___ miles * $ .20/mile = $ ___
Toll Tax = ___ cases * $ 2.00/case = $ ___
Layover = ___ days * $75.00/day = $ ___

___ $/case
* (Selling price)

∴ $ ___ − ___ = $ ___
(Revenue) (Total Exp.)

= $ ___
(Net Profit)

- - - - - - - - - - - - - - - - - - - - - - - - - - - - - - - - - -

**Day 6**

Cases Carried ___

Route
Fr ___
To ___

___ cases
(Offered for sale)

Operating Cost = ___ miles * $ .20/mile = $ ___
Toll Tax = ___ cases * $ 2.00/case = $ ___
Layover = ___ days * $75.00/day = $ ___

___ $/case
* (Selling price)

∴ $ ___ − ___ = $ ___
(Revenue) (Total Exp.)

= $ ___
(Net Profit)

DRIVER'S BONUS (10%)

TOTAL PROFIT

MANAGEMENT DECISION SIMULATIONS

EXHIBIT V

| CITY | DAY 1 | | DAY 2 | | DAY 3 | | DAY 4 | | DAY 5 | |
|---|---|---|---|---|---|---|---|---|---|---|
| | $C_1$ | $P_1$ | $C_2$ | $P_2$ | $C_3$ | $P_3$ | $C_4$ | $P_4$ | $C_5$ | $P_5$ |
| San Francisco | | | | | | | | | | |
| Phoenix | | | | | | | | | | |
| Dallas | | | | | | | | | | |
| New Orleans | | | | | | | | | | |
| St. Louis | | | | | | | | | | |
| Denver | | | | | | | | | | |
| Chicago | | | | | | | | | | |
| Atlanta | | | | | | | | | | |
| Pittsburgh | | | | | | | | | | |
| New York City | | | | | | | | | | |

NOTE: There is no column for the sixth day because the price is constant at $50 per case in New York City (where all trucks should be on the sixth day) and each team may only sell the 60 cases as contracted.

## (10) HOLIDAY TREE COMPANY

*Introduction*    Holiday Tree Company is a management game requiring marketing and economic decisions. The purpose of this game is to work with and demonstrate linear programming and incremental analysis. The simplicity designed into the game play can only be realized by preparation. Participants should review linear programming material found in the Appendix.

Realism has not been sacrificed for simplicity, but the game has been abridged to fit within time constraints. The game can be played by five teams for three periods (15 calculation runs) in about two hours.

*Background*    The Holiday Tree Company is a proprietorship with limited capital. Its business consists of buying

Christmas trees in the tree-growing areas of the Western United States and shipping them to markets in five cities where they are retailed.

The operation consists of purchasing options for trees during the summer months at four tree-growing areas located in Washington, Oregon, northern California (Shasta), and central California (Tahoe). The markets consist of leased lots in the five following cities: Seattle, Portland, San Francisco, Los Angeles, and Phoenix. Freight charges per tree have been determined from each tree-growing area to each possible city and are related to the distance involved.

In this simulation, the trees will be purchased, shipped, and sold as "average trees." In reality the company might buy, ship, and sell at different prices based on the size and type of tree. Also, for simplicity, the purchase price, freight charge, and sales price have been preestablished and the participants cannot change these. (The sensitivity of these variables can be tested in subsequent variations of this game.)

The decision, therefore, consists of determining the quantity of trees to be purchased, cut, and shipped from each growing area to each market area and to ship these trees by the most economical transportation available to minimize the total transportation and other costs.

The following information is given for the first season of play. This same information is repeated in Schedule 1, which the participants complete in order to play the first season.

A. Number of trees available by location on which purchase options have been purchased. These purchase options (of $.10 per tree) do not have to be exercised.

B. Freight charges per tree:

| TO:<br>FROM: | Seattle | Portland | San Francisco | Los Angeles | Phoenix |
|---|---|---|---|---|---|
| Washington | $ .60 | $ .70 | $1.20 | $1.45 | $1.90 |
| Oregon | .80 | .60 | 1.10 | 1.15 | 1.80 |
| Shasta | 1.05 | .90 | .85 | 1.00 | 1.70 |
| Tahoe | 1.35 | 1.15 | .65 | .95 | 1.65 |

C. The fixed set-up cost (SU) of establishing retail tree lots is as follows:

| | |
|---|---|
| Seattle | $1000 |
| Portland | 600 |
| San Francisco | 1000 |
| Los Angeles | 1500 |
| Phoenix | 700 |

D. The variable selling cost (SC) for each tree is determined by the number of trees delivered to each market multiplied by the following factors:

| | |
|---|---|
| Seattle | $.25 |
| Portland | .25 |
| San Francisco | .28 |
| Los Angeles | .30 |
| Phoenix | .30 |

E. The sales price (SP) at each location is initially established as follows:

| | |
|---|---|
| Seattle | $3.25 |
| Portland | 3.00 |
| San Francisco | 4.00 |
| Los Angeles | 5.00 |
| Phoenix | 6.00 |

F. The total cash expenditure budget is initially $29,000.

G. The demand by city is given in ten percent (10%) probability ranges (see Schedule 1).

H. The cost of the purchase option is ten cents ($.10) per tree.

I. The additional cost of cutting and processing each tree ordered is sixty-five cents ($.65). Thus, the total purchase price of a tree is $.75 and any unused options cost you $.10 each.

The above items will be given on additional schedules for each subsequent season. The amounts of some of the items will be changed from season to season.

Since the demand is stated as a probability, it will be determined by a Monte

## MANAGEMENT DECISION SIMULATIONS

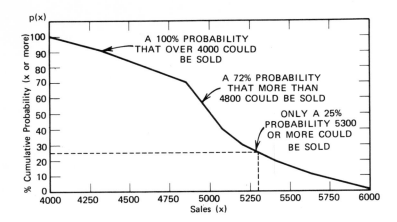

Carlo selection. The actual demand at each location will be announced after the teams have completed the matrix showing their shipment allocations.

Highest profit is the scoring objective. Unit sales in each city is either the number of trees delivered or the Monte Carlo generated demand, *whichever is less.*

The Christmas-tree market is highly speculative and dominated by small operators. Therefore, credit is extremely difficult to obtain and the initial cash budget must provide the funds to purchase options and trees, cover set-up costs in all five cities, and pay all transportation costs. If the cash budget is exceeded by the shipping allocation proposed, the shipments will be reduced until costs are within the budget. If this occurs, the trees that cannot be shipped were still cut and must be purchased and are therefore considered losses.

*Player instructions*

1. Forecast expected demand in each of the market areas and record on the transportation matrix.

2. Allocate available trees to specific market areas by filling in the matrix and then optimize this allocation by any known method. (See the Appendix.)

3. Compute all costs including purchases and your purchase options and compare with your capital resource limit. In the computer-scored version this is automatically calculated and small penalties are assigned for overexpenditure.

4. After actual demands are provided by the administrator, compute net profit. In the computer-scored version this is automatically computed and the results are printed out.

OPERATING RESULTS FOR TEAM # 1

TREES SOLD:

|  | UNITS | REVENUE |
|---|---|---|
| SEATTLE | 5215 | $18252.5 |
| PORTLAND | 2925 | 8043.7 |
| SAN FRANCISCO | 1900 | 9500.0 |
| LOS ANGELES | 3000 | 20250.0 |
| PHOENIX | 1000 | 6250.0 |
| TOTAL REVENUE |  | 62296.2 |

| COSTS: | |
|---|---|
| TREES PURCHASED | $12000.00 |
| EXPIRED OPTIONS | -50.00 |
| SET UP COST | 5600.00 |
| SELLING EXPENSE | 4350.00 |
| TRANSPORTATION | 12685.00 |
| TOTAL COSTS | 34585.00 |

MANAGEMENT DECISION GAMES

SCHEDULE 1

PERIOD 1   Team

| Tree farms \ Markets | Seattle | Portland | San Francisco | Los Angeles | Phoenix | Trees available for purchase options |
|---|---|---|---|---|---|---|
| Washington | .60 | .70 | 1.20 | 1.45 | 1.90 | 2,000 |
| Oregon | .80 | .60 | 1.10 | 1.15 | 1.80 | 8,500 |
| Shasta | 1.05 | .90 | .85 | 1.00 | 1.70 | 3,000 |
| Tahoe | 1.35 | 1.15 | .65 | .95 | 1.65 | 1,500 |
| Deliveries | | | | | | 15,000 |

Budget ............................................................ $29,000

Cost per tree (including $.10 option cost) ............... $  .75

| | Seattle | Portland | San Francisco | Los Angeles | Phoenix |
|---|---|---|---|---|---|
| Sales price (SP) | $3.25 | $3.00 | $4.00 | $5.00 | $6.00 |
| Set up (SU) | 1000 | 600 | 1000 | 1500 | 700 |
| Selling cost (SC) | .25 | .25 | .28 | .30 | .30 |

| Projected demand (10% ranges) | | | | | |
|---|---|---|---|---|---|
| <4350 | <2350 | <1725 | <3000 | <890 |
| 4600 | 2600 | 1850 | 3500 | 940 |
| 4800 | 2800 | 1950 | 3800 | 980 |
| 4925 | 2925 | 1975 | 3900 | 990 |
| 5000 | 3000 | 2000 | 4000 | 1000 |
| 5075 | 3075 | 2050 | 4200 | 1030 |
| 5200 | 3200 | 2100 | 4400 | 1060 |
| 5400 | 3400 | 2175 | 4700 | 1090 |
| 5650 | 3650 | 2275 | 5000 | 1120 |
| 6000 | 4000 | 2400 | 5500 | 1200 |

| E = | 5000 | 3000 | 2000 | 4000 | 1000 |

MANAGEMENT DECISION SIMULATIONS

SCHEDULE 2

PERIOD 2   Team

| Tree farms \ Markets | Seattle | Portland | San Francisco | Los Angeles | Phoenix | Trees available for purchase options |
|---|---|---|---|---|---|---|
| Washington | .60 | .70 | 1.25 | 1.50 | 1.95 | 2,000 |
| Oregon | .80 | .60 | 1.15 | 1.20 | 1.85 | 8,000 |
| Shasta | 1.10 | .95 | .85 | 1.00 | 1.75 | 3,200 |
| Tahoe | 1.40 | 1.20 | .65 | .95 | 1.70 | 1,800 |
| Deliveries | | | | | | 15,000 |

Budget      $29,500

Cost per tree
   (including $.10      $ .75
   option cost)

| | Seattle | Portland | San Francisco | Los Angeles | Phoenix |
|---|---|---|---|---|---|
| Sales price (SP) | $3.25 | $3.00 | $4.50 | $6.00 | $6.00 |
| Set up (SU) | 1000 | 600 | 1200 | 1800 | 700 |
| Selling cost (SC) | .25 | .25 | .30 | .35 | .30 |

| Projected demand (10% ranges) | | | | | |
|---|---|---|---|---|---|
| <4350 | <2400 | <1600 | <2400 | <990 |
| 4600 | 2600 | 1800 | 3000 | 1040 |
| 4800 | 2800 | 1900 | 3500 | 1080 |
| 4925 | 2925 | 1950 | 3900 | 1090 |
| 5000 | 3000 | 2000 | 4000 | 1100 |
| 5075 | 3075 | 2050 | 4200 | 1130 |
| 5200 | 3200 | 2100 | 4400 | 1160 |
| 5400 | 3400 | 2200 | 4700 | 1190 |
| 5650 | 3600 | 2300 | 5100 | 1220 |
| 6000 | 3800 | 2400 | 5600 | 1300 |

| E = | 5000 | 3000 | 1970 | 3875 | 1100 |
|---|---|---|---|---|---|

SCHEDULE 3

PERIOD 3

| Markets / Tree farms | Seattle | Portland | San Francisco | Los Angeles | Phoenix | Trees available |
|---|---|---|---|---|---|---|
| Washington | .65 | .75 | 1.25 | 1.50 | 1.95 | 2,000 |
| Oregon | .85 | .65 | 1.15 | 1.20 | 1.85 | 8,000 |
| Shasta | 1.10 | .95 | .90 | 1.05 | 1.75 | 3,000 |
| Tahoe | 1.40 | 1.20 | .70 | 1.00 | 1.30 | 1,500 |
| | | | | | | 14,500 |
| Deliveries | | | | | | |

Budget      $31,000

Cost per tree (including $.10 option cost)      .80

| | Seattle | Portland | San Francisco | Los Angeles | Phoenix |
|---|---|---|---|---|---|
| Sales price (SP) | $3.50 | $2.75 | $5.00 | $6.75 | $6.25 |
| Set up (SU) | 1,200 | 600 | 1,400 | 2,100 | 800 |
| Selling cost (SC) | .28 | .25 | .35 | .40 | .32 |

| Projected demand (10% ranges) | <4550 | <2400 | <1900 | <2900 | <990 |
|---|---|---|---|---|---|
| | 4800 | 2600 | 2100 | 3500 | 1040 |
| | 5000 | 2800 | 2200 | 4000 | 1080 |
| | 5125 | 2925 | 2250 | 4400 | 1090 |
| | 5200 | 3000 | 2300 | 4500 | 1100 |
| | 5275 | 3075 | 2350 | 4700 | 1130 |
| | 5400 | 3200 | 2400 | 4900 | 1160 |
| | 5600 | 3400 | 2500 | 5200 | 1190 |
| | 5850 | 3600 | 2600 | 5600 | 1220 |
| | 6200 | 3800 | 2700 | 6100 | 1300 |
| E = | 5200 | 3000 | 2270 | 4375 | 1100 |

## MANAGEMENT DECISION SIMULATIONS

### (11) DORN CORPORATION

A SPARES ALLOCATION STRATEGY GAME

*Introduction* Determination of optimal policies for stockpiling of spare parts has significant economic importance for many industries. The products developed by some companies are used in a variety of activities at geographically dispersed locations and in various stages of the product's life. Providing spare parts at the proper locations can mean significant savings, especially where contracts include schedule delay penalties.

If a limited number of spares are available at any one time, many variables must be considered in determining optimum allocation of these spares. These variables include the probability of failure at each site, shipping, warehousing, replacement, and repair costs. This simulation is designed to heighten the awareness of the interaction of the variables that must be considered in deciding a spare-parts allocation strategy.

*Background* The Rocket Development Division of Dorn Corporation is reviewing a particular logistics problem.

This division produces large rocket engines. These engines are shipped to facilities in California, Louisiana, Mississippi, and Florida. Activities at the various sites are explained in Exhibit I.

The division president has expressed concern over the excessive cost to the division of supplying replacement parts to field sites when failures occur. At present, a spare-parts inventory is kept only at the Coppel Facility. When a failure occurs at any other site, a replacement part must be sent from the Coppel Facility to the field site. This often results in heavy penalties because of failure to meet government schedule requirements.

*Objective and procedure* The objective of this game is to minimize the total costs caused by component failures at each of the five site locations shown in Exhibit I. The probabilities of component failures at each site are given in Exhibit II. The spares available at the beginning of play are all located at Site 1 and are listed in Column "M" of Form 1, the Site Inventory.

Each team of 3 to 4 participants is to distribute the components to the sites in order to minimize the total expected cost. The shipping and warehousing costs are shown in Exhibit III and are to be used

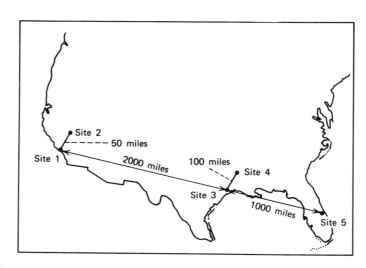

Exhibit I

to calculate the cost of the allocations.

After the allocations or reallocations have been made, random failures will be generated using the probabilities shown in Exhibit II. Costs incurred by responding to these failures are computed and recorded on Form 2. The cost data are given in Exhibits III and IV.

When an item fails, the choice is as follows:

1. Repair the item on site (charge site with repair cost and delays for repair and installation) or

2. Replace the item with a spare (charge site with cost of spare, shipping cost, if not at site, and delay days for shipping from another site plus installation days). The failed part may be discarded or repaired (add repair cost) and put into spares inventory at site. It may not be stored unless it is first repaired.

The decision cycle can be repeated for as many periods as time will allow. The cumulative costs summary will reveal the "winner." The rationale of the winner should be explored in postgame discussion.

TEAM

PERIOD 1

## SPARES ALLOCATION OR REALLOCATION

(Time Allowed 30 Minutes)

The spares listed in Column M are available at Site 1. Within the time allowed determine where to store these items. If items are to be stored at other sites, determine shipping costs to these sites. There are no time-delay penalties during this period. Assume stored items will remain in warehouse for entire period to determine warehouse costs. At the beginning of each period a new supply of components will be made available at Site 1.

| | Component Name | M | No. of Components Stored at Sites: | | | | | Warehousing Costs | Shipping Costs |
|---|---|---|---|---|---|---|---|---|---|
| | | | 1 | 2 | 3 | 4 | 5 | | |
| A | Thrust Chamber | 1 | | | | | | | |
| B | Turbopump | 1 | | | | | | | |
| C | Gas Generator | 4 | | | | | | | |
| D | Oxidizer Valve | 4 | | | | | | | |
| E | Fuel Valve | 4 | | | | | | | |
| F | Heat Exchanger | 2 | | | | | | | |
| G | High Pressure Duct | 2 | | | | | | | |
| H | Injector | 1 | | | | | | | |
| | Totals | $ | | + | $ | | = | | $ |

MANAGEMENT DECISION SIMULATIONS

EXHIBIT II. PROBABILITY OF FAILURE

| | | | Probability of Failure at Site | | | | |
|---|---|---|---|---|---|---|---|
| Qty | | Component | 1 | 2 | 3 | 4 | 5 |
| (1) | A | *Thrust chamber* | | | | | |
| | | A1 failure mode 1 | .1 | .4 | .1 | .2 | .1 |
| | | A2 failure mode 2 | .0 | .05 | .0 | .05 | .0 |
| (1) | B | *Turbopump* | | | | | |
| | | B1 failure mode 1 | .1 | .1 | .2 | .2 | .1 |
| | | B2 failure mode 2 | .0 | .1 | .1 | .1 | .1 |
| (4) | C | *Gas generator* | .4 | .1 | .2 | .1 | .2 |
| (4) | D | *Oxidizer valve* | .4 | .1 | .2 | .1 | .2 |
| (4) | E | *Fuel valve* | .4 | .1 | .2 | .1 | .2 |
| (2) | F | *Heat exchanger* | .1 | .1 | .1 | .1 | .1 |
| (2) | G | *High pressure duct* | .2 | .1 | .1 | .1 | .1 |
| (1) | H | *Injector* | | | | | |
| | | H1 failure mode 1 | .1 | .1 | .0 | .1 | .0 |
| | | H2 failure mode 2 | .0 | .1 | .0 | .1 | .0 |

Failures occurring in each period will be generated according to the above probabilities.

NOTE: Repaired items may be reinstalled immediately (after repair delay) or put in spares inventory. Items not repaired are scrapped. Failure mode 1 indicates component is *always* repaired if it fails. It is then subject to Failure mode 2; i.e., failure of a repaired component must be replaced. It cannot be repaired again.

EXHIBIT III. ADDITIONAL COST DATA

Warehouse costs per period $/ft² (See Exhibit IV for component space requirements)

| | Sites | | | | |
|---|---|---|---|---|---|
| Square feet required | 1 | 2 | 3 | 4 | 5 |
| 0– 50 | $2.00 | $3.50 | $2.50 | $2.50 | $3.50 |
| 51–200 | 1.50 | 2.50 | 2.00 | 2.00 | 2.50 |
| 200 | 1.00 | 2.00 | 1.50 | 1.50 | 2.00 |

Shipping costs (See Exhibit IV for volumes and weights of components)

| | Miles | | |
|---|---|---|---|
| Transportation | 0–100 | 101–1500 | > 1500 |
| By truck ($/ft.³-mile) | $ .003 | $ .002 | $ .001 |
| By air ($/lb.-mile) | — | .003 | .002 |

Shipping time requirements

| | |
|---|---|
| By truck: | One-day shipment up to 300 miles, e.g., 305 miles requires two days. |
| By air: | Cannot be used for shipment less than 200 miles.<br>One-day shipment up to 1900 miles.<br>Two days required over 1900 miles. |

Delay penalties (Use only delay days of limiting component at a site, i.e., if two components fail, one with 3 delay days, the other with 2 delay days the number of delay days would be 3.)

| Sites 1 and 2: | $ 200/day |
|---|---|
| 3 and 4: | $1000/day |
| 5 | $2000/day |

MANAGEMENT DECISION SIMULATIONS

EXHIBIT IV. COMPONENT CONFIGURATION AND COST DATA

| Component | On Site Repair Cost | Days Req'd for Repair | Basic Cost of Spare | Days Req'd for Installation | Weight (lbs) | Volume (ft³) | Storage Requirement (ft²) |
|---|---|---|---|---|---|---|---|
| A Thrustchamber | | | | | 10,000 | 1,000 | 100 |
|   Failure mode 1 | $5,000 | 1 | | 14 | | | |
|   Failure mode 2 | Impossible | | $50,000 | 14 | | | |
| B Turbopump | | | | | 3,000 | 100 | 20 |
|   Failure mode 1 | 10,000 | 5 | | 3 | | | |
|   Failure mode 2 | Impossible | | 50,000 | 3 | | | |
| C Gas generator | 10,000 | 5 | 10,000 | 1 | 300 | 50 | 20 |
| D Oxidizer valve | 2,000 | 5 | 5,000 | 1 | 150 | 30 | 10 |
| E Fuel valve | 2,000 | 5 | 5,000 | 1 | 150 | 30 | 10 |
| F Heat exchanger | 3,000 | 6 | 10,000 | 1 | 400 | 100 | 20 |
| G High pressure duct | 2,500 | 5 | 5,000 | 1 | 600 | 100 | 50 |
| H Injector | | | | | 2,000 | 300 | 30 |
|   Failure mode 1 | 2,000 | 1 | | 5 | | | |
|   Failure mode 2 | Impossible | | 15,000 | 5 | | | |

TEAM

PERIOD  0

—SAMPLE—

SPARES ALLOCATIONS OR REALLOCATIONS

(Time Allowed 15 Minutes/Period)

Additional spares as listed in Column M are now available at Site 1. Determine where these items should be shipped and stored. Spares may be moved from one site to another at this time. There are no time delays during this period. Assume stored items remain in warehouses for entire period to determine costs.

| | Component name | M | No. of components stored at sites: | | | | | Warehousing costs | Shipping costs |
| | | | 1 | 2 | 3 | 4 | 5 | | |
|---|---|---|---|---|---|---|---|---|---|
| A | Thrust chamber | 1 | 1 | | | | | 150 | 0 |
| B | Turbopump | 1 | 1 | | | | | 40 | 0 |
| C | Gas generator | 4 | 2 | | 1 | | 1 | 200 | 250 |
| D | Oxidizer valve | 4 | 2 | | 1 | | 1 | 100 | 150 |
| E | Fuel valve | 4 | 2 | | 1 | | 1 | 100 | 150 |
| F | Heat exchanger | 2 | 1 | | | | 1 | 110 | 300 |
| G | High pressure duct | 2 | 1 | | 1 | | | 250 | 200 |
| H | Injector | 1 | 1 | | | | | 60 | 0 |

Totals $1010.00   +   $1050.00   =   $2060.00

Form 1

MANAGEMENT DECISION SIMULATIONS

TEAM<br>
PERIOD   2

## SPARES ALLOCATIONS OR REALLOCATIONS

### (Time Allowed 15 Minutes/Period)

Additional spares as listed in Column M are now available at Site 1. Determine where these items should be shipped and stored. Spares may be moved from one site to another at this time. There are no time delays during this period. Assume stored items remain in warehouses for entire period to determine costs.

| Component name | M | No. of components stored at sites: | | | | | Ware-housing costs | Shipping costs |
|---|---|---|---|---|---|---|---|---|
| | | 1 | 2 | 3 | 4 | 5 | | |
| A   Thrust chamber | 1 | | | | | | | |
| B   Turbopump | 1 | | | | | | | |
| C   Gas generator | 4 | | | | | | | |
| D   Oxidizer valve | 4 | | | | | | | |
| E   Fuel valve | 4 | | | | | | | |
| F   Heat exchanger | 2 | | | | | | | |
| G   High pressure duct | 2 | | | | | | | |
| H   Injector | 1 | | | | | | | |

Totals     $_____   +   $_____   =   $_____

Form 1

MANAGEMENT DECISION GAMES

TEAM
PERIOD 3

SPARES ALLOCATIONS OR REALLOCATIONS

(Time Allowed 15 Minutes/Period)

Additional spares as listed in Column M are now available at Site 1. Determine where these items should be shipped and stored. Spares may be moved from one site to another at this time. There are no time delays during this period. Assume stored items remain in warehouses for entire period to determine costs.

| Component name | M | No. of components stored at sites: | | | | | Warehousing costs | Shipping costs |
|---|---|---|---|---|---|---|---|---|
| | | 1 | 2 | 3 | 4 | 5 | | |
| A  Thrust chamber | 1 | | | | | | | |
| B  Turbopump | 1 | | | | | | | |
| C  Gas generator | 4 | | | | | | | |
| D  Oxidizer valve | 4 | | | | | | | |
| E  Fuel valve | 4 | | | | | | | |
| F  Heat exchanger | 2 | | | | | | | |
| G  High pressure duct | 2 | | | | | | | |
| H  Injector | 1 | | | | | | | |

Totals    $_____   +   $_____   =   $_____

Form 1

TEAM _____

## COMPONENT FAILURES AND ADDED LOGISTICS COSTS

|  | PERIOD 1 | | | | PERIOD 2 | | | | PERIOD 3 | | | |
|---|---|---|---|---|---|---|---|---|---|---|---|---|
| Site | Failed Units | Repair/ Spare $ | Delay $ | Added Shipping $ | Failed Units | Repair/ Spare $ | Delay $ | Added Shipping $ | Failed Units | Repair/ Spare $ | Delay $ | Added Shipping $ |
| 1 |  |  |  |  |  |  |  |  |  |  |  |  |
| 2 |  |  |  |  |  |  |  |  |  |  |  |  |
| 3 |  |  |  |  |  |  |  |  |  |  |  |  |
| 4 |  |  |  |  |  |  |  |  |  |  |  |  |
| 5 |  |  |  |  |  |  |  |  |  |  |  |  |
| Subtotals | $ | $ | $ | $ | $ | $ | $ | $ | $ | $ | $ | $ |

Added logistics cost (above)     $ _____ , _____     $ _____ , _____     $ _____ , _____
Initial logistics cost (form 1)    + $ _____ , _____    + $ _____ , _____    + $ _____ , _____
Previous cumulative cost        + $ _____ , _____    + $ _____ , _____    + $ _____ , _____
Cumulative logistics cost       = $ _____ , _____    = $ _____ , _____    = $ _____ , _____

Form 2

124

# Reliability

## (12) SUBMARINE P3 RELIABILITY AND SPARES PROVISIONING UNDER A VOLUME CONSTRAINT

*Introduction* This System Reliability is designed to provide the participant with an understanding of the problems and constraints associated with part reliability considerations under conditions of space restraints. This game applies to any situation in which the lead time and reliability of components is so critical as to endanger the total project's success.

The objective of the game is to apply reliability concepts to decisions regarding spare parts quantities under conditions in which space is limited. In other situations a dollar constraint or other restriction could be imposed.

The navigation officer on board a submarine has the primary responsibility for its Electronic Navigational System (ENS). This responsibility includes the spares provisioning, periodic checkouts, and maintenance program for the ENS. When on a mission, if the ENS becomes inoperative for any reason the mission is aborted and the sub must return to its base before the end of the designated cruise. To you, the navigation officer, an abort would be calamitous and shatter any chances you have at present for adding another stripe to your sleeve.

*Objective* The ENS must be operational at all times during a cruise. Therefore, any malfunctioning item within the system must be able to be replaced with a spare. If there are insufficient spares for an item, a subsystem becomes inoperative and may terminate the cruise. Therefore, all that is required is to carry enough spares so that any item that fails can be replaced. However, a submarine

has rather limited storage space and only 205 cubic feet is alloted for the spares.

*Rules and conditions*

1. The Electronic Navigation System (ENS) consists of three subsystems. Each subsystem consists of plug-in items which randomly fail.

2. The system is to be operational 24 hours per day for the chosen cruise of 60 days or 1440 hours.

3. Exhibit I shows the MTBF for each item and the probability of using more than the spares indicated during the cruise. (For example, in 98 out of 100 cruises of 1440 hours each, there would be 5 or less failures of Item A. The probability that the original and 5 spares would fail is about 2%).

4. The data in Exhibit I indicates that items with low MTBF's are more prone to failure that those with high MTBF's. From these data the spares quantity of each item is selected for Exhibit II. This Exhibit lists the items and their cubic feet of volume. Multiplying the item quantity by the volume per item yields the space required. The sum

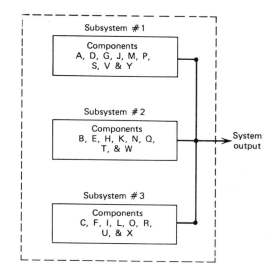

## EXHIBIT I
### NUMBER OF SPARES VERSUS PROBABILITY OF A STOCKOUT

| Item | MTBF | m | Spares 1 | 2 | 3 | 4 | 5 | 6 |
|------|------|---|----|----|----|----|----|----|
| A | 686 | 2.1 | 60% | 35% | 16% | 6% | 2% | .5% |
| B | " | " | " | " | " | " | " | " |
| C | 800 | 1.8 | 52% | 27% | 11%[a] | 4% | 1% | — |
| D | " | " | " | " | " | " | " | — |
| E | 960 | 1.5 | 44% | 20% | 6% | 2% | .5% | — |
| F | " | " | " | " | " | " | " | — |
| G | 1200 | 1.2 | 35% | 12% | 4% | 1% | — | — |
| H | " | " | " | " | " | " | — | — |
| I | " | " | " | " | " | " | — | — |
| J | " | " | " | " | " | " | — | — |
| K | " | " | " | " | " | " | — | — |
| L | " | " | " | " | " | " | — | — |
| M | 1600 | .9 | 22% | 6% | 2% | .2% | — | — |
| N | " | " | " | " | " | " | — | — |
| O | " | " | " | " | " | " | — | — |
| P | " | " | " | " | " | " | — | — |
| Q | " | " | " | " | " | " | — | — |
| R | 2400 | .6 | 12% | 1% | .3% | .1% | — | — |
| S | " | " | " | " | " | " | — | — |
| T | " | " | " | " | " | " | — | — |
| U | 4800 | .3 | 3% | .3% | — | — | — | — |
| V | " | " | " | " | — | — | — | — |
| W | " | " | | | | | | |
| X | " | " | | | | | | |
| Y | " | " | | | | | | |

[a] From the cumulative Poisson where:
$$P(x) = \Sigma p(x) = \Sigma m^x e - m/x!$$
$$P(3) = p(0) + p(1) + p(2) + p(3)$$
$.89 = .165 + .296 + .267 + .160 = $ Prob. that no more than 3 of item C will fail during 1440 hours. Conversely; Prob. will require 3 spares $= (1 - P_3) = 11\%$

**EXHIBIT II**
**WORK SHEET**

| Item | MTBF | Ft³/Item | Quantity | Ft³ | Quantity | Ft³ | Quantity | Ft³ |
|------|------|----------|----------|-----|----------|-----|----------|-----|
| A | 686 | 8 | | | | | | |
| B | " | 6 | | | | | | |
| C | 800 | 3 | | | | | | |
| D | " | 6 | | | | | | |
| E | 960 | 9 | | | | | | |
| F | " | 4 | | | | | | |
| G | 1200 | 3 | | | | | | |
| H | " | 3 | | | | | | |
| I | " | 5 | | | | | | |
| J | " | 2 | | | | | | |
| K | " | 4 | | | | | | |
| L | " | 6 | | | | | | |
| M | 1600 | 1 | | | | | | |
| N | " | 3 | | | | | | |
| O | " | 3 | | | | | | |
| P | " | 2 | | | | | | |
| Q | " | 5 | | | | | | |
| R | 2400 | 7 | | | | | | |
| S | " | 6 | | | | | | |
| T | " | 3 | | | | | | |
| U | 4800 | 2 | | | | | | |
| V | " | 4 | | | | | | |
| W | " | 1 | | | | | | |
| X | " | 2 | | | | | | |
| Y | " | 3 | | | | | | |

TOTALS          101                    _____

EXHIBIT III

GAME SHEET

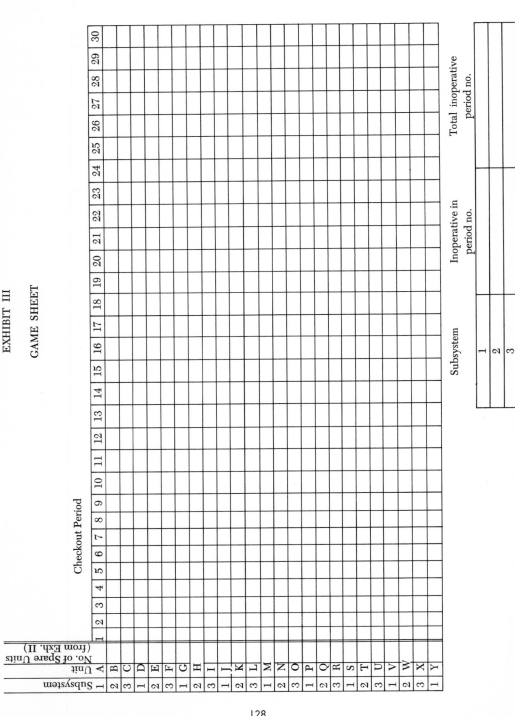

Checkout Period

| Subsystem | Unit | No. of Spare Units (from Exh. II) | 1 | 2 | 3 | 4 | 5 | 6 | 7 | 8 | 9 | 10 | 11 | 12 | 13 | 14 | 15 | 16 | 17 | 18 | 19 | 20 | 21 | 22 | 23 | 24 | 25 | 26 | 27 | 28 | 29 | 30 |
|---|---|---|---|---|---|---|---|---|---|---|---|---|---|---|---|---|---|---|---|---|---|---|---|---|---|---|---|---|---|---|---|---|
| 1 | A | | | | | | | | | | | | | | | | | | | | | | | | | | | | | | | |
| 2 | B | | | | | | | | | | | | | | | | | | | | | | | | | | | | | | | |
| 3 | C | | | | | | | | | | | | | | | | | | | | | | | | | | | | | | | |
| 1 | D | | | | | | | | | | | | | | | | | | | | | | | | | | | | | | | |
| 2 | E | | | | | | | | | | | | | | | | | | | | | | | | | | | | | | | |
| 3 | F | | | | | | | | | | | | | | | | | | | | | | | | | | | | | | | |
| 1 | G | | | | | | | | | | | | | | | | | | | | | | | | | | | | | | | |
| 2 | H | | | | | | | | | | | | | | | | | | | | | | | | | | | | | | | |
| 3 | I | | | | | | | | | | | | | | | | | | | | | | | | | | | | | | | |
| 1 | J | | | | | | | | | | | | | | | | | | | | | | | | | | | | | | | |
| 2 | K | | | | | | | | | | | | | | | | | | | | | | | | | | | | | | | |
| 3 | L | | | | | | | | | | | | | | | | | | | | | | | | | | | | | | | |
| 1 | M | | | | | | | | | | | | | | | | | | | | | | | | | | | | | | | |
| 2 | N | | | | | | | | | | | | | | | | | | | | | | | | | | | | | | | |
| 3 | O | | | | | | | | | | | | | | | | | | | | | | | | | | | | | | | |
| 1 | P | | | | | | | | | | | | | | | | | | | | | | | | | | | | | | | |
| 2 | Q | | | | | | | | | | | | | | | | | | | | | | | | | | | | | | | |
| 3 | R | | | | | | | | | | | | | | | | | | | | | | | | | | | | | | | |
| 1 | S | | | | | | | | | | | | | | | | | | | | | | | | | | | | | | | |
| 2 | T | | | | | | | | | | | | | | | | | | | | | | | | | | | | | | | |
| 3 | U | | | | | | | | | | | | | | | | | | | | | | | | | | | | | | | |
| 1 | V | | | | | | | | | | | | | | | | | | | | | | | | | | | | | | | |
| 2 | W | | | | | | | | | | | | | | | | | | | | | | | | | | | | | | | |
| 3 | X | | | | | | | | | | | | | | | | | | | | | | | | | | | | | | | |
| 1 | Y | | | | | | | | | | | | | | | | | | | | | | | | | | | | | | | |

| Subsystem | Inoperative in period no. | Total inoperative period no. |
|---|---|---|
| 1 | | |
| 2 | | |
| 3 | | |

128

of the space requirements must not exceed 205 ft$^3$.

5. After transposing the chosen spares' quantities to Exhibit III, the cruise is begun. Every two days the system is 'checked out' by your men to detect failures and assure system capability.

6. If an item failed, you must be able to replace it with a spare from your stores. The subsystem becomes inoperative if you are not able to replace an item that has failed.

7. In subsequent checkouts, if you are unable to maintain at least *two* subsystems operational, the mission is aborted and the submarine must return to port—and there goes your stripe.

8. All three subsystems must be supported by spares provisioning. Therefore if *any* subsystem fails within the first 10 checkouts, the mission is aborted.

9. Failed items cannot be repaired on board—only replaced.

10. None of the items is interchangeable with any of the other items.

*Background*    The major objective of this logistics simulation is to operate in an environment that only has a pass or fail outcome and also severe resource constraints, in this case physical volume or space. Inherent in the simulation the participant is required to understand and utilize reliability concepts such as Mean-Time-Between-Failure (MTBF).

In the case of a submarine patrol or any plane, ship, or other mission, the equipment system on board would be expected to be operational for a period of say "$X$" hours. However, during the mission, individual items may fail and must be replaced with a spare. If there is no spare remaining, the subsystem requiring this item becomes inoperative. There is sufficient redundancy of the three subsystems in this case such that two of the three subsystems must be inoperative before the total system becomes useless.

To understand how the MTBF of an item is derived, assume the manufacturer selects a sample of 10 units of the same item and each is to be tested until it fails. All 10 units start the test simultaneously and the elapsed time when each of the 10 fails is recorded. The hours until the failure of each are added and divided by 10, the sample size. The result is the estimated MTBF for this particular item. Because any MTBF is an average, the life of some units (33%) will exceed this figure, whereas others (67%) will not reach it.

The MTBF can be used to determine the average number of failures of an item one may expect in a given number of operating hours. For example, Item A of an equipment system may be *expected* to have 2.1 failures in a mission of 1440 hours if its MTBF was 686 hours.

$$m_A = \frac{\text{Expected}}{\text{failures of } A} = \frac{\text{Operating Time}}{\text{MTBF of Item } A} \text{ i.e., } \frac{1440 \text{ hrs}}{686 \text{ hr/failure}} = 2.1 \text{ failures}$$

Given the MTBF's, the expected number of failures of each of the components in a system operating for $T$ hours can be computed. The expected number of spares of each item to keep the subsystem operating is equal to the expected number of failures. This would result in providing for an expected number of failures without regard to the element of probability (randomness of failures) on either side of the MTBF. Strict adherence to this

provisioning policy also ignores secondary and induced failures, which will be referred to as double-failures during the simulation. Therefore, it is desirable to carry more than the amount of spares indicated by the above computation in order to reduce the probability of incurring a "stockout."

Exhibit I is a tabulation of $(1 - Pc)$, the complement of the cumulative Poisson distribution. For example, if the

## MANAGEMENT DECISION SIMULATIONS

mean is 1.8 failures, then the probability that *2 or less* failures would occur is $p(0) + p(1) + p(2) = .73 = P(2)$. There is a 27% chance $(1 - .73)$ that more than 2 failures would occur. Therefore, at least 3 of the items (original + 2 spares) would be required 27% of the time.

An item called on to operate for at least its MTBF has only about a 37% chance of doing so. Therefore, its reliability for attaining its MTBF is only 37%. (Setting $m = 1$ is .37). Stated another way, the probability of a component having 0 failures before its MTBF is 37%. Conversely, there is a 73% chance of an item failing before its MTBF. Again referring to Exhibit I, Item C has an MTBF of 800. There is only 37% confidence that a C item will last 800 hours, much less 1440 hours. However, we have a 73% confidence that the total life of 3 C items will last the 1440 hours as $P(3) = .16 + .30 + .27 = .73$.

### Procedure[1]

1. Using the probability guides in Exhibit I, use Exhibit II to determine the quantity of spares to be attempted during a simulated cruise. The cubic feet must not exceed 205. Transcribe these quantities to Column 3 of Exhibit III.

2. Chips or key tags representing the failures will be drawn (with replacement) at occasions simulating the 30 checkout periods (every 48 hours). The 100 tags are marked with the letters of the items they represent. The quantity of each marked tag is in proportion to the probability of incurring a failure of that item. Therefore, there are fewer tags for items with high MTBF's. (For example, there are 7 "A" tags since 2.1 A's should be drawn on the average from the 30 draws $\therefore$ 2.1:30 = 7:100.)

3. Mark the drawn "failure" on Exhibit III opposite the item and time period. When the total "failures" of an item exceeds its

---

[1] This portion may be performed with a random number generation at the discretion of the administrator.

spares, the respective subsystem is inoperative (e.g., 3 spares and 4 failures of an item constitutes a subsystem failure).

4. There is a 7% probability of no failure occurring as well as a 7% probability of a double failure whereby 2 additional chips are drawn for that period.

5. Continue the simulation until a second subsystem fails in which case the mission is aborted. Record which subsystems failed and the period in which they failed in Exhibit III.

6. Performance in one round of a simulation is independent of subsequent rounds if more than one cruise is simulated. The failures are random, each item having its proportional opportunity or chance to fail.

*Further applications*    This type of logistics support is becoming rather commonplace. A submarine was chosen, but a manned space vehicle or a space platform could have been chosen as well. Airborne and other systems could be simulated using dollar, weight, or other constraints instead of space as was used in this simulation.

### (13) CORDELL COMPANY

A COMPETITIVE BIDDING AND PRICING GAME

*Introduction*    This game is designed to provide the participant with a challenging opportunity to plan and implement a strategy under a simulated competitive bidding and pricing situation. Each team is required to make competitive decisions by bidding for raw materials, converting them to finished goods through production, and then offering them at a price that will sell. Each team keeps a record of cash balance, a P&L, and an inventory record for each quarter.

These competitive bids begin with a customer's request for a bid. A firm will have to quickly analyze its resources and the market environment and put together a feasible strategy consistent with its resources and objectives. The company's strategists and financial planners must react to the opportunity by organizing responsibilities and delegating important tasks to integrate their efforts toward success in the bid and contract. Thus, the players on each team will be under stress to prepare the bids and select pricing alternatives with the utmost care—as in the real world. Time, budgeting, and organization of effort are of the essence.

*Objective*   The team achieving the greatest net profit after taxes in the final quarter of play will be the winner. Each team will play four quarters or more as determined by the time allotted for the game.

*Background*   This company is a manufacturing concern with a long history of developing and marketing quality products. Over the past few years the market in which it sells its products has become increasingly competitive. Profit growth has leveled off and even declined in some quarters. You and your planning team are responsible to the President in matters of material purchases and product marketing and pricing. He has stated that he expects a minimum after-tax rate of return on equity of 15% per year.

*Material, bidding, purchasing, and manufacturing costs*   Because of the nature of the product line, the raw materials to

be purchased are in limited supply. Material is acquired on the basis of a competitive bid.

The following table shows the average availability of raw material per quarter over the past two years.

| Y − 2 | Units | Y − 1 | Units |
|---|---|---|---|
| Quarter 1 | 60 | Quarter 1 | 61 |
| Quarter 2 | 75 | Quarter 2 | 78 |
| Quarter 3 | 62 | Quarter 3 | 65 |
| Quarter 4 | 60 | Quarter 4 | 58 |

The difference from the mean, for each quarter, is a normal distribution with a standard deviation of two units.

*Bidding*   The minimum acceptable raw materials bid is $400 per unit. Bids may be submitted in $50 increments only.

*Awards*   Raw Material will be awarded on the following basis:

(a) If the demand for material exceeds availability, each team will receive at least *five units* unless its bid price is less than one-half of the highest bid submitted, in which case it receives none. The remaining material will be allocated in accordance with the rankings of the bids (see Exhibit I).

(b) In the event of a duplicate bid price (e.g., Team 1 and Team 4) each team will receive a percentage of the available units. This percentage is as follows:

$$\text{Team 1's Quantity} = \frac{\#1\text{'s Bid Qty} \times (\text{Units Available for } \#1 \& \#4)}{\#1\text{'s Bid Qty} + \#4\text{'s Bid Qty}}$$

$$\text{Team 4's Quantity} = \frac{\#4\text{'s Bid Qty} \times (\text{Units Available for } \#1 \& \#4)}{\#1\text{'s Bid Qty} + \#1 \text{ Bid Qty}}$$

Sample Calculation of a duplicate bid price situation:

After initial allocation of five units to all teams within 50 percent of top prices, the units of material available = 8.
Team 1 bid 9 units @ $500 therefore

$$5 + \frac{9 \times 8}{9 + 20} = 5 + 3 = 8 \text{ units total.}$$

Team 4 bid 20 units @ $500 therefore

$$5 + \frac{20 \times 8}{9 + 20} = 5 + 5 = 10 \text{ units total.}$$

(c) If demand is less than availability, each team will receive the amount requested at the bid price.

*Manufacturing Costs*   Manufacturing Costs are computed in the following manner:

Raw Materials
  at bid price        $ XXX
Fixed Cost
  includes:           $3000/Quarter
  Overhead
  Depreciation
  General &
    administrative
Labor                 $ 700/Unit
Inventory Carrying
  Costs               $ 300/Unit/Quarter

NOTE: Material costs are incurred on a First In-First Out (FIFO) basis. It is therefore important that careful records of inventory be maintained. A Raw Material Inventory Record Worksheet is provided for this purpose. The teams have the option of carrying their inventory in the form of raw material and/or finished goods. Whether inventory is carried as raw material or finished goods, there is an inventory carrying cost of $300/unit for each quarter.

## Cash flow

1. Sales Revenue—One-half of the amount sold during any period will be collected in the period of that sale while the remaining one-half will be collected in the following period.

2. Raw materials must be paid for in the quarter following the quarter in which they were purchased.

3. Fixed costs are to be paid in the quarter after they are incurred.

4. Labor cost must be paid in the quarter incurred.

5. Income taxes (50%) must be paid at the end of each quarter. In the event a loss is incurred in a subsequent quarter, no tax refund will be paid.

*Plant capacity*  In the short run, plant capacity is fixed at a maximum of 14 units per quarter.

*Borrowing*  The company has a line of credit up to $10,000. The interest charge is 4% per quarter.

*Sales*  The product is sold in a competitive market with limited demand. The following table shows the average sales demand experienced over the past two years.

| Y-2 Sales | | Y-1 Sales | |
|---|---|---|---|
| Quarter | Units | Quarter | Units |
| 1 | 50 | 1 | 55 |
| 2 | 58 | 2 | 63 |
| 3 | 70 | 3 | 79 |
| 4 | 60 | 4 | 65 |

A team's sales will be determined in the following manner:

1. If supply is greater than demand for the product, each team whose quoted price is not more than 120% of lowest quoted price will be allowed to sell five units. A price quote greater than 120% of the lowest will prevent the team from selling anything that quarter. Demand remaining after the sale of five units per team will be allocated on the basis of lowest quote first (see Exhibit II).

2. In the event of a duplicate sales price quoted (e.g., Team 1 and Team 3), each team will receive a percentage of the units demanded. This percentage is derived from the following:

$$\text{Team 1's Sales} = \frac{\#1\text{'s offering} \times (\text{Sales available for }\#1 \ \& \ \#3)}{\#1\text{'s offering} + \#3\text{'s offering}}$$

Sample calculation of a duplicate selling price offering: After the initial allocation of 5 units to all teams within 120% of the lowest quoted price, assume a demand remaining of 11 units.

Team 1 quotes $1000 for 30 units. Thus

$$5 + \left(\frac{30}{10+30}\right)(11) = 5 + 8 = 13 \text{ units}$$

sold.

EXHIBIT I

MATERIAL ALLOCATION SCORE SHEET
(Sample)

0    Quarter

0    Quarter Availability 59

Minimum Acceptable Bid = 50% of Highest Bid
∴ Minimum Bid = $450.00

| Team | Bid Price/Unit | Bid Qty. | 1st Alloc. | 2nd Alloc. | Total |
|------|---------------|----------|------------|------------|-------|
| 3 | $900.00 | 12 | 5 | 7 | 12 |
| 4 | $800.00 | 9 | 5 | 4 | 9 |
| 1 | $700.00 | 11 | 5 | 6 | 11 |
| 2 | $550.00 | 12 | 5 | 7 | 12 |
| 5 | $450.00 | 10 | 5 | 5 | 10 |
| 6 | $400.00 | 10 | 0 | 5 | 5 |
| TOTAL | | 64 | 25 | 34 | 59 |

EXHIBIT II

SALES ALLOCATION SCORE SHEET
(Sample)

0    Quarter Demand 64

Maximum Acceptable Price = 120% of Lowest Price
Maximum Price = $2,500.00

| Team | Price/Unit | Qty. Offered | 1st Alloc. | 2nd Alloc. | Total |
|------|-----------|--------------|------------|------------|-------|
| 2 | $2100.00 | 14 | 5 | 9 | 14 |
| 4 | $2150.00 | 12 | 5 | 7 | 12 |
| 1 | $2250.00 | 13 | 5 | 8 | 13 |
| 5 | $2300.00 | 11 | 5 | 6 | 11 |
| 6 | $2400.00 | 10 | 5 | 5 | 10 |
| 3 | $2550.00 | 14 | 0 | 4 | 4 |
| TOTAL | | 74 | 25 | 39 | 64 |

## MANAGEMENT DECISION SIMULATIONS

EXHIBIT III
Cordell Company
BALANCE SHEET
(End of Prior Period)

| CURRENT ASSETS | | CURRENT LIABILITIES | |
|---|---|---|---|
| Cash | $15,000 | Accounts Payable | $10,000 |
| Receivables | 5,000 | | |
| Raw Materials 5 units @ $500 per unit | 2,500 | | |
| | $22,500 | | $10,000 |

| LONG TERM ASSETS | | LONG TERM LIABILITIES AND CAPITAL | |
|---|---|---|---|
| Factory | $80,000 | Debt | $12,500 |
| less: Cumulative Depreciation | (30,000) | | |
| | $50,000 | Common Stock | 50,000 |
| Land | 10,000 | Rt'd. Earnings | 10,000 |
| | $60,000 | | $72,500 |
| | $82,500 | | $82,500 |

Team 3 quotes $1000 for 10 units. Thus

$$5 + \left( \frac{10}{10 + 30} \right) (11) = 5 + 3 = 8 \text{ units}$$

sold.

3. If supply is less than demand, each team will sell the product it offers at its quoted price.

4. The minimum sales price is $1600. There is no maximum price.

### Rules of Play

Each team has 4 forms as follows:

Form 1—BID SHEET AND INVEN-
    TORY RECORD
Form 2—CASH FLOW
Form 3—QUARTERLY PROFIT & LOSS
    STATEMENT
Form 4—MATERIAL    ALLOCATION
    SCORE SHEET

1. Each team starts the game with a $15,000 cash balance, plus a first quarter cash inflow from receivables. Each team has a beginning raw material inventory of five units at $500 each, or $2500 worth. The *only cash inflow* is from receivables.

2. The only source for additional cash is from profitable sales and/or bank loans up to $10,000.

3. Prior to the beginning of each quarter, your team will submit your raw materials bid to the Administrator on the bid sheet (Form 1). A seasonal index on raw material availability can be developed from its past history.

4. The Administrator determines the total number of raw material units available for that quarter (by means of a random number selection process). The Administrator also computes the number of units your team has purchased, according to the rules previously outlined. The number of units you

# BID SHEET—RAW MATERIAL, PRODUCTION AND F/F TRANSACTION LEDGER

TEAM _____

|  | Quarter #1 | Quarter #2 | Quarter #3 | Quarter #4 |
|---|---|---|---|---|

## RAW MATERIALS

a. Balance forward

b. Quantity bid for

c. Bid price/unit

d. Quantity able to buy

e. Raw material available

f. Raw material procesed

g. Raw material balance

## PRODUCTION

h. Quantity processed

i. F/G balance forward

j. F/G available

## SALES

k. Quantity offered

l. Asking price/unit

m. Qty. sold & revenue

n. F/G balance

Form #1

CASH FLOW      TEAM _____

| | Quarter #1 | Quarter #2 | Quarter #3 | Quarter #4 |
|---|---|---|---|---|
| **CASH ON HAND** | $15,000 | $ ____ | $ ____ | $ ____ |
| **RECEIPTS** | | | | |
| One-half last Qtr. sales | $ 5,000 | $ ____ | $ ____ | $ ____ |
| One-half this Qtr. sales | $ ____ | $ ____ | $ ____ | $ ____ |
| Bank loans | $ ____ | $ ____ | $ ____ | $ ____ |
| Total receipts | $ ____ | $ ____ | $ ____ | $ ____ |
| **EXPENDITURES** | | | | |
| R/M (bought last qtr.) | $10,000 | $ ____ | $ ____ | $ ____ |
| Carrying cost ($300/unit) | $ ____ | $ ____ | $ ____ | $ ____ |
| Labor ($700/unit) | $ ____ | $ ____ | $ ____ | $ ____ |
| Fixed costs | $ 3,000 | $ 3,000 | $ 3,000 | $ 3,000 |
| Bank payment | $ ____ | $ ____ | $ ____ | $ ____ |
| Bank interest | $ ____ | $ ____ | $ ____ | $ ____ |
| Tax (50% of profit) | $ ____ | $ ____ | $ ____ | $ ____ |
| Total expenditures | $ ____ | $ ____ | $ ____ | $ ____ |
| **CASH Balance** | $ ____ | $ ____ | $ ____ | $ ____ |

Form #2

# QUARTERLY PROFIT AND LOSS STATEMENT

TEAM _____

| | Quarter #1 | Quarter #2 | Quarter #3 | Quarter #4 |
|---|---|---|---|---|
| A. SALES REVENUE: (Q × R) | $_____ | $_____ | $_____ | $_____ |
| B. DIRECT COST: | | | | |
| R/M used (FIFO) | $_____ | $_____ | $_____ | $_____ |
| Labor (Q × $700) | $_____ | $_____ | $_____ | $_____ |
| Total | −$_____ | −$_____ | −$_____ | −$_____ |
| C. GROSS PROFIT: | $_____ | $_____ | $_____ | $_____ |
| D. OPERATING EXPENSES: | | | | |
| Inv. carrying cost[a] | $_____ | $_____ | $_____ | $_____ |
| Fixed expense | $ 3,000 | $ 3,000 | $ 3,000 | $ 3,000 |
| Bank interest (4%/qtr.) | $_____ | $_____ | $_____ | $_____ |
| Total | −$_____ | −$_____ | −$_____ | −$_____ |
| E. OPERATING PROFIT: | $_____ | $_____ | $_____ | $_____ |
| F. INCOME TAX: | −$_____ | −$_____ | −$_____ | −$_____ |
| G. NET PROFIT: | $_____ | $_____ | $_____ | $_____ |
| H. PROFITS BROUGHT FWD. | +$_____ | +$_____ | +$_____ | +$_____ |
| I. CUMULATIVE PROFIT: | $_____ | $_____ | $_____ | $_____ |

[a] Carrying cost = ( R/M Inv. Bal. + F/G Inv. Bal. ) × $300.

Form #3

137

were able to purchase will be recorded on your "bid sheet" and returned to you. (See Exhibit II for an example of this procedure.)

5. Based on the resources available, determine the number of units you should produce and sell in order to realize a profit.

6. At the halfway point of each quarter's play, your team will submit to the Administrator, on your sales record (Form 1), the number of the finished units you are offering to sell and at what quoted price. A seasonal index of finished units demand, based on past history, may be helpful.

7. The Administrator will determine the total demand for finished units by means of a random number selection process. The Administrator then determines the number of finished units your team has sold according to the rules previously outlined. Your bid sheet form with the number of finished units your team sold will then be returned.

8. Based on your experience in the first quarter, you are now asked to submit a bid for raw materials for the next quarter.

9. In order to help determine your material bids and sales prices for subsequent quarters, maintain copies of the bid sheet and inventory record, cash inflow, and the profit and loss forms for each quarter.

10. At the end of the fourth quarter your final profit and loss statement should be turned over to the Administrator together with all of the other forms used throughout the four quarters.

11. The winner of the game will be determined by the greatest profit achieved at the end of four quarters of play.

12. A schedule should be placed on the blackboard delineating the clock time at which to:

(a) Start each quarter's play.
(b) Submit raw material bids in each quarter.
(c) Submit quarter sales offers in each quarter.
(d) Complete each quarter's financial statements.

## (14) POWERS COMPANY

*Introduction* The Powers Company situation is designed to simulate the management activity known as project management. The game applies planning and control techniques in order to integrate the areas of production, tooling, engineering, quality control, and materials. It focuses on the interrelations between these various production activities and provides a technique (status index) for analyzing each area in order to determine if satisfactory progress is being made toward the desired objective.

*Background* This game has been designed to give the participant an opportunity to perform certain critical project management functions (i.e., planning, controlling, fiscal management and cost control plus profit maintenance). The objectives are to minimize the cost of the project and to complete the project within a specified period.

Each team assumes the management role for a program that is half completed. Based on historical data, future trends, shop feedback, etc., the team decides how to allocate resources to the project in order to finish on time. Allocation decisions are submitted to the referee each quarter. The referee, using pregenerated actual times, provides each player with data to determine the actual progress for that period. This procedure is repeated for four quarters. At completion, the project is evaluated for units completed and profits or loss.

*Participant's Instructions* The Air Force has awarded Powers Company a contract for Project Afterburner. It is a $25-million contract for the production of 100 units in a two-year period. The project is estimated to cost $20 million with a negotiated fee of $5 million. Thus, although the target cost is $20 million, costs could go to $25 million before a loss is incurred. The contract is therefore a fixed price of $25 million.

A penalty clause is written into the contract which makes it vital to meet the two-year time limit for the 100 units.

For every unit NOT made, a penalty of $300,000 is charged against project cost.

1. *Present status of project*    In Exhibit I a "Manager's Data Sheet" has been prepared to show the past history of the project. At the present time, the project is one year old and has one year to go. The status index can be utilized to determine progress thus far and is computed from the following:

$$\frac{\text{Actual Progress (wks)}}{\text{Scheduled Progress (wks)}} \times \frac{\text{Planned Budget (\$)}}{\text{Actual Expenditure (\$)}} = \text{Status Index}[1]$$

If actual progress can be measured by earned dollars, then the index can be expressed as
$$\frac{\text{cumulative earned \$}}{\text{cumulative spent \$}} = \text{Status Index}$$

This concept is a significant aspect in the formulation of policy decisions by management.

According to the data sheet, Project Afterburner has a total contract value of $20 million, with $9.2 million planned for the first year and $10.8 million for the second year.

Also, from the data sheet it can be seen that $10 million has been spent to date with only $6.7 million worth of work accomplished. Thus, the project is $3.3 million overrun (beyond its plan). The actual value of work to go is $13.3 million. The present cost of the project, plus planned work to go, is $23.3 million at completion.

From the slack column it can be seen that the total project is 15 weeks behind schedule. The extent to which each element of the project is behind can also be determined from the data sheet.

In summary, after one year, Project Afterburner has spent half of its funds ($10 million), and is 15 weeks behind schedule. It has produced only one-third of the output value ($6.7 million) required.

This present project status can be attributed to the problems of the various task departments (engineering, tooling, production, quality control, and materials). These are discussed below.

2. *Department problems*    The basic problem in Project Afterburner is that *Engineering* is having difficulty designing a product that is easily manufactured and of high quality. At this point, however, the engineering changes in the project have been completed and the Engineering Dept. is confident that a significant and valuable breakthrough is in the immediate future—provided management supplies the men and money necessary.

The *Tooling Dept.* is having trouble using Engineering's designs to build tools. The present tools are only capable of producing quality work for a short while. New tools will be needed for production.

*Production* has the problem that it cannot build good afterburners from inadequate designs and tools. However, production feels that it is a superior department and could build *300* units a year with its present allocation.

In *Quality Control* and *Material* the problem involves close quality limits and large wastage. In this project Q.C. is directly related to production, and all adjustments that improve production also improve Q.C. During the second year, material will also be directly related to production. Thus a poor production index will be reflected in a poor material usage index and vice versa.

[1] See J. S. Baumgartner, *Project Management*, R. D. Irwin.

## MANAGEMENT DECISION SIMULATIONS

3. *Instructions*    In this game your prime duty as project manager is to establish a list of priorities regarding the capabilities and needs of the various departments involved in the project (engineering, tooling, production, quality control, and materials). Basically these decisions revolve around the allocation of funds to various departments and, more importantly, the time at which these funds are to be allocated. It is the responsibility of the project manager to determine, based on knowledge of the production process, where immediate al-location of funds are necessary in order to have the greatest positive impact on the project. As feedback of results are obtained, the manager can then chart his progress toward completion of the project and shift his attention to those departments that now require attention.

An example of the allocation sheet to be used by the participant (project manager) is as follows:

If participants set up a production budget of $0.8 million for first quarter of Year 2, the return might be:

| | 1st Quarter | | Cumulative 1st Year & 1st Qtr | | | |
|---|---|---|---|---|---|---|
| | Input | Output Earned[a] | Budget | Spent | Output Earned | SI |
| Production | 0.8 | 0.6 | 4.1 | 4.3 | 3.0 | 70% |
| Tooling | | | | | | |
| Engineering | | | | | | |
| Quality Control | | | | | | |
| Material | | | | | | |
| TOTAL | | | | | | |

[a] Referee's output of project based on previous year's and additional input.

If insufficient funds are allocated over the four quarters, the project will not be able to produce afterburners as required and will have a penalty for underproduction. The project management team must meet the contract for afterburners and at the same time deliver a satisfactory profit to the company.

4. *Procedures*    The following are suggested procedures for the game:

(a) Review the data sheet (Exhibit I) for project status and forecasts. Status Index Values should be checked by participants.

(b) Review department problems described in the case.

(c) Based on your analysis determine a one-year budget by quarters for each of the five areas and post to Form 1.

(d) Now allocate 1st quarter expenditures.

(e) Using predetermined data the referee will tell each team how much output was accomplished for each allocated input.

(f) Best results in this game will come from using the Status Index after every quarter's earned results are given. By this method,

## EXHIBIT I

## MANAGER'S DATA SHEET

| Function | Total Contract Value (A) | 1st Yr. Budget (B) | 1st Yr. Actuals (C) | 1st Yr. Value Earned (D) | 1st Year Progress (Wk) (E) | 1st Yr. Slack (E-52) | Status Index (SI) | 2nd Yr. Budget (A − B) | $ Value Work to Go (A − D) | Projected at Completion A + (C − D) |
|---|---|---|---|---|---|---|---|---|---|---|
| PRODUCTION | $10.0 | $3.3 | $ 3.5 | $2.4 | 38 weeks | −14 wk. | .69 | $ 6.7 | $ 7.6 | $11.1 |
| TOOLING | 2.7 | 2.5 | 2.5 | 1.6 | 33 | −19 | .64 | 0.2 | 1.1 | 3.6 |
| ENGINEERING | 1.8 | 1.5 | 2.0 | 1.0 | 35 | −17 | .50 | 0.3 | 0.8 | 2.8 |
| QUAL. CON. | 1.5 | 0.5 | 0.6 | 0.3 | 37 | −15 | .50 | 1.0 | 1.2 | 1.8 |
| MATERIAL | 4.0 | 1.4 | 1.4 | 1.4 | 52 | 0 | 1.00 | 2.6 | 2.6 | 4.0 |
| PROJECT | $20.0 | $9.2 | $10.0 | $6.7 | 38 weeks | −14 wk. | .67 | $10.8 | $13.3 | $23.3 |

$ in millions

Sample *Status Index* Calculation:

Function: Prod'n. $\dfrac{38}{52} \times \dfrac{3.3}{3.5} = 0.69$

or $\dfrac{2.4}{3.5} = .69$

$Progress \text{ (wks)} = \dfrac{\text{Cum. Earned (\$)}}{\text{Cum. Budget (\$)}} \times \text{Sch. WKS}$

$= \dfrac{2.4}{3.3} \times 52 \text{ (end of 1st. yr.)}$

$= 38$

## DECISION AND FEEDBACK SHEET

| Function | | Quarter 4 Sched. Wks. = 104 Addn. | Cum. | S.I./Prog. | Quarter 3 Sched. Wks. = 91 Addn. | Cum. | S.I./Prog. | Quarter 2 Sched. Wks. = 78 Addn. | Cum. | S.I./Prog. | Quarter 1 Sched. Wks. = 65 Addn. | Cum. | S.I./Prog. | Quarter 4 Sched. Wks. = 52 Addn. | Cum. | S.I./Prog. |
|---|---|---|---|---|---|---|---|---|---|---|---|---|---|---|---|---|
| Prod. | Budget | | 10.0 | | | | | | | | | | | 1.00 | 3.30 | |
| | Spent | | | | | | | | | | | | | 1.10 | 3.50 | .69 |
| | Earned | | | | | | | | | | | | | 0.70 | 2.40 | 38W |
| Tool. | Budget | | 2.7 | | | | | | | | | | | 0.70 | 2.50 | |
| | Spent | | | | | | | | | | | | | 0.60 | 2.50 | .63 |
| | Earned | | | | | | | | | | | | | 0.40 | 1.60 | 33W |
| Eng. | Budget | | 1.8 | | | | | | | | | | | 0.50 | 1.50 | |
| | Spent | | | | | | | | | | | | | 0.70 | 2.00 | .50 |
| | Earned | | | | | | | | | | | | | 0.50 | 1.00 | 35W |
| Q.C. | Budget | | 1.5 | | | | | | | | | | | 0.20 | 0.50 | |
| | Spent | | | | | | | | | | | | | 0.10 | 0.60 | .50 |
| | Earned | | | | | | | | | | | | | 0.10 | 0.30 | 37W |
| Matl. | Budget | | 4.0 | | | | | | | | | | | 0.40 | 1.40 | |
| | Spent | | | | | | | | | | | | | 0.40 | 1.40 | 1.0 |
| | Earned | | | | | | | | | | | | | 0.40 | 1.40 | 52W |
| Total | Budget | | 20.0 | | | | | | | | | | | 2.80 | 9.20 | |
| | Spent | | | | | | | | | | | | | 2.90 | 10.00 | .62 |
| | Earned | | | | | | | | | | | | | 2.10 | 6.70 | 38W |

Equiv. Units Completed = Earned Value (V)/$200,000 = (M) = _____     Fixed Price (F) = $25,000,000

Production Penalty = 100 − Equiv. Units (M)   = _____ × $300,000 (R)   = $ _____

Total $ Spent (S)   $ _____

Progress is computed as follows:     Profit = Price − Penalty − Spent

SI is computed as follows:

$$\frac{\text{Cum. Budget}}{\text{Cum. Spent}} \times \frac{\text{Cum. Earned}^{[a]}}{\text{Cum. Budget}} = SI$$

$$\frac{\text{Cum. Earned}^{[a]}}{\text{Cum. Budget}} \times \text{Sched. Wks.}^{[a]}$$

Spent = (F − R − S) = $ _____

[a] An equivalence of earned value to weeks accomplished is assumed. Scheduled weeks are given for each quarter.

Form 1

a quick decision can be made as to what expenditure allocation should be given each department in subsequent quarters. In computing the Status Index, 13 weeks should be added to the planned progress for every quarter.

(g) At the end of four quarters the players should determine their total costs on the bottom of Form 1. By subtracting costs from $25 million, net fee (profit) can be obtained and the winner of the game determined. Failure to complete any function in terms of progress (104 weeks) results in cancellation of the contract and the team is thereby disqualified.

## (15) DAVIS ENGINEERING

*Introduction*    The purpose of the Davis Engineering game is to present to the student a situation in which PERT network analysis can be utilized to effectively plan and control a project to meet a sucessful completion. The game will enable the student to study the trade-offs that exist between costs and time in the scheduling of a production operation. As a result of participation in the game, the student will have increased his awareness of the problems surrounding resource allocation decisions within the business environment. In addition, the familiarity he will gain in the area of PERT planning and control will serve as a valuable tool aiding his ability to solve such problems.

In addition to the game a short appendix is included in order to provide a review of some of the basic concepts behind PERT.

*Background*    This simulation consists of analyzing a PERT Network that represents a particular business project and then utilizing the network to control the accomplishment of the project. The objective is to minimize the total project costs when the project is viewed at various stages of completion. It is necessary

to plan a reasonable probability of completing the work by a specified date. After allocating the in-house and subcontractable *resources* to the required *activities* in order to attain the specified probability of a completion date, it is expected that the network be utilized for control and replanning. Reaction to actual conditions is initiated by reallocating the resources available to minimize the total project cost.

This simulation is designed to teach concepts, applications, and use of PERT in planning and controlling complex projects. It is suggetsed that the reference material be studied preceding the actual simulation. A PERT network has been charted and contains a number of complex interdependencies of the events such that the participant is forced to use a step-by-step analysis instead of a visual analysis of the network. The step-by-step analysis may seem tedious as characterized by the manual method, but there is no substitute for this in the learning process as the participant will hasten to admit.

The first objective of the simulation is to understand the network model that charts the activities in their proper sequence as per the project requirements. This has been done in Exhibit I and is called the PERT network. Each activity in this network can be accomplished in either of two alternate ways. Only two alternates for each activity have been suggested and the time estimates made. The estimates for "normal" operations are considered Condition I and the "expeditious" estimates are identified as Condition II. The expected activity times under Condition II in Exhibit II have been left blank for purposes of participant calculation practice. This requires the solution of:

$$t = \frac{t_0 + 4t_m + t_p}{6}$$

by Pertographs or manual methods.

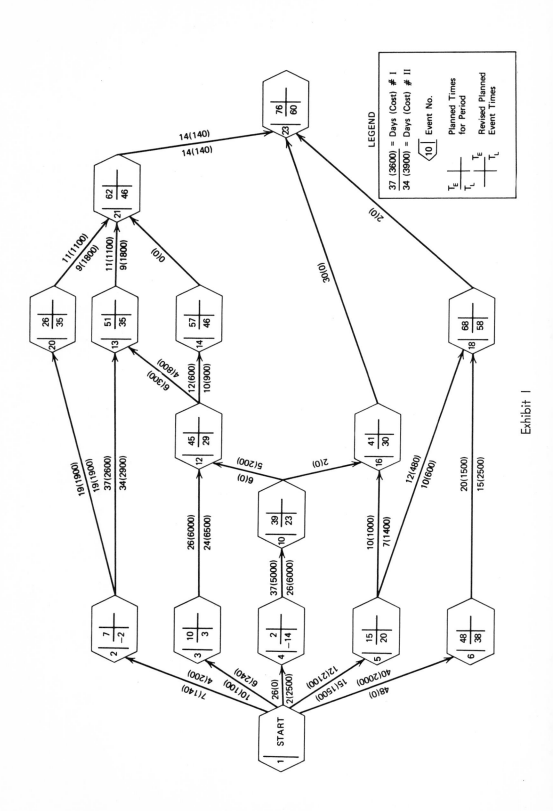

Exhibit I

LEGEND

| | |
|---|---|
| 37 (3600) = Days (Cost) # I | |
| 34 (3900) = Days (Cost) # II | |

⟨10⟩ Event No.

Planned Times
for Period

$T_E$ | $T_L$

Revised Planned
Event Times

# EXHIBIT II

## BASIC DATA FOR COST AND RESOURCE ALLOCATION

Est. of Variance $\sigma_i^2 = d_i^2 = \left(\dfrac{t_p - t_0}{6}\right)^2$

Est. of Std. Dev. $= \sigma_i = d_i = \dfrac{t_p - t_0}{6}$

| Activity | | Resource Allocation Under Condition #1 | | | | | | | | Resource Allocation Under Condition #2 | | | | | | | |
| --- | --- | --- | --- | --- | --- | --- | --- | --- | --- | --- | --- | --- | --- | --- | --- | --- | --- |
| Prec. | Succ. | $t_0$ | $t_m$ | $t_p$ | $t$ | $(t_p-t_0)$ | $d^2=\dfrac{(t_p-t_0)^2}{36}$ | Cost | Rate | $t_0$ | $t_m$ | $t_p$ | $t$ | $(t_p-t_0)$ | $\dfrac{(t_p-t_0)^2}{36}$ | Cost | Rate |
| 1 | 2 | 5 | 7 | 9 | 7 | 4 | .4 | 140 | 20 | 3 | 4 | 5 | 4 | 2 | .1 | 200 | 50 |
|  | 3 | 5 | 10 | 15 | 10 | 10 | 2.8 | 100 | 10 | 4 | 6 | 8 |  | 4 | .4 | 240 | 40 |
|  | 4 | 20 | 25 | 40 | 26 | 20 | 11.1 | 0 | 0 | 1 | 2 | 3 | 2 | 2 | .1 | 2500 | fixed cost |
|  | 5 | 10 | 15 | 20 | 15 | 10 | 2.8 | 1500 | 100 | 9 | 12 | 15 |  | 6 | 1.0 | 2100 | 175 |
|  | 6 | 40 | 45 | 70 | 48 | 30 | 25.0 | 0 | 0 | 35 | 38 | 53 |  | 18 | 9.0 | 2000 | 50 |
| 2 | 20 | 12 | 20 | 22 | 19 | 10 | 2.8 | 1900 | 100 | 30 | 34 | 38 |  | 8 | 1.8 | 2900 | 85 |
|  | 13 | 30 | 36 | 45 | 37 | 15 | 6.4 | 2600 | 70 | 20 | 23 | 30 | 24 | 10 | 2.8 | 6500 | 270 |
| 3 | 12 | 20 | 25 | 35 | 26 | 15 | 6.4 | 6000 | 230 | 22 | 25 | 35 | 26 | 13 | 4.7 | 6000 | 230 |
| 4 | 10 | 30 | 35 | 50 | 37 | 20 | 11.1 | 5000 | 135 | 3 | 5 | 7 |  | 4 | .4 | 200 | fixed price |
|  | 12 | 4 | 6 | 8 | 6 | 4 | .4 |  |  |  |  |  |  |  |  |  |  |
| 12 | 13 | 5 | 6 | 7 | 6 | 2 | .1 | 300 | 50 | 3 | 4 | 5 | 4 | 2 | .1 | 800 | 200 |
| 12 | 14 | 10 | 12 | 15 | 12 | 5 | .7 | 600 | 50 | 9 | 10 | 11 |  | 2 | .1 | 900 | 90 |
| 13 | 21 | 10 | 11 | 12 | 11 | 2 | .1 | 1100 | 100 | 8 | 9 | 10 |  | 2 | .1 | 1800 | 200 |
| 20 | 21 | 10 | 11 | 12 | 11 | 2 | .1 | 1100 | 100 | 8 | 9 | 10 | 9 | 2 | .1 | 1800 | 200 |
| 14 | 21 | 0 | 0 | 0 |  |  |  |  |  |  |  |  |  |  |  |  |  |
| 21 | 23 | 12 | 14 | 16 | 14 | 4 | .4 | 140 | 100 |  |  |  |  |  |  |  |  |
| 10 | 16 | 1 | 2 | 3 | 2 | 2 | .1 | 1000 | 100 |  |  |  |  |  |  |  |  |
| 5 | 16 | 8 | 10 | 12 | 10 | 4 | .4 | 0 | 0 |  |  |  |  |  |  |  |  |
| 16 | 23 | 25 | 29 | 45 | 30 | 20 | 11.1 |  |  | 6 | 7 | 9 |  | 3 | .2 | 1400 | 200 |
| 5 | 18 | 10 | 12 | 14 | 12 | 4 | .4 | 480 | 40 | 8 | 10 | 12 |  | 4 | .4 | 600 | 60 |
| 6 | 18 | 16 | 20 | 25 | 20 | 9 | 2.3 | 1500 | 75 | 12 | 15 | 18 |  | 5 | .7 | 2500 | 167 |
| 18 | 23 | 1 | 2 | 3 | 2 | 2 | .1 |  |  |  |  |  |  |  |  |  |  |

## MANAGEMENT DECISION SIMULATIONS

The second objective of the simulation is to allocate manpower and other resources to the project activities in order to reduce total project time so that there will be a 20% or greater probability that the scheduled date (60 days) can be met. This requires the calculation of earliest and latest *event* times for the network and the critical path. As soon as a participating team has selected the I or II Conditions for each activity that will lead to at least a 20% probability of meeting the schedule, this plan for resource allocation is submitted to the Administrator.

The individual team is then given the actual times for *activities* that have been wholly or partially completed as of a specified date. Estimate revisions are given to the team and they are now charged with reviewing the project plan at the end of this Period 1. The review may mean a change in plans such as Condition I to II which will add costs but is necessary to maintain the 20% or higher probability of meeting schedule.

The new resource allocation or plan is submitted with the required information for the next period's play. Again the Administrator provides the actual times for the submitted alternatives and provides any time revisions. This process is continued for the three or more periods of play until the project is deemed completed.

*Participant instructions*   Your company recently prepared a bid in competition with other contractors to refurbish a substantial number of ground power units that are currently in use by a defense customer. The bid was supported by a PERT network that is shown in Exhibit I. It indicates that a total time of 100 days is required from the award date of the contract to the start of production. Production time could vary between 60 and 90 days and will depend on the customer's shipment of units for processing.

Word has been received through your Sales Department that your company was awarded the contract, but that the schedule is highly critical. The customer insists that the project must be completed and production must start within 60 days. A penalty clause has been written into the contract for extension past that date, as shown below:

$$61\text{–}70 \text{ days} = \quad\quad \$200/\text{day} \quad S_n = -1 \text{ to} -10$$
$$71\text{–}75 \text{ days} = \$2000 + \$300/\text{day} \quad S_n = -11 \text{ to} -15$$
$$75\text{–over} \quad = \$3500 + \$500/\text{day} \quad S_n = -16 \text{ to} -\infty$$

Furthermore, the customer requires a PERT network to be used and an evaluation made of the probability of meeting schedule. Since the schedule is highly critical, the customer expects at least a probability of 0.20 that the project will be completed in 60 days or less before the contract will be formally awarded. For business reasons, it is important that your company perform this contract.

The PERT network (Exhibit I) and the Time and Cost Sheet (Exhibit II) are being reviewed at the present time to determine what steps can be taken to shorten the critical path. The critical path activities are shown by the negative slack in Exhibit I and numerically in Exhibit III. In the first staff meeting on this job, Engineering offers the following suggestion:

"Since Engineering is overloaded and will not be free from present commitments for from 20 to 40 days, engineering design could be subcontracted for which arrangements could be completed in 1 to 3 days and save 24 days in the network by not having to staff the project. The added costs would be $2500."

The added cost of this proposal ($105/day) is more than offset by the reduction in penalty costs ($200/day). These data are fed into the network and the new times are shown in Exhibit III as Alternative 1. ($t_{1-4} = 2$, the expected time for activity 1–4). This has been accomplished in sample period O of the Time and Cost Analysis Report.

This reduces the project finish time from 100 to 76 days or to within 16 days of the required 60-day completion time. For this alternative the probability of making schedule is computed. This is shown at the bottom of Exhibit III. However, the chances of this alternative plan meeting the schedule are remote, as indicated by Exhibit IV, the Probability Table, where $Pr < 1\%$ for a normal deviate between 2.2 & $\infty$.

The next suggestion made to reduce the project time was to authorize overtime for the subcontract engineering (activity 4–10) at an added cost of $1000. This would bring the estimates for the design time into the range $t_o = 22$, $t_m = 25$, $t_p = 35$. Based on this new input $t_4 - 10$ is to be calculated, this alternative economically evaluated and the new probability of meeting schedule determined. Other alternatives are submitted by responsible staff groups. These are tabulated and shown in Exhibit II as Condition II.

As project management, you are required to carry the contract to a successful conclusion. Your performance will be judged on your ability to minimize total project cost. The plan/actual cost report (Exhibit III) is to be submitted at the end of each period's play. This report brings together the probable schedule and cost to complete plus the actual costs and accomplishments to date.

The simulation consists essentially of two phases: (1) The start phase in which each participant obtains familiarity with the network and the determination of a plan permitting at least 20% probability of making schedule with the original input estimates. (2) The second phase utilizes the network to control the project as actual time progresses and events are accomplished. The procedure is as follows:

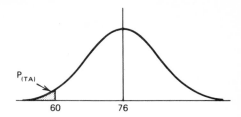

1. Analyze the network and submit the network decision on the Time and Cost Control Report, Form PM 2, indicating which Condition has been selected for each activity (a = Condition II). The expenditure rate for each activity is governed by the condition selected. Conditions chosen may be changed except if work has begun on the activity.

2. The probability of accomplishing the network as of Period 1's decisions is computed and entered at the bottom of the appropriate column.

3. The actual time fed back for each activity completed or partially completed after a stimulated elapsed time or period will be determined by a random choice from the time distribution of the individual activities. These times will come from the Condition I or Condition II distributions depending on the choice of activity condition. After each period these actual times will be announced by the Administrator and entered on the Control Report, Form PM 2.

4. The actual times and the rates for the conditions selected will be used to calculate the cost of each activity completed or partially completed to date.

5. Based on the actual times for the activities in the first period, the network should be reevaluated, Condition changes for remaining activities made, and the network decisions submitted with the new probability of making schedule stated. This step can be done by crosshatching out what has been accomplished on Form PM-1 and concentrating on the remainder. Another method would be to redraw this network for the activities remaining.

6. Estimates on activities remaining can change at the discretion of the Administrator, which simulates an actual project environment. The participant must naturally react to these new estimates as they affect their project cost.

MANAGEMENT DECISION SIMULATIONS

EXHIBIT III

TIME AND COST ANALYSIS REPORT

Period # _____          Period # _____

| Activity Prec. Succ. | $t$ or $t_a$ | $T_E$ | $T_L$ | $S$ | $d^2$ | Est. Cost | Actual Cost | $t$ or $t_a$ | $T_E$ | $T_L$ | $S$ | $d^2$ | Est. Cost | Actual Cost |
|---|---|---|---|---|---|---|---|---|---|---|---|---|---|---|
| 1– 2 | | | | | | | | | | | | | | |
| 1– 3 | | | | | | | | | | | | | | |
| 1– 4 | | | | | | | | | | | | | | |
| 1– 5 | | | | | | | | | | | | | | |
| 1– 6 | | | | | | | | | | | | | | |
| 2–20 | | | | | | | | | | | | | | |
| 2–13 | | | | | | | | | | | | | | |
| 3–12 | | | | | | | | | | | | | | |
| 4–10 | | | | | | | | | | | | | | |
| 10–12 | | | | | | | | | | | | | | |
| 12–13 | | | | | | | | | | | | | | |
| 12–14 | | | | | | | | | | | | | | |
| 13–21 | | | | | | | | | | | | | | |
| 20–21 | | | | | | | | | | | | | | |
| 14–21 | | | | | | | | | | | | | | |
| 21–23 | | | | | | | | | | | | | | |
| 10–13 | | | | | | | | | | | | | | |
| 5–16 | | | | | | | | | | | | | | |
| 16–23 | | | | | | | | | | | | | | |
| 5–18 | | | | | | | | | | | | | | |
| 6–18 | | | | | | | | | | | | | | |
| 18–23 | | | | | | | | | | | | | | |
| | | | | | | | | | | | | | | |

| Period # _____ | Begin | End |
|---|---|---|
| 1. Est. to Complete | | |
| 2. Actuals to Date | | |
| 3. Est. at Completion | | |
| 4. Schedule Penalties | | |
| 5. Est. Project Cost | | |
| 6. Fixed Price | | |
| 7. Contr. to O'hd & Pr. $T_E - T_L/\sqrt{\Sigma\ d^2}$ | | |
| 8. Prob. of Making Sched. _____ _____ | | |

a Condition II

| Period # _____ | Begin | End |
|---|---|---|
| 1. Est. to Complete | | |
| 2. Actuals to Date | | |
| 3. Est. at Completion | | |
| 4. Schedule Penalties | | |
| 5. Est. Project Cost | | |
| 6. Fixed Price | | |
| 7. Contr. to O'hd & Pr. | | |
| 8. Prob. of Making Sched. _____ _____ | | |

a Condition II

Form PM-2

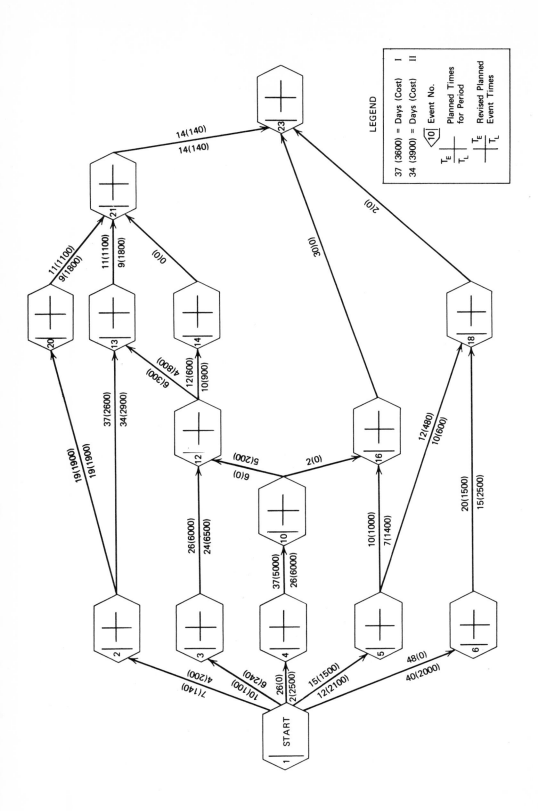

MANAGEMENT DECISION SIMULATIONS

## EXHIBIT III

### TIME AND COST ANALYSIS REPORT

Period #                              Period #

| Activity Prec. Succ. | $t$ or $t_a$ | $T_E$ | $T_L$ | $S$ | $d^2$ | Est. Cost | Actual Cost | $t$ or $t_a$ | $T_E$ | $T_L$ | $S$ | $d^2$ | Est. Cost | Actual Cost |
|---|---|---|---|---|---|---|---|---|---|---|---|---|---|---|
| 1– 2 | | | | | | | | | | | | | | |
| 1– 3 | | | | | | | | | | | | | | |
| 1– 4 | | | | | | | | | | | | | | |
| 1– 5 | | | | | | | | | | | | | | |
| 1– 6 | | | | | | | | | | | | | | |
| 2–20 | | | | | | | | | | | | | | |
| 2–13 | | | | | | | | | | | | | | |
| 3–12 | | | | | | | | | | | | | | |
| 4–10 | | | | | | | | | | | | | | |
| 10–12 | | | | | | | | | | | | | | |
| 12–13 | | | | | | | | | | | | | | |
| 12–14 | | | | | | | | | | | | | | |
| 13–21 | | | | | | | | | | | | | | |
| 20–21 | | | | | | | | | | | | | | |
| 14–21 | | | | | | | | | | | | | | |
| 21–23 | | | | | | | | | | | | | | |
| 10–16 | | | | | | | | | | | | | | |
| 5–16 | | | | | | | | | | | | | | |
| 16–23 | | | | | | | | | | | | | | |
| 5–18 | | | | | | | | | | | | | | |
| 6–18 | | | | | | | | | | | | | | |
| 18–23 | | | | | | | | | | | | | | |

|  | Period # | Begin | End |  | Period # | Begin | End |
|---|---|---|---|---|---|---|---|
| 1. | Est. to Complete | | | 1. | Est. to Complete | | |
| 2. | Actuals to Date | | | 2. | Actuals to Date | | |
| 3. | Est. at Completion | | | 3. | Est. at Completion | | |
| 4. | Schedule Penalties | | | 4. | Schedule Penalties | | |
| 5. | Est. Project Cost | | | 5. | Est. Project Cost | | |
| 6. | Fixed Price | | | 6. | Fixed Price | | |
| 7. | Contr. to O'hd & Pr. $T_E - T_L/\sqrt{\Sigma d^2}$ | | | 7. | Contr. to O'hd & Pr. | | |
| 8. | Prob. of Making Sched. | | | 8. | Prob. of Making Sched. | | |

[a] Condition II            [a] Condition II

Form PM-2

## EXHIBIT IV

### TABLE OF THE NORMAL DISTRIBUTION

$$Z = \frac{T_S - T_L}{\sqrt{\Sigma d^2}} = \frac{T_S - T_L}{\sigma_T} = \frac{60 - 76}{3.5} = \frac{-16}{3.5} = -4$$

| Z | $P(T_A \leq T_S < T_E)^a$ | Z | $P(T_A \leq T_S > T_E)^b$ |
|---|---|---|---|
| Normal Deviate | Probability | Normal Deviate | Probability |
| −0.0 | .50 | 0.0 | .50 |
| −0.1 | .46 | 0.1 | .54 |
| −0.2 | .42 | 0.2 | .58 |
| −0.3 | .38 | 0.3 | .62 |
| −0.4 | .34 | 0.4 | .66 |
| −0.5 | .31 | 0.5 | .69 |
| −0.6 | .27 | 0.6 | .73 |
| −0.7 | .24 | 0.7 | .76 |
| −0.8 | .21 | 0.8 | .79 |
| −0.9 | .18 | 0.9 | .82 |
| −1.0 | .16 | 1.0 | .84 |
| −1.1 | .14 | 1.1 | .86 |
| −1.2 | .12 | 1.2 | .88 |
| −1.3 | .10 | 1.3 | .90 |
| −1.4 | .08 | 1.4 | .92 |
| −1.5 | .07 | 1.5 | .93 |
| −1.6 | .05 | 1.6 | .95 |
| −1.7 | .04 | 1.7 | .96 |
| −1.8 | .04 | 1.8 | .96 |
| −1.9 | .03 | 1.9 | .97 |
| −2.0 | .02 | 2.0 | .98 |
| −2.1 | .02 | 2.1 | .98 |
| −2.2 | .01 | 2.2 | .99 |
| −2.3 | .01 | 2.3 | .99 |
| −2.4 | .01 | 2.4 | .99 |
| −2.5 | .01 | 2.5 | .99 |

[a] Probability that actual completion time ($T_A$) will be equal to or less than a scheduled date ($T_S$) which is less than predicted earliest completion date ($T_E$).
[b] Probability that the actual completion date will be equal to or less than a scheduled date ($T_S$) which is greater than predicted earliest completion date ($T_E$).

# 6

# Briefing Material

The sections to follow are designed to provide specific theoretical quantitative material that may be helpful in formulating strategy and making decisions in various functional areas. Through the use of these briefings the participants should be capable of approaching a game in a more disciplined manner, make more knowledgeable and rational decisions, and apply some theoretical concepts, models, or equations to rather specific situations.

Briefing materials that can be referenced to specific games included in the text are as follows:

| Game | Briefing Material |
|------|-------------------|
| Clean Air Petroleum | Pricing |
| Davis Engineering | PERT |
| Holiday Tree | Transportation Model Incremental Analysis |
| Powers Company | Project Management |
| Submarine P3 | Reliability |
| Taylor Manufacturing | Lot Size/Reorder Point |
| Water Recreation | Queuing |

The instructor has the option of assigning this appendix material prior or subsequent to playing the game. In some cases the briefings are specific to the decisions areas involved and may be more appropriate as debriefing material to be discussed after game play. This would be true of the Pricing, Transportation Model, and Lot Size/Reorder Point material.

## MANAGEMENT DECISION SIMULATIONS

When participants design games, the fruits of their research into an area should be similarly documented in briefings and distributed to their colleagues.

### Briefing on Pricing

The main consideration in a firm's pricing decision is the effect that the price will have on the demand for the product. This relationship is called the *elasticity* and refers to the change in demand that will take place for a given change in price. Normally we expect demand for a product to increase as we lower price, and conversely, the demand to drop if price is increased.

What is really of interest to the business manager is the effect of this elasticity on revenue and ultimately on profit. If the price of a product is lowered, the demand is often increased. However, if the added volume sold does not offset the lower price obtained on each unit, the total revenue may fall.

The pricing decision then is one of determining the relative degree of elasticity with respect to a product and then selecting a price that will maximize profit. For example, assume that the demand function is represented by the linear equation:

$$D = 50,000 - 25p \quad \text{where } D = \text{demand} \\ p = \text{price} \tag{1}$$

if demand equals 0, the price equals $2000; which means no one will buy at this price. If the firm has $25,000 of fixed costs and a variable cost/unit of $50.00 the total cost is the sum of the fixed and variable costs or:

$$C = 25,000 + 50D \tag{2}$$

Substituting the demand function from (1), the total cost becomes:

$$C = 25,000 + 50 (50,000 - 25p) \\ = 2,525,000 - 1250p \tag{3}$$

The revenue to be obtained from the product would be given by the expression:

$$\text{Revenue} = \text{Demand} \times \text{Price, or } R = D \cdot p$$

Again substituting the demand function from (1):

$$R = (50,000 - 25p)p. \tag{4}$$

From the demand function, a price of $0 would result in selling 50,000 units, each one having a variable cost of $50.00. In addition, the firm bears $25,000 in fixed expenses. This gives a total cost of $2,525,000.

As indicated earlier, the firm is ultimately concerned with the maximization of profit. The profit for the chosen product is expressed by:

$$\text{Profit} = \text{Revenue} - \text{Total Cost}$$

which is:

$$Z = (50,000 - 25p)p \\ - 2,525,000 - 1250p \tag{5}$$

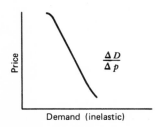

Demand (inelastic)

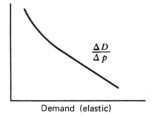

Demand (elastic)

This simplifies to:

$$Z = 50{,}000p - 25p^2 - 2{,}525{,}000 + 1250p$$
$$or$$
$$Z = 51{,}250p - 25p^2 - 2{,}525{,}000 \qquad (6)$$

We desire to know the point at which this profit equation reaches its maximum. This is the point at which the slope is

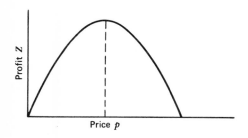

Price $p$

equal to zero or where a slight change in price has no effect on profit. Thus, taking the first derivative of the profit equation (slope) and setting it equal to zero will define the peak of the profit curve. The price corresponding to this maximum profit point is the optimum price.

$$\frac{dZ}{dp} = 51{,}250 - 50p = 0 \qquad (7)$$

solving for $p$ we find $p = \$102.50$ which would be the price at which we would maximize profit.

This problem could also be solved utilizing marginal revenue and marginal cost concepts. The point at which a firm would want to operate is where its marginal revenue equals its marginal cost. If marginal revenue is greater than marginal cost, a company could increase profit by continuing to increase production. If, on the other hand, marginal cost is greater than marginal revenue, the firm has gone beyond the point of maximum contribution to profit.

This point can be determined by utilizing equations (3) and (4):

$$R = 50{,}000p - 25p^2$$
$$C = 2{,}525{,}000 - 1250p$$

The marginal revenue

$$= \frac{dR}{dp} = 50{,}000 - 50p$$

marginal cost $\qquad = \frac{dC}{dp} = -1250$

Equating these two expressions gives:

$$50{,}000 - 50p = -1250$$
$$50p = 51{,}250$$
$$p = 102.50$$

### Briefing on Lot Size and Reorder Points

Two groups of opposing forces act in the formulation of decisions with regard to amounts of stock to order and store. Ordering and carrying smaller amounts is desirable because there is:

1. Less stock investment.
2. Less insurance charges and taxes.
3. Less depreciation, deterioration, and obsolescence.
4. Less space required to rent, clean, and heat.

Larger amounts are desirable to order and stock because there are:

1. Fewer numbers of orders to write and invoices to pay.
2. Fewer receivables in Receiving Department; less handling costs.
3. Less individual receiving inspections.
4. Fewer deliveries to stock room.

To strike a balance between these two opposing views, it is possible to derive some fundamental equations that result in minimizing the total cost of inventory procurement and investment. The result obtained from these equations is known as the Economic Lot Size—a quantity or

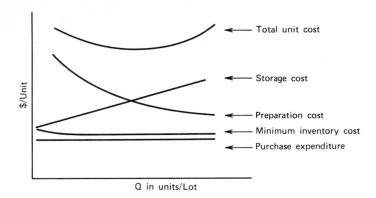

Q in units/Lot

number of units that should be *purchased, manufactured,* or *processed* if the *least cost* is to be incurred from the time the preparations for production or purchase are started until material is issued out of storage area. This quantity, again, is only the quantity to be purchased or produced and *added to* the inventory and not the optimum inventory itself. It does, however, minimize the cost of the inventory carried.

### DERIVATION OF ECONOMIC LOT SIZE

Let: $Q$ = Economic lot size.

$C$ = Purchase price or production price per unit.

$S$ = Set-up or preparation cost or procurement cost per order.

$I$ = Sum of percentage rates of interest, taxes, obsolescence, depreciation, and insurance per time period (year).

$B$ = Reserve, minimum, or emergency stock.

$A$ = Number of units required per time period.

$T$ = Total cost of a time period's supply.

The case of the Minimum Cost Purchase Quantity.

$T$ = Purchasing Expenditure + Procurement Charges + Carrying Charge.

$$T = AC + \frac{AS}{Q}$$

$$+ I\left[\left(C + \frac{S}{Q}\right)^1\left(B + \frac{Q}{2}\right)\right]$$

$$= AC + \frac{AS}{Q} + ICB + \frac{ICQ}{2} + \frac{ISB}{Q} + \frac{IS}{2}$$

Differentiating with respect to $Q$ and setting the first derivative equal to zero to obtain the minimum on the curve:

$$\frac{dT}{dQ} = \frac{-AS}{Q2} + \frac{IC}{2} - \frac{ISB}{Q^2} = 0$$

(1) Solving, it is found that

$$Q = \sqrt{\frac{2S(A + IB)}{CI}}$$

Figure 3 illustrates how the inventory might vary for one particular item. The minimum inventory is emergency material, determined by past experience, company policy, or statistical techniques. They all attempt to prevent, minimize, or control the out-of-stock situations. The maximum inventory is the greatest amount of material that may be on hand at any one time and is a quantity in the neighborhood of the minimum inventory plus the quantity ordered.

The order point is usually expressed

[1] Total unit cost, including proration of set-up costs.

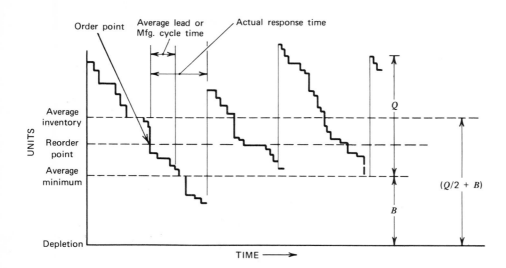

as the number of units in inventory at which the next economic lot order is to begin being processed. The time interval between the time of ordering and the receipt of material is the lead time in the case of supplier or vendor activities or the manufacturing cycle time in the case of materials produced in the plant itself.

## PREREQUISITES TO ECONOMIC LOT SIZE APPLICATION

The following are some of the prerequisites that should be met if the theory is to replace practical, "seat-of-the-pants" methods in inventory control:

1. The rate of consumption must be able to be represented by a mean or median. The items must be placed in and withdrawn from storage in order to attach a storage cost to them.

2. Labor, material, and overhead costs must be relatively stable and determinable.

3. Preparation or set-up costs are real and determinable.

4. Storage costs must reflect sound accounting methods.

### The Average Rate of Consumption

In the case where parts are ordered and, on receipt, are immediately sent to the first operation, it is easily seen that since there is no storage there can be no average inventory, therefore no economic lot size.

Determining the time period to be used in the computation of average consumption can present some difficulty. If the item is seasonal, there would be different usage each month and each quarter. Should, therefore, the average monthly demand be computed on the basis of a year's demand?

A general rule could be used to resolve this situation such as:

If one uses the average monthly demand based on an entire year and the solution to the formula shows a lot size less than one year's demand, then the solution should be recalculated for each quarter's demand.

If the lot size is less than a quarter's demand, then the calculations should be repeated using the average monthly demand on a quarterly basis.

If the solution is less than a monthly demand, then one should challenge this pro-

## MANAGEMENT DECISION SIMULATIONS

cedure and establish contract or regular replenishment commitments.

### Material, Labor, and Overhead Costs

Knowledge of these costs is imperative in correctly applying economic lot size theory to production.

Material costs are assumed to be constant during the period the formula is to cover. These costs are rather easy to obtain.

The labor cost to be used is usually based on more rash assumptions. These include such assumptions as: the men assigned to the job are of equal pay and productivity or an average representative rate covering all who are to work on this job can be used. The method used is important in that it affects the direct labor cost.

The overhead figure should not include costs that have already been assigned in the formula, i.e., preparation, production control, and storage costs, unless these costs are a small percentage of the overhead figure. This figure or rate is, of course, a function of the plant accounting system. The actual *burden* rate when the plant is operating at full capacity is likely to be smaller than the rate used at partial capacity. Usually, one overhead rate is used throughout the year. Therefore, the economic lot size is computed on the basis of one overhead rate irrespective of the plant capacity and thus

contributes somewhat to an unrealistic quantity.

### Preparation or Set-Up Costs

Customary usage of economic lot size computations include under the above classification those costs that are constant no matter what the order size and only those costs that are incurred up to the time the material is received in stock. If the costs incurred after receipt of the material could be more easily obtained, then they too would theoretically be included.

The preparation costs for obtaining material outside the plant would normally include writing a requisition, contacting a supplier, issuing a purchase order, and recording this information. If the item is supplied by our own production facilities, then the set-up charges normally include all costs associated with tearing down and setting up for production, including writing a shop order, scheduling, dispatching, follow-up reports, dismantling, return of tools, getting new tools, and installation.

### Storage Charges

A simple method of dealing with these charges would be to establish a percentage of the value of an item to represent the total cost of storing that item. One would find very likely that there would be great variation from one company to another. One report states:

| | | |
|---|---|---|
| Interest, depreciation, and obsolescence | 6 to 8%/year | 15 to 20%/year |
| Taxes and insurance | 1/2% | 1-1/2% |
| Storage facilities and handling | 1-1/2 to 3-1/2% | 3-1/2 to 8% |
| Average total | 10%/year | 25%/year |

The determination of storage charge composition and amount is a rather complete problem in itself involving careful analysis of accounting data. It is apparent

with the inherent accounting limitations that the averages, approximations, and assumptions again contribute to the "inaccuracy" of the final result.

## REORDER POINTS AND SAFETY STOCK

If the demand is constant and lead time is known and constant, the reorder point is simply usage during lead time.

$$R = U \cdot L$$

If $U = 11$, $L = 10$, then $R = 110$ units.

However, this provides no margin of safety if demand or lead time vary. If the past demand can be statistically analyzed, a safety stock could be computed that would help prevent stockouts. For example, if $\overline{U} =$ average weekly demand, $\sigma_U =$ standard deviation of the demand, then for over 99% protection against stockouts resulting from variable demand during an inventory cycle, establish the reorder point as follows:

$$R = U \cdot L + B$$

where $B = 3 \cdot \sigma_u$

If $\sigma_U = 4$, then $R = 110 + 12$ or 122 units.

If demand is constant but the lead time is variable, it too should be statistically analyzed. For example,

If $\overline{L} =$ average lead time in weeks

$\sigma_L =$ standard deviation of the lead times

Then for over 99% protection against stockouts during an inventory cycle due to long lead times, the reorder point would be established as follows:

$R = \overline{U} \cdot \overline{L} + B$ where $B = \overline{U} \cdot 3\sigma_L$

If $\sigma_L = 3$ weeks, then

$$R = 110 + 11 \cdot 3 \cdot 3 = 209 \text{ units}$$

Often both demand and lead time are variable, but the chances of maximum demand occurring during maximum lead time are small. The concept of additivity of variances can be used to resolve the combinatorial effect of both variable lead times and variable demand. Thus,

$$\sigma_{UL}^2 = \sigma_U^2 + (\overline{U}\sigma_L)^2$$

gives the variance in units.

and $R = \overline{U} \cdot \overline{L} + B$ where

$$B = \sqrt{\sigma_u^2 + (U\sigma_2)^2}$$

If $U = 11$, $L = 10$, $\sigma_u = 4$ and

$$\sigma_L = 3, \text{ then}$$

$$R = 110 + 3\sqrt{16 + 900}$$

$$= 110 + 91 = 201$$

Thus there should be no more than one stockout in 100 inventory ordering cycles when using a reorder point of 200. Less protection may be desired with correspondingly less carrying costs for safety stock.

### Briefing on Queuing Theory

Sometimes referred to as waiting-line problems. queuing theory deals with the situation in which customers seek service from one or more facilities. If the facilities are not able to accommodate all customers on their arrival, a waiting line or queue will develop. The basic decision required is to determine the number of facilities to operate in order to service the arrival patterns of the customers with an acceptable level of service.

Several different arrival and service patterns exist or can be approximated in practice; i.e., constant arrival rates with constant service time, Poisson arrivals with exponential service time, or Poisson arrivals with nonexponential service time, and other combinations.

There are many excellent references in this area that deal with the analytical solutions of waiting-line problems. However, if the arrival and service distributions are not known or the mathematics are seemingly too complex, Monte Carlo analysis of waiting-line problems is a very pragmatic method. Utilizing this method also helps obtain a true understanding of the problems associated with queuing problems. This technique enables the participant to simulate the behavior and operating cost of a system over some

## MANAGEMENT DECISION SIMULATIONS

period of time and to compare the behavior or outcome when the variables are changed.

Monte Carlo analysis as applied to waiting-line problems requires no assumptions concerning arrival times or service time requirements. Thus the shape of the distribution curve for these parameters do not influence the method of analysis. To proceed with a Monte Carlo analysis the decision maker should have some idea through data gathering of the arrival rate of customers either in arrivals/period or interval between arrivals *and* the amount of time a customer will spend in the service facility. A set of probability distributions might take the following form.

### PROBABILITY

When a unit arrives it will move directly into the facility (if the facility is vacant); if the facility is being utilized the unit will form a queue until it can be served. Given the frequency distribution of arrivals and service times the objective of the Monte Carlo technique is to simulate the operation over some period of time and to determine the most effective (least cost) system to employ.

If a single channel service facility is assumed, the Monte Carlo analysis might follow this pattern:

Assign blocks of numbers to each of the arrival- and service-time possibilities. These numbers must represent the respective probabilities of each demand (arrival) and service time.

| Time Between Arrivals | | | Service Time | | |
|---|---|---|---|---|---|
| Min. | Prop. | R.N. | Min. | Prob. | R.N. |
| 4 | .05 | 1–5 | 2 | .10 | 1–10 |
| 5 | .20 | 6–25 | 3 | .30 | 11–40 |
| 6 | .70 | 26–95 | 4 | .50 | 41–90 |
| 7 | .05 | 96–00 | 5 | .10 | 91–00 |

The next step in the process will be to generate random numbers which are utilized to represent the actual time between arrivals and the service times during some predetermined number of periods.

Assume the following numbers have been generated representing "time between arrivals":

| R.N. | | Time Between Arrivals (B) |
|---|---|---|
| 17 | = | 2 min. |
| 42 | = | 6 min. |
| 3 | = | 4 min. |
| 30 | = | 6 min. |

In addition, the following numbers represent service times:

| R.N. | | Service Time (S) |
|---|---|---|
| 50 | = | 4 min. |
| 96 | = | 5 min. |
| 7 | = | 2 min. |
| 37 | = | 3 min. |

These four events may be graphed in Figure 6.

Suppose that waiting cost is estimated to be $0.25/min. and that it costs $0.30/

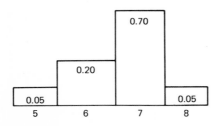

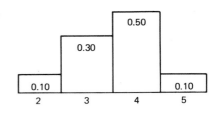

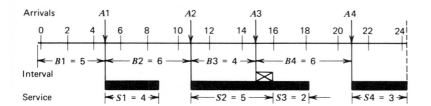

min. to provide the service capability as described by the service-time distribution, the total cost of the above system might be

$$\text{System Cost/Min.} = \text{Total Minutes} \times \text{Cost/Min.} + \underset{\text{Service} +}{\underset{\text{in Queue}}{\text{Minutes in}}} \times \underset{\text{Cost}}{\text{Waiting}}$$

$$= (24 \times .30 + 15 \times 0.25)/24$$

$$= \$15.75/24 \text{ min. or } \$.657/\text{min.}$$

Larger sampling from this particular system would produce a more representative cost. Sensitivity analysis can be performed by repeating the Monte Carlo samplings and calculations for other arrival and service distributions.

### Briefing on the Transportation Model

This special case of linear programming is often called the Transportation Model. It has been applied to the problem of distributing goods from a set of origin points to multiple destinations at a minimum cost. There are basic requirements that have to be met which are generally as follows:

1. Source capacities and demands must be expressed in the same units of the commodity.
2. The problem can be expressed in a set of linear equations.
3. The exchange of resource commodities among sources and consumers is on a one-for-one basis.
4. No negative amounts of the resource commodity can be allocated.

A simple model $(2 \times 2)$ can be set up as follows:

*Cost Matrix*

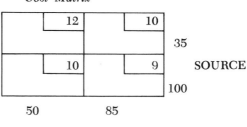

DESTINATION

I. *An Initial Feasible Solution*

1. Find the smallest cost in the matrix.

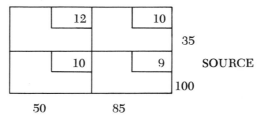

DESTINATION

2. Allocate as much of the resource as possible into the cell. (A log-

# MANAGEMENT DECISION SIMULATIONS

ical maneuver.) The amount may be restricted by either the satisfaction of column's demand or the exhaustion of a row's capacity. If the row capacity (or column demand) restricts the allocation, delete temporarily all cells in this (or column) from further consideration in developing the initial solution.

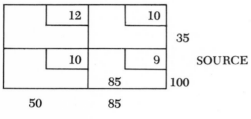

DESTINATION

3. Proceed to the next smallest cost cell remaining for consideration and again allocate as in Steps 1 and 2. In case of ties, arbitrarily choose one cell for allocation and proceed.

COSTS

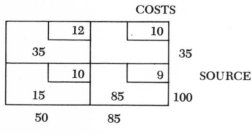

DESTINATION

4. When allocation is complete, check for row and column balance throughout. This is then an initial, feasible solution.

*Cost Evaluation*

| | |
|---|---|
| Cost added | + 10 |
| Cost sub | − 12 |
| Cost added | + 10 |
| Cost sub | − 9 |
| | |
| Net | − 1 (Cost Reduction) |

5. Before testing for improvement, it is wise to check if sufficient cells have had an allocation by computing number of rows + number of columns less 1. If the allocated cells total less than this, the solution is degenerate and reference should be made to Part IV.

## II. *Testing for Solution Improvement*

1. The incremental steppingstone tests can begin by selecting a nonallocated or vacant cell and determining the advisability of shifting some of the allocation into this vacant cell.

2. In determining this advisability, add one unit into the vacant cell, subtract from a cell having an allocation in the same row (or column), add one to another allocated cell, etc., until all columns and rows are again in balance. Only the *chosen vacant* cell can be modified by the incremental unit. All other modified cells are cells with allocations. Often the evaluation pattern is a rectangle but occasionally the "plus-minus one" route through the matrix may involve 5, 7, or even more allocated cells before returning to the cell being evaluated.

3. Algebraically add the incremental costs, that is, the cost of adding or deleting one unit in the modified cells. If the net cost is positive, this would have an adverse effect on cost. If net cost is negative, costs can be reduced by a shift in the present allocation toward the vacant cell.

4. Perform this vacant cell evaluation for all vacant cells.

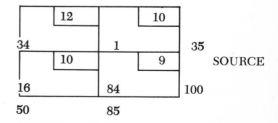

DESTINATION

5. Choose the vacant cell having the most potential cost saving and shift the maximum amount possible into this cell following the same route pattern as with one unit evaluation procedure. All rows and columns must remain in balance with no negative cells. This is an improved solution by the amount shifted multiplied by the net cost saving when one unit is shifted.

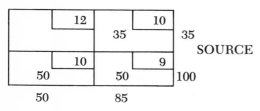

SOURCE

DESTINATION

## III. *The Iterative Process Toward Optimization*

Repeat Steps 2 through 5 in Section II until no further improved solution can be obtained. This final allocation is an optimum solution.

## IV. *Degeneracy*

Occasionally one finds an insufficient number of allocated cells available, thereby preventing the above testing procedure to be followed. In order to allow the vacant-cell evaluation to proceed which may involve more than one row vacant cell, an insignificant amount "$e$" is inserted in a particular vacant cell. The "$e$" cell is chosen to permit the evaluation patterns to be completed and is treated as an allocated cell and not as a vacant cell.

### Briefing on Incremental Analysis*

Given a number of units, if one more unit is added to the production scheme, there will be an increase in cost, called the incremental cost. It is the difference

* This material drawn from *Analysis for Production Management*, Bowman and Fetter, Erwin 1961:310-320.

between total cost before the unit is added and total cost after the unit is added. The addition of one unit to the production scheme should also permit some benefit or gain. This gain, associated with the additional unit, is the incremental gain.

Comparing the incremental cost with the incremental gain reveals the net contribution due to the additional unit. As a logical extension of this idea, units should be added to the scheme until the incremental cost ($\Delta C$) equals the incremental gain ($\Delta G$). That is, a contribution can be made until $\Delta C = \Delta G$.

The use of probability with incremental analysis may also be used. The more units purchased, the better are the chances of having enough units on hand to meet a possible demand. On the other hand, the more units bought, the better are the chances of having too many units on hand that might not be sold. The former is analogous to incremental gain, the latter to incremental cost. Figure 7 represents the cumulative probability distribution of sales that could possibly be experienced by a company. With this distribution and knowledge of unit costs and profits, the equation of condition is as follows:

$$E(\Delta C) = E(\Delta G)$$

Thus, when the expected value of the incremental cost equals the expected value of the incremental gain, no further

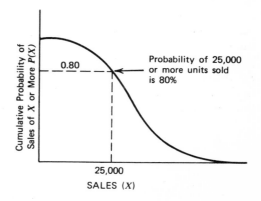

## MANAGEMENT DECISION SIMULATIONS

contribution can be made by an additional unit.

$C$ = cost of unit

$M$ = margin or profit made on each unit

$P(X)$ = probability of being able to sell a given quantity or more (whether or not the units are available) and thus gain additional profits

$1 - P(X)$ = probability of not being able to sell a given quantity or more and thus incurring extra costs.

Thus incremental cost $E(\Delta C) = (1 - P(X)) * C$ and incremental gain $E(\Delta G) = P(X) * M$. The solution for optimum $P(X)$ is:

$$(1 - P(X))C = P(X)M$$
$$C - P(X)C = P(X)M$$
$$C = P(X)M + P(X)C$$
$$C = P(X)(M + C)$$
$$P(X) = \frac{C}{M + C}$$

### Briefing on Reliability*

Figure 1 illustrates the three ways in which reliability data may be graphed.

During the useful portion of the life of many electronic equipments (after burn-in and prior to wear out), failures tend to occur randomly and the equipment exhibits relatively constant failure rates. Since it is also assumed that these failures are single, discrete, independent events in time, the probability of exactly $i$ failures, when the expected (average) number of failures is $m$, is given by the Poisson distribution:

$$p(i) = \frac{m^i e^{-m}}{i!}$$

* Reliability prediction T.C. Qecires ASME paper 60-MB-1 Feb. 1960.

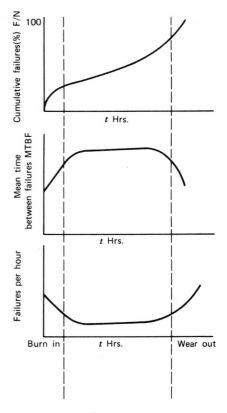

Figure 1

For $N$ items in operation, each item having an average failure rate, $\lambda$, the average expected number of failures, $m$, during operating time $t$ is:

$$m = N \cdot t \cdot \lambda$$

The average failure rate is also the reciprocal of the $MTBF$. If it is assumed that only one item is to be operating at any one time ($N = 1$), then $m$ is calculated as follows:

$$M = \left(\frac{t}{MTBF}\right).$$

If $c$ spares are available, we wish to know the probability, $P_c$, that there will be $c$ or fewer failures during the required operating time period. If $c$ units fail, the system will still be operational be-

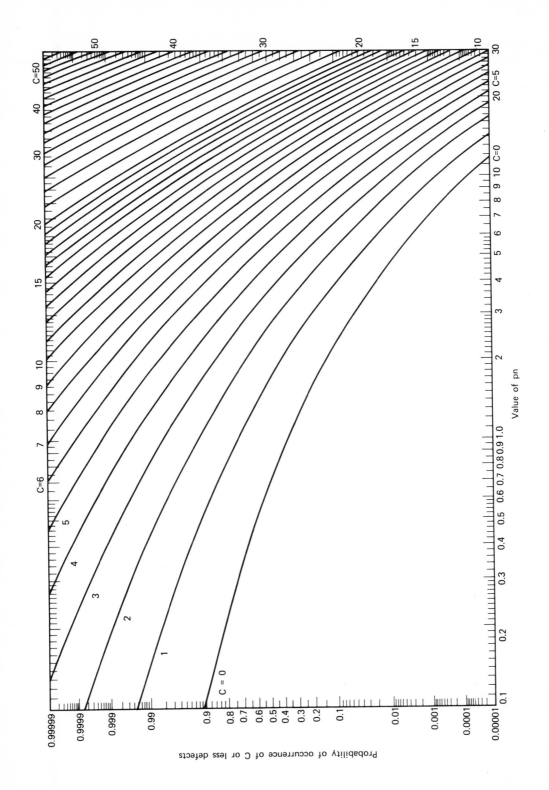

Value of pn

Probability of occurrence of C or less defects

# MANAGEMENT DECISION SIMULATIONS

cause the total units available include the original unit $(N = C + 1)$

$$P_c = p(0) + p(1) + p(2) + \ldots + p(c)$$

$$= \frac{m^0 e^{-m}}{0!} + \frac{m^1 e^{-m}}{1!} + \frac{m^2 e^{-m}}{2!}$$

$$+ \ldots + \frac{m^c e^{-m}}{c!}$$

$$= \sum_{i=0}^{c} p(i) = e^{-m} \sum_{i=0}^{c} \frac{m^i}{i!}$$

$P_c$, the probability of $c$ or fewer failures, is equivalent to the confidence level for any particular spares provisioning situation. For any calculated value of $m$, the average number of failures $(t/MTBF)$, and a specified level of confidence, $P_c$, we can use the Poisson distribution to determine $c$, the required number of spares to provide this confidence. $P_c$, the Poisson probability that an event (failure) occurs $c$ or less times in a large group of trials for which the average number of occurrences is $m$ is plotted in Figure 9.

To illustrate the use of this graph, consider the case where $m = 1.5$ and the desired confidence level, $P_c$, is 99%, or .99. To determine $c$, the required number of spares, note the coordinate of $P_c = .99$ and $m = 1.5$. This point falls between the curves for $c = 4$ and $c = 5$. Since it is required that $P_c$ be at least .99, and $c$ must be an integer, we move to the upper curve and choose the value 5. Thus for $m = 1.5$, there will be greater than .99 probability that 5 or less failures will occur. Thus we have better than 99% confidence that no more than 5 spares will be required to support the system. Conversely, there is less than a 1% chance that the original and 4 spares will fail.

If the calculated value of $m$ or average numbers of failures exceeds the tabulated values for the given confidence level, a good approximation is available to calculate the number of spares, $c$. The approximation is based on the premise that the Poisson distribution for large values of $m$ approaches the normal distribution. For the normal distribution, the probability (confidence) that a given value will not be exceeded is a function of the mean and standard deviation.

For example, the 99% confidence value for $c = m + 2.32\sigma$, where $m$ is the mean and $\sigma$ the standard deviation. Since the standard deviation for the Poisson distribution is equal to the square root of the mean, the following formula can be used:

$$c = \text{integer of } (m + k\sqrt{M} + .5)$$

where $k$ is a factor dependent on the specified confidence level (i.e., $k = 2.3$ if $P_c = 99\%$). The 0.5 is added as a continuity correction because of the discreteness of the Poisson distribution.

### Briefing on Project Management and the Status Index*

Project management is a management activity encompassing the planning, controlling, development, manufacturing, and supervision of a program or project. The individual manager or management team has specific program objectives which, when achieved, mean the conclusion of the job function. To illustrate the many challenges, activities, and problems facing project management, the Powers Co. simulation gives the participants an opportunity to perform some of the critical decisions within a project.

## THE PROJECT MANAGER

The project manager is at the focal point of the major program problem areas. How the manager "manages" these problems has a direct bearing on whether his project is successfully completed. By training or experience, or both, the project manager is usually knowledgeable in scheduling and budgeting techniques, general planning, and getting things done

* Material drawn in part from Project Management, J. S. Baumgartner, Irwin, 1963: p. 48-58.

through people. He has a general understanding of marketing, contracting, and control, as well as some of the technology involved. He knows and understands the major contract points as much as possible, and he maintains his company's interests while meeting the customer's requirements. Through the course of his job, the manager encounters many problem areas. Some of these are project planning, project control, fiscal management, cost control, and profit maintenance. Other areas include project team development and customer relations. A brief discussion on some of these problem areas is presented.

### Project Planning

The activity that has the most far-reaching effect on the project is the extent, detail, and realism of project plans. Many of the problems that develop on a project can be traced back to faulty planning in scheduling, budgeting, contingency planning, forecasting, etc.

### Project Control

Project control means taking action where deviations from plan begin to develop and avoiding or minimizing anticipated trouble spots. The project manager is faced with the responsibility for controlling operations toward achievement of project objectives. In fact, after the basic plan is developed, project control is his primary function.

The project manager is not necessarily within his budget if progress is behind schedule, since getting on schedule may require costs in excess of budget. Similarly, he is not necessarily within budget and on schedule if technical accomplishment is considerably less than it should be, because to achieve the required performance may cost more than the time and dollars allotted. The project manager must simultaneously consider all factors for effective control.

### Fiscal Management and Profit Maintenance

The manager should seek to maximize the profit to be derived from the project. Funds must be made available as needed and current project status information should be avaliable for control by top management.

### STATUS INDEX

This index is an analytical and interpretive tool that fulfills the project manager's need for cost-progress correlation. It relates actual progress and costs to the project plan. It provides a means for ranking problem areas by degree of criticality. In addition, it anticipates schedule slippages, overruns, and underruns.

This status index is calculated from the formula:

$$\frac{\text{Actual Progress}}{\text{Scheduled Progress}} \times \frac{\text{Planned \$ Budgets}}{\text{Actual \$ Expenditures}} = \text{Status Index}$$

An index of 1.0 is "par," while anything above indicates better-than-expected progress for the dollars expended. For instance, if a project has progressed 15 weeks but should be 20 weeks per the schedule, while the budget is \$40,000 and actual expenditures are \$30,000, the status index is:

$$\frac{15 \text{ weeks}}{20 \text{ weeks}} \times \frac{\$40,000}{\$30,000} = 1.0$$

The above calculation indicates that although progress is behind schedule, the progress accomplished is in line with the cost at that point. It should be noted that a major problem in the status index is that it is often difficult to measure work in process. In many cases arbitrary milestones are established and do give an indication of the work in process. The status index is only *one* tool and should be recognized as such.

## MANAGEMENT DECISION SIMULATIONS

By applying the index calculation over a series of tasks, the project manager can determine which areas are in trouble. For example, in Exhibit I, production is exceeding expectations whereas the other functions are behind.

EXHIBIT I

| Task | Status Index |
|------|--------------|
| Production | 1.2 |
| Tooling | .9 |
| Engineering | .5 |
| Quality control | .8 |

By plotting the status index for each task versus elapsed time, the project manager can evaluate the progress of the subprojects (See Exhibit II).

A past history of status indices can also be used to forecast cost to completion. (Graphing or least squares or other curve fitting techniques may be used for project.) In Exhibit III the completion forecast curve intersects the scheduled completion time at a status index of about 0.85. This means that the actual cost will be 118% (1.0/.85) of the original estimated cost. Thus approximately an 18% overrun should be expected at the com-

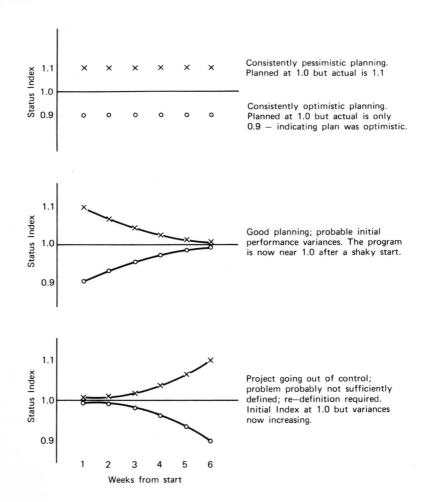

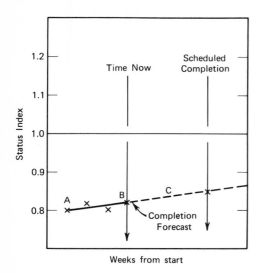

Weeks from start

pletion of the project. By using this method, a realistic estimate of cost at completion is possible.

### Briefing on Program Evaluation and Review Technique (PERT)

### INTRODUCTION

PERT, or the Program Evaluation and Review Technique, was first used on the Polaris program in 1958. After proving its value in assisting to manage this large and complex project, PERT's use spread throughout industry. Hailed at first as a cure-all for management's ills, which it is not, it has gradually found its place as an effective aid to help focus management's attention on the real problems in project planning and control. Literature abounds with PERT material but a brief treament of this subject follows.

PERT is a planning and control mode for defining and integrating what must be done to accomplish the objectives of a program or project.

Small PERT networks of approximately 100 events can be readily processed by hand. Occasions may arise, even with larger networks, when it is desirable to

calculate a critical path quickly without going through the task of providing input cards and arranging for a computer run. The following is a review of the hand computation procedure, which is essentially the same procedure as that built into computer programs.

### Activities, Events, Networks, and Numbering

The network of *activities* and their *events* is the foundation of the PERT concept and the construction of this network becomes in effect the project plan. An *event* is a point in time signifying the completion of one or more time-consumed elements called *activities*. Events should be numbered sequentially for hand computation of the network. Sequential numbering means that the predecessor event of an activity always has a lower number than the successor event of the same activity. This is shown in the example PERT Network in Exhibit IV.

Sequential numbering speeds up the calculation process and reduces the likelihood of errors. However, sequential numbering is not absolutely necessary; it is simply a convenience.

### Sorting the Activities

The first step in sorting the activities is to lay out a calculation table such as the one shown in Exhibit V. Each row of figures in the table represents an activity, identified by its predecessor and successor events. The activities should be listed in order according to the following suggestions.

(a) No activity should be listed until all its predecessors have been listed.

(b) All activities terminating in a common event should be grouped together in the listing.

The sequential numbering system makes it easy to follow these rules. The predecessor event listed is the first event

## MANAGEMENT DECISION SIMULATIONS

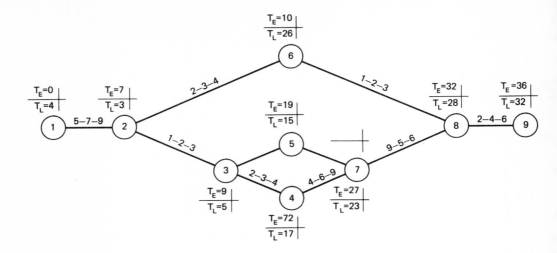

of the network. Then its successor events are listed in order in the successor event column. This process is repeated until all events have been listed in numerical order in the predecessor event column.

### Calculating the Expected Time of an Activity ($\hat{t}$)

Time estimates are an essential part of the plan and PERT.

Recognizing the uncertainty in planning, three time estimates are often used:

*Optimistic Estimate ($t_o$)*
Minimum time in an activity if everything goes well. The probability of meeting this time is considered to be 0.01.

*Most Likely Estimate ($t_m$)*
This estimate reflects the estimator's judgment of the time that would be most often required if the project were done repetitively under normal circumstances.

*Pessimistic Estimate ($t_p$)*
If everything could and did go wrong, this estimate would represent the longest time required to complete an activity.

*Expected Activity Time ($\hat{t}$)*
For calculation purposes in the PERT network, it is necessary to work with the time value which is expected to occur 50% of

the time. Skewed distributions are the rule instead of the exception and it was found that the beta distribution most nearly approximates the conditions encountered in actual practice. The expected activity time can be calculated by the following formula:

$$\hat{t} = \frac{t_o + 4\,(t_m) + t_p}{6}$$

The use of $\hat{t}$ is the most convenient way to adjust the bias introduced if the most likely times were to be accepted as expected times.

### Calculating the Earliest Expected Time ($T_E$)

Another PERT term is the earliest expected time ($T_E$) to achieve an event. It is the sum of the expected times along the longest path from the beginning of the network to the event in question. The adjective "earliest" indicates that it is assumed that all activities are started as early as possible, regardless of the amount of slack they may have. Slack is the time between when an activity can start and must start. To determine the expected time to complete the network, it is necessary to number the events and sum the expected times through the net-

EXHIBIT V

| Predecessor Event | Successor Event | Optimistic $t_o$ | Most Likely $t_m$ | Pessimistic $t_p$ | Expected $\hat{t}$ | Earliest Start $T_E$ | Latest Start $T_L$ | Slack S |
|---|---|---|---|---|---|---|---|---|
| 1 | 2 | 5 | 7 | 9 | 7 | 7 | 3 | −4 ← |
| 2 | 6 | 2 | 3 | 4 | 3 | 10 | 26 | +16 |
|   | 3 | 1 | 2 | 3 | 2 | 9 | 5 | −4 ← |
| 3 | 5 | 6 | 10 | 14 | 10 | 19 | 15 | −4 ← |
|   | 4 | 2 | 3 | 4 | 3 | 12 | 17 | +5 |
| 5 | 7 | 4 | 8 | 12 | 8 | (27) | 23 | −4 ← |
| 4 | 7 | 4 | 6 | 9 | 6 | ~~18~~ | 23 | +5 |
| 6 | 8 | 1 | 2 | 3 | 2 | ~~12~~ | 28 | +16 |
| 7 | 8 | 3 | 5 | 6 | 5 | (32) | 28 | −4 ← |
| 8 | 9 | 2 | 4 | 6 | 4 | [36] | [32] | −4 ← |

critical path = ←

Earliest expected completion date

Desired or estimated completion date

work in a systematic manner. Exhibit IV, shown earlier, presented a simple PERT network with three time estimates shown for each activity. The calculation portion on Exhibit IV indicates the expected time computed for each activity and the cumulative completion time for each event in the network ($T_E$).

When a successor event has more than one predecessor, two or more different $T_E$ figures will generally appear. *The highest* of these figures should be circled and used in calculating $T_E$ for succeeding activities. These are shown on the Network Analysis Sheet, Exhibit IV.

As an example, to accomplish Event 7, it is necessary to trace the time required to go from Events 1 to 2, 2 to 3, 3 to 4, and 4 to 7, which is 18 days. The alternative branch must also be investigated, which is 1 to 2, 2 to 3, 3 to 5, and 5 to 7.

This second branch takes 27 days and the $T_E$ for Event 7 is, therefore, limited by the path 1 —2—3—5—7. Analysis of the total network indicates that the "critical path" also goes through Events 5 and 7. All events on this critical path require close management attention. The total network time is 36 days from Event 1 to Event 9.

### Calculating the Latest Allowable Time ($T_L$)

The next step is to assign an end date to the last event and then work back through the network, assigning a completion date (latest allowable event time = $T_L$) to each event. At times, in order to find the critical path, $T_E$ for the last event is set equal to $T_L$ for the last event when a schedule date is not preassigned.

The latest allowable time ($T_L$) is the time by which an event must be achieved in order to avoid missing the scheduled date for completion of the entire project. To calculate the latest allowable time for a particular event, subtract from the scheduled length of the project the length of the longest path from the end of the network back to the event in question.

When an event has two or more succeeding activities, two or more $T_L$ figures will be calculated. The *lowest* of these figures is limiting and should be used.

### Calculating Slack

Slack time is a very important part of the PERT concept in that it highlights areas for management attention. Negative slack time indicates the amount by which the time to complete the event must be shortened in order not to delay the entire project. It highlights the areas for management attention. Positive slack time indicates that excess time is available to complete the event and these areas, therefore, do not require close management attention.

The slack for each successor event should be calculated by means of the following formula:

$$\text{Slack} = T_L - T_E$$

In our example, an end completion date of 32 days has been specified. The slack time is calculated accordingly and is shown in Exhibit IV in the last column of the calculation section.

### Identifying the Critical Path

The critical path is readily identified as the sequence of activities that has the *least* amount of slack. In the example shown in Exhibit IV, the critical path is indicated by the heavy black lines and requires a total of 36 days. All events on the critical path have a negative slack of $-4$. No other events have more negative slack or, conversely, less slack.

### Calculating the Probability of Meeting a Scheduled Time

Associated with each activity on the network is a certain degree of uncertainty resulting from the fact that the elapsed time estimates for each activity are themselves uncertain.

The standard deviation is a measure of the uncertainty of a statistical climate. Stated another way, it is a measure of the spread of the probability distribution. The larger the standard deviation, the greater the uncertainty of the estimate and the spread of the distribution.

The standard deviation of the earliest expected time, $T_E$ for a particular event depends on the spread between the optimistic and pessimistic time estimates for all the activities on the longest path from the origin of the network to the particular event. If there are wide ranges between the two extreme time estimates, there is a high degree of uncertainty, which is reflected in a high value for the standard deviation.

There is only a 50% probability of achieving an event on or before its earliest expected time, $T_E$, since this time splits the distribution in half. The PERT analysis, however, provides a way of calculating the time associated with any given probability. If a 98% probability of achieving an event on or before $T_E$ is desired, for example, a factor can be calculated and added to the earlier expected time. This factor is equal to two standard deviations. For the normal distribution, an actual time will exceed the expected time by more than two standard deviations in only about 2% of all cases. Therefore, there is a 98% probability of achieving the event in question by this time. Two and one-half standard deviations must be used to obtain a 99% probability.

The normal distribution is symmetrical, so the probability of achieving a particular event before the earliest expected

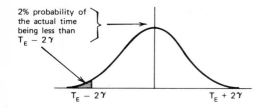

2% probability of the actual time being less than $T_E - 2\gamma$

$T_E - 2\gamma$        $T_E + 2\gamma$

time can also be calculated. For example, there is a 2% probability of achieving the event two standard deviations before the earliest expected time.

The following is a step-by-step procedure for manual computation of the probability of achieving an event:

1. *Calculate the Sum of Squares of the Differences Between the Optimistic and Pessimistic Times for Each Activity Along Critical Path = $\Sigma (Range)^2$*
   In the example, this sum of squares is 180.

2. *Calculate the Variance*
   Estimate of the critical path or sum of variance of the critical path's activities.

$$\sigma_T^2 = \Sigma \sigma_i^2 = \Sigma \left( \frac{Ri}{6} \right)^2$$

$$= \Sigma \frac{(Ri)^2}{36} = \frac{180}{36} = 5.0$$

   where $\sigma i$ is the estimated approximation of 1/6th of the range.

3. *Calculate the Square Root of the Variance*
   The square root of the variance is the standard deviation, therefore:

$$\sigma_T = \sqrt{5} = 2.24$$

4. *Calculate the Difference Between the Scheduled Time and the Earliest Expected Time*
   In the example, the scheduled time is 32 and the earliest expected time is 36. Therefore:

$$S = 32 - 36 = -4$$

5. *Calculate the Ratio of This Difference to the Standard Deviation*
   This ratio, denoted by Z is called a normal deviate. Thus,

$$Z = \frac{S}{\sigma_T} = -4/2.24 = -1.8$$

6. *Look Up the Probability Corresponding to the Value of the Normal Deviate*
   The normal distribution is extensively tabulated in standard handbooks and textbooks of statistics. A condensed table is contained in the Exhibit VI. The probability corresponding to a normal deviate of $-4.5$ is not shown on the table and, therefore, indicates less than 0.01 probability of making schedule.

The probability corresponding to a normal deviate of $-1.8$ is .04. Therefore, there is a 4% probability of meeting the scheduled completion date. If the normal deviate was $-2.2$ or more, there would be little probability of meeting schedule. In a like manner, if the schedule could be extended to the 34 instead of 32 days, the normal deviate $-.9$ or $(-2/2.24)$, would yield an 18% chance of meeting this new schedule.

As time progresses a reevaluation of the project status, estimate-to-complete and other monitoring data is to be compiled. Referring to the original PERT network in Exhibit IV, a jagged vertical line will connote the accomplishment to date after, say 20 days. The actual times taken in the activities can be stated and the changes in the table noted. One can look at the network to the right of the jagged line as a new network and treat it accordingly. Since one of the activities, 3—5, is only partially completed, another event can be created, namely 3a, which represents the beginning of the remainder of the activity.

Obviously, the old time scale or schedule scale could remain or a new scale be used which ignores the prior completions

MANAGEMENT DECISION SIMULATIONS

EXHIBIT VI.   TABLE OF THE NORMAL DISTRIBUTION

| Z<br>Normal<br>Deviate | $P(T_A \leqslant T_S \leqslant T_E)$ [a]<br>Probability | Z<br>Normal<br>Deviate | $P(T_A \leqslant T_S \geqslant T_E)$ [b]<br>Probability |
|---|---|---|---|
| −0.0 | .50 | 0.0 | .50 |
| −0.1 | .46 | 0.1 | .54 |
| −0.2 | .42 | 0.2 | .58 |
| −0.3 | .38 | 0.3 | .62 |
| −0.4 | .34 | 0.4 | .66 |
| −0.5 | .31 | 0.5 | .69 |
| −0.6 | .27 | 0.6 | .73 |
| −0.7 | .24 | 0.7 | .76 |
| −0.8 | .21 | 0.8 | .79 |
| −0.9 | .18 | 0.9 | .82 |
| −1.0 | .16 | 1.0 | .84 |
| −1.1 | .14 | 1.1 | .86 |
| −1.2 | .12 | 1.2 | .88 |
| −1.3 | .10 | 1.3 | .90 |
| −1.4 | .08 | 1.4 | .92 |
| −1.5 | .07 | 1.5 | .93 |
| −1.6 | .05 | 1.6 | .95 |
| −1.7 | .04 | 1.7 | .96 |
| −1.8 | .04 | 1.8 | .96 |
| −1.9 | .03 | 1.9 | .97 |
| −2.0 | .02 | 2.0 | .98 |
| −2.2 | .01 | 2.2 | .99 |
| −2.3 | .01 | 2.3 | .99 |
| −2.4 | .01 | 2.4 | .99 |
| −2.5 | .01 | 2.5 | .99 |

[a] Probability that actual completion time ($T_A$) will be equal to or less than a scheduled date ($T_S$) which is less than predicted earliest completion date ($T_E$).

[b] Probability that the actual completion date will be equal to or less than a scheduled date ($T_S$) which is greater than predicted earliest completion date ($T_E$).

and looks only at what remains to be accomplished. The new scale reduces the scheduled time by the time elapsed to date. Thus, the 20 days elapsed leave a scheduled completion day of 32−20 or 12 days remaining. The $T_L$'s are computed accordingly. For the $T_E$'s the earliest times begin with a reference of today's date being zero. Since the same slack time results by either method, there is no particular advantage in changing the schedule reference scale.

# 7

## Appendices

## MANAGEMENT DECISION SIMULATIONS

5%

### ANNUAL COMPOUND INTEREST TABLE
#### EFFECTIVE RATE = 5%    i = .05

5%

| | 1 Amount of $1 at Compound Interest | 2 Accumulation of $1 per Period | 3 Sinking Fund Factor | 4 Pres. Value Reversion of $1 | 5 Present Value Ord. Annuity $1 per Period | 6 Instalment to Amortize $1 | n YEARS |
|---|---|---|---|---|---|---|---|
| YEARS | | | | | | | |
| 1 | 1.050000 | 1.000000 | 1.000000 | .952381 | .952381 | 1.050000 | 1 |
| 2 | 1.102500 | 2.050000 | .487805 | .907029 | 1.859410 | .537805 | 2 |
| 3 | 1.157625 | 3.152500 | .317209 | .863838 | 2.723248 | .367209 | 3 |
| 4 | 1.215506 | 4.310125 | .232012 | .822702 | 3.545951 | .282012 | 4 |
| 5 | 1.276282 | 5.525631 | .180975 | .783526 | 4.329477 | .230975 | 5 |
| 6 | 1.340096 | 6.801913 | .147017 | .746215 | 5.075692 | .197017 | 6 |
| 7 | 1.407100 | 8.142008 | .122820 | .710681 | 5.786373 | .172820 | 7 |
| 8 | 1.477455 | 9.549109 | .104722 | .676839 | 6.463213 | .154722 | 8 |
| 9 | 1.551328 | 11.026564 | .090690 | .644609 | 7.107822 | .140690 | 9 |
| 10 | 1.628895 | 12.577893 | .079505 | .613913 | 7.721735 | .129505 | 10 |
| 11 | 1.710339 | 14.206787 | .070389 | .584679 | 8.306414 | .120389 | 11 |
| 12 | 1.795856 | 15.917127 | .062825 | .556837 | 8.863252 | .112825 | 12 |
| 13 | 1.885649 | 17.712983 | .056456 | .530321 | 9.393573 | .106456 | 13 |
| 14 | 1.979932 | 19.598632 | .051024 | .505068 | 9.898641 | .101024 | 14 |
| 15 | 2.078928 | 21.578564 | .046342 | .481017 | 10.379658 | .096342 | 15 |
| 16 | 2.182875 | 23.657492 | .042270 | .458112 | 10.837770 | .092270 | 16 |
| 17 | 2.292018 | 25.840366 | .038699 | .436297 | 11.274066 | .088699 | 17 |
| 18 | 2.406619 | 28.132385 | .035546 | .415521 | 11.689587 | .085546 | 18 |
| 19 | 2.526950 | 30.539004 | .032745 | .395734 | 12.085321 | .082745 | 19 |
| 20 | 2.653298 | 33.065954 | .030243 | .376889 | 12.462210 | .080243 | 20 |
| 21 | 2.785963 | 35.719252 | .027996 | .358942 | 12.821153 | .077996 | 21 |
| 22 | 2.925261 | 38.505214 | .025971 | .341850 | 13.163003 | .075971 | 22 |
| 23 | 3.071524 | 41.430475 | .024137 | .325571 | 13.488574 | .074137 | 23 |
| 24 | 3.225100 | 44.501999 | .022471 | .310068 | 13.798642 | .072471 | 24 |
| 25 | 3.386355 | 47.727099 | .020952 | .295303 | 14.093945 | .070952 | 25 |
| 26 | 3.555673 | 51.113454 | .019564 | .281241 | 14.375185 | .069564 | 26 |
| 27 | 3.733456 | 54.669126 | .018292 | .267848 | 14.643034 | .068292 | 27 |
| 28 | 3.920129 | 58.402583 | .017123 | .255094 | 14.898127 | .067123 | 28 |
| 29 | 4.116136 | 62.322712 | .016046 | .242946 | 15.141074 | .066046 | 29 |
| 30 | 4.321942 | 66.438848 | .015051 | .231377 | 15.372451 | .065051 | 30 |
| 31 | 4.538039 | 70.760790 | .014132 | .220359 | 15.592811 | .064132 | 31 |
| 32 | 4.764941 | 75.298829 | .013280 | .209866 | 15.802677 | .063280 | 32 |
| 33 | 5.003189 | 80.063771 | .012490 | .199873 | 16.002549 | .062490 | 33 |
| 34 | 5.253348 | 85.066959 | .011755 | .190355 | 16.192904 | .061755 | 34 |
| 35 | 5.516015 | 90.320307 | .011072 | .181290 | 16.374194 | .061072 | 35 |
| 36 | 5.791816 | 95.836323 | .010434 | .172657 | 16.546852 | .060434 | 36 |
| 37 | 6.081407 | 101.628139 | .009840 | .164436 | 16.711287 | .059840 | 37 |
| 38 | 6.385477 | 107.709546 | .009284 | .156605 | 16.867893 | .059284 | 38 |
| 39 | 6.704571 | 114.095023 | .008765 | .149148 | 17.017041 | .058765 | 39 |
| 40 | 7.039989 | 120.799774 | .008278 | .142046 | 17.159086 | .058278 | 40 |
| 41 | 7.391988 | 127.839763 | .007822 | .135282 | 17.294368 | .057822 | 41 |
| 42 | 7.761588 | 135.231751 | .007395 | .128840 | 17.423208 | .057395 | 42 |
| 43 | 8.149667 | 142.993339 | .006993 | .122704 | 17.545912 | .056993 | 43 |
| 44 | 8.557150 | 151.143006 | .006616 | .116861 | 17.662773 | .056616 | 44 |
| 45 | 8.985008 | 159.700156 | .006262 | .111297 | 17.774070 | .056262 | 45 |
| 46 | 9.434258 | 168.685164 | .005928 | .105997 | 17.880067 | .055928 | 46 |
| 47 | 9.905971 | 178.119422 | .005614 | .100949 | 17.981016 | .055614 | 47 |
| 48 | 10.401270 | 188.025393 | .005318 | .096142 | 18.077158 | .055318 | 48 |
| 49 | 10.921333 | 198.426663 | .005040 | .091564 | 18.168722 | .055040 | 49 |
| 50 | 11.467400 | 209.347996 | .004777 | .087204 | 18.255925 | .054777 | 50 |
| 51 | 12.040770 | 220.815395 | .004529 | .083051 | 18.338977 | .054529 | 51 |
| 52 | 12.642808 | 232.856165 | .004294 | .079096 | 18.418016 | .054294 | 52 |
| 53 | 13.274949 | 245.498974 | .004073 | .075330 | 18.493403 | .054073 | 53 |
| 54 | 13.938696 | 258.773922 | .003864 | .071743 | 18.565146 | .053864 | 54 |
| 55 | 14.635631 | 272.712618 | .003667 | .068326 | 18.633472 | .053667 | 55 |
| 56 | 15.367412 | 287.348249 | .003480 | .065073 | 18.698545 | .053480 | 56 |
| 57 | 16.135783 | 302.715662 | .003303 | .061974 | 18.760519 | .053303 | 57 |
| 58 | 16.942572 | 318.851445 | .003136 | .059023 | 18.819542 | .053136 | 58 |
| 59 | 17.789701 | 335.794017 | .002978 | .056212 | 18.875754 | .052978 | 59 |
| 60 | 18.679186 | 353.583718 | .002828 | .053536 | 18.929290 | .052828 | 60 |

Reprinted by permission, from *Ellwood's Tables for Real Estate Appraising and Financing* (Ridgewood, N.J.: published by the author, 1959).

6%        ANNUAL COMPOUND INTEREST TABLE        6%
          EFFECTIVE RATE = 6%    i = .06

| | 1<br>Amount of $1<br>at Compound<br>Interest | 2<br>Accumulation<br>of $1<br>per Period | 3<br>Sinking<br>Fund<br>Factor | 4<br>Pres. Value<br>Reversion<br>of $1 | 5<br>Present Value<br>Ord. Annuity<br>$1 per Period | 6<br>Instalment<br>to<br>Amortize $1 | |
|---|---|---|---|---|---|---|---|
| YEARS | | | | | | | n<br>YEARS |
| 1 | 1.060000 | 1.000000 | 1.000000 | .943396 | .943396 | 1.060000 | 1 |
| 2 | 1.123600 | 2.060000 | .485437 | .889996 | 1.833393 | .545437 | 2 |
| 3 | 1.191016 | 3.183600 | .314110 | .839619 | 2.673012 | .374110 | 3 |
| 4 | 1.262477 | 4.374616 | .228591 | .792094 | 3.465106 | .288591 | 4 |
| 5 | 1.338226 | 5.637093 | .177396 | .747258 | 4.212364 | .237396 | 5 |
| 6 | 1.418519 | 6.975319 | .143363 | .704961 | 4.917324 | .203363 | 6 |
| 7 | 1.503630 | 8.393838 | .119135 | .665057 | 5.582381 | .179135 | 7 |
| 8 | 1.593848 | 9.897468 | .101036 | .627412 | 6.209794 | .161036 | 8 |
| 9 | 1.689479 | 11.491316 | .087022 | .591898 | 6.801692 | .147022 | 9 |
| 10 | 1.790848 | 13.180795 | .075868 | .558395 | 7.360087 | .135868 | 10 |
| 11 | 1.898299 | 14.971643 | .066793 | .526788 | 7.886875 | .126793 | 11 |
| 12 | 2.012196 | 16.869941 | .059277 | .496969 | 8.383844 | .119277 | 12 |
| 13 | 2.132928 | 18.882138 | .052960 | .468839 | 8.852683 | .112960 | 13 |
| 14 | 2.260904 | 21.015066 | .047585 | .442301 | 9.294984 | .107585 | 14 |
| 15 | 2.396558 | 23.275970 | .042963 | .417265 | 9.712249 | .102963 | 15 |
| 16 | 2.540352 | 25.672528 | .038952 | .393646 | 10.105895 | .098952 | 16 |
| 17 | 2.692773 | 28.212880 | .035445 | .371364 | 10.477260 | .095445 | 17 |
| 18 | 2.854339 | 30.905653 | .032357 | .350344 | 10.827603 | .092357 | 18 |
| 19 | 3.025600 | 33.759992 | .029621 | .330513 | 11.158116 | .089621 | 19 |
| 20 | 3.207135 | 36.785591 | .027185 | .311805 | 11.469921 | .087185 | 20 |
| 21 | 3.399564 | 39.992727 | .025005 | .294155 | 11.764077 | .085005 | 21 |
| 22 | 3.603537 | 43.392290 | .023046 | .277505 | 12.041582 | .083046 | 22 |
| 23 | 3.819750 | 46.995828 | .021278 | .261797 | 12.303379 | .081278 | 23 |
| 24 | 4.048935 | 50.815577 | .019679 | .246979 | 12.550358 | .079679 | 24 |
| 25 | 4.291871 | 54.864512 | .018227 | .232999 | 12.783356 | .078227 | 25 |
| 26 | 4.549383 | 59.156383 | .016904 | .219810 | 13.003166 | .076904 | 26 |
| 27 | 4.822346 | 63.705766 | .015697 | .207368 | 13.210534 | .075697 | 27 |
| 28 | 5.111687 | 68.528112 | .014593 | .195630 | 13.406164 | .074593 | 28 |
| 29 | 5.418388 | 73.639798 | .013580 | .184557 | 13.590721 | .073580 | 29 |
| 30 | 5.743491 | 79.058186 | .012649 | .174110 | 13.764831 | .072649 | 30 |
| 31 | 6.088101 | 84.801677 | .011792 | .164255 | 13.929086 | .071792 | 31 |
| 32 | 6.453387 | 90.889778 | .011002 | .154957 | 14.084043 | .071002 | 32 |
| 33 | 6.840590 | 97.343165 | .010273 | .146186 | 14.230230 | .070273 | 33 |
| 34 | 7.251025 | 104.183755 | .009598 | .137912 | 14.368141 | .069598 | 34 |
| 35 | 7.686087 | 111.434780 | .008974 | .130105 | 14.498246 | .068974 | 35 |
| 36 | 8.147252 | 119.120867 | .008395 | .122741 | 14.620987 | .068395 | 36 |
| 37 | 8.636087 | 127.268119 | .007857 | .115793 | 14.736780 | .067857 | 37 |
| 38 | 9.154252 | 135.904206 | .007358 | .109239 | 14.846019 | .067358 | 38 |
| 39 | 9.703507 | 145.058458 | .006894 | .103056 | 14.949075 | .066894 | 39 |
| 40 | 10.285718 | 154.761966 | .006462 | .097222 | 15.046297 | .066462 | 40 |
| 41 | 10.902861 | 165.047684 | .006059 | .091719 | 15.138016 | .066059 | 41 |
| 42 | 11.557033 | 175.950545 | .005683 | .086527 | 15.224543 | .065683 | 42 |
| 43 | 12.250455 | 187.507577 | .005333 | .081630 | 15.306173 | .065333 | 43 |
| 44 | 12.985482 | 199.758032 | .005006 | .077009 | 15.383182 | .065006 | 44 |
| 45 | 13.764611 | 212.743514 | .004700 | .072650 | 15.455832 | .064700 | 45 |
| 46 | 14.590487 | 226.508125 | .004415 | .068538 | 15.524370 | .064415 | 46 |
| 47 | 15.465917 | 241.098612 | .004148 | .064658 | 15.589028 | .064148 | 47 |
| 48 | 16.393872 | 256.564529 | .003898 | .060998 | 15.650027 | .063898 | 48 |
| 49 | 17.377504 | 272.958401 | .003664 | .057546 | 15.707572 | .063664 | 49 |
| 50 | 18.420154 | 290.335905 | .003444 | .054288 | 15.761861 | .063444 | 50 |
| 51 | 19.525364 | 308.756059 | .003239 | .051215 | 15.813076 | .063239 | 51 |
| 52 | 20.696885 | 328.281422 | .003046 | .048316 | 15.861393 | .063046 | 52 |
| 53 | 21.938698 | 348.978308 | .002866 | .045582 | 15.906974 | .062866 | 53 |
| 54 | 23.255020 | 370.917006 | .002696 | .043001 | 15.949976 | .062696 | 54 |
| 55 | 24.650322 | 394.172027 | .002537 | .040567 | 15.990543 | .062537 | 55 |
| 56 | 26.129341 | 418.822348 | .002388 | .038271 | 16.028814 | .062388 | 56 |
| 57 | 27.697101 | 444.951689 | .002247 | .036105 | 16.064919 | .062247 | 57 |
| 58 | 29.358927 | 472.648790 | .002116 | .034061 | 16.098980 | .062116 | 58 |
| 59 | 31.120463 | 502.007718 | .001992 | .032133 | 16.131113 | .061992 | 59 |
| 60 | 32.987691 | 533.128181 | .001876 | .030314 | 16.161428 | .061876 | 60 |

Reprinted by permission, from *Ellwood's Tables for Real Estate Appraising and Financing* (Ridgewood, N.J.: published by the author, 1959).

# MANAGEMENT DECISION SIMULATIONS

8% ANNUAL COMPOUND INTEREST TABLE 8%
EFFECTIVE RATE = 8%    i = .08

| | 1 Amount of $1 at Compound Interest | 2 Accumulation of $1 per Period | 3 Sinking Fund Factor | 4 Pres. Value Reversion of $1 | 5 Present Value Ord. Annuity $1 per Period | 6 Instalment to Amortize $1 | |
|---|---|---|---|---|---|---|---|
| YEARS | | | | | | | n YEARS |
| 1 | 1.080000 | 1.000000 | 1.000000 | .925926 | .925926 | 1.080000 | 1 |
| 2 | 1.166400 | 2.080000 | .480769 | .857339 | 1.783265 | .560769 | 2 |
| 3 | 1.259712 | 3.246400 | .308034 | .793832 | 2.577097 | .388034 | 3 |
| 4 | 1.360489 | 4.506112 | .221921 | .735030 | 3.312127 | .301921 | 4 |
| 5 | 1.469328 | 5.866601 | .170456 | .680583 | 3.992710 | .250456 | 5 |
| 6 | 1.586874 | 7.335929 | .136315 | .630170 | 4.622880 | .216315 | 6 |
| 7 | 1.713824 | 8.922803 | .112072 | .583490 | 5.206370 | .192072 | 7 |
| 8 | 1.850930 | 10.636628 | .094015 | .540269 | 5.746639 | .174015 | 8 |
| 9 | 1.999005 | 12.487558 | .080080 | .500249 | 6.246888 | .160080 | 9 |
| 10 | 2.158925 | 14.486562 | .069029 | .463193 | 6.710081 | .149029 | 10 |
| 11 | 2.331639 | 16.645487 | .060076 | .428883 | 7.138964 | .140076 | 11 |
| 12 | 2.518170 | 18.977126 | .052695 | .397114 | 7.536078 | .132695 | 12 |
| 13 | 2.719624 | 21.495297 | .046522 | .367698 | 7.903776 | .126522 | 13 |
| 14 | 2.937194 | 24.214920 | .041297 | .340461 | 8.244237 | .121297 | 14 |
| 15 | 3.172169 | 27.152114 | .036830 | .315242 | 8.559479 | .116830 | 15 |
| 16 | 3.425943 | 30.324283 | .032977 | .291890 | 8.851369 | .112977 | 16 |
| 17 | 3.700018 | 33.750226 | .029629 | .270269 | 9.121638 | .109629 | 17 |
| 18 | 3.996019 | 37.450244 | .026702 | .250249 | 9.371887 | .106702 | 18 |
| 19 | 4.315701 | 41.446263 | .024128 | .231712 | 9.603599 | .104128 | 19 |
| 20 | 4.660957 | 45.761964 | .021852 | .214548 | 9.818147 | .101852 | 20 |
| 21 | 5.033834 | 50.422921 | .019832 | .198656 | 10.016803 | .099832 | 21 |
| 22 | 5.436540 | 55.456755 | .018032 | .183941 | 10.200744 | .098032 | 22 |
| 23 | 5.871464 | 60.893296 | .016422 | .170315 | 10.371059 | .096422 | 23 |
| 24 | 6.341181 | 66.764759 | .014978 | .157699 | 10.528758 | .094978 | 24 |
| 25 | 6.848475 | 73.105940 | .013679 | .146018 | 10.674776 | .093679 | 25 |
| 26 | 7.396353 | 79.954415 | .012507 | .135202 | 10.809978 | .092507 | 26 |
| 27 | 7.988061 | 87.350768 | .011448 | .125187 | 10.935165 | .091448 | 27 |
| 28 | 8.627106 | 95.338830 | .010489 | .115914 | 11.051078 | .090489 | 28 |
| 29 | 9.317275 | 103.965936 | .009619 | .107328 | 11.158406 | .089619 | 29 |
| 30 | 10.062657 | 113.283211 | .008827 | .099377 | 11.257783 | .088827 | 30 |
| 31 | 10.867669 | 123.345868 | .008107 | .092016 | 11.349799 | .088107 | 31 |
| 32 | 11.737083 | 134.213537 | .007451 | .085200 | 11.434999 | .087451 | 32 |
| 33 | 12.676050 | 145.950620 | .006852 | .078889 | 11.513888 | .086852 | 33 |
| 34 | 13.690134 | 158.626670 | .006304 | .073045 | 11.586934 | .086304 | 34 |
| 35 | 14.785344 | 172.316804 | .005803 | .067635 | 11.654568 | .085803 | 35 |
| 36 | 15.968172 | 187.102148 | .005345 | .062625 | 11.717193 | .085345 | 36 |
| 37 | 17.245626 | 203.070320 | .004824 | .057986 | 11.775179 | .084924 | 37 |
| 38 | 18.625276 | 220.315945 | .004539 | .053690 | 11.828869 | .084539 | 38 |
| 39 | 20.115298 | 238.941221 | .004185 | .049713 | 11.878582 | .084185 | 39 |
| 40 | 21.724521 | 259.056519 | .003860 | .046031 | 11.924613 | .083860 | 40 |
| 41 | 23.462483 | 280.781040 | .003561 | .042621 | 11.967235 | .083561 | 41 |
| 42 | 25.339482 | 304.243523 | .003287 | .039464 | 12.006699 | .083287 | 42 |
| 43 | 27.366640 | 329.583005 | .003034 | .036541 | 12.043240 | .083034 | 43 |
| 44 | 29.555972 | 356.949646 | .002802 | .033834 | 12.077074 | .082802 | 44 |
| 45 | 31.920449 | 386.505617 | .002587 | .031328 | 12.108401 | .082587 | 45 |
| 46 | 34.474085 | 418.426067 | .002390 | .029007 | 12.137409 | .082390 | 46 |
| 47 | 37.232012 | 452.900152 | .002208 | .026859 | 12.164267 | .082208 | 47 |
| 48 | 40.210573 | 490.132164 | .002040 | .024869 | 12.189136 | .082040 | 48 |
| 49 | 43.427419 | 530.342737 | .001886 | .023027 | 12.212163 | .081886 | 49 |
| 50 | 46.901613 | 573.770156 | .001743 | .021321 | 12.233485 | .081743 | 50 |
| 51 | 50.653742 | 620.671769 | .001611 | .019742 | 12.253227 | .081611 | 51 |
| 52 | 54.706041 | 671.325510 | .001490 | .018280 | 12.271506 | .081490 | 52 |
| 53 | 59.082524 | 726.031551 | .001377 | .016925 | 12.288432 | .081377 | 53 |
| 54 | 63.809126 | 785.114075 | .001274 | .015672 | 12.304103 | .081274 | 54 |
| 55 | 68.913856 | 848.923201 | .001178 | .014511 | 12.318614 | .081178 | 55 |
| 56 | 74.426965 | 917.837058 | .001090 | .013436 | 12.332050 | .081090 | 56 |
| 57 | 80.381122 | 992.264022 | .001008 | .012441 | 12.344491 | .081008 | 57 |
| 58 | 86.811612 | 1072.645144 | .000932 | .011519 | 12.356010 | .080932 | 58 |
| 59 | 93.756540 | 1159.456755 | .000862 | .010666 | 12.366676 | .080862 | 59 |
| 60 | 101.257064 | 1253.213296 | .000798 | .009876 | 12.376552 | .080798 | 60 |

Reprinted by permission, from *Ellwood's Tables for Real Estate Appraising and Financing* (Ridgewood, N.J.: published by the author, 1959).

10%       ANNUAL COMPOUND INTEREST TABLE      10%
EFFECTIVE RATE = 10%     i = .10

| YEARS | 1<br>Amount of $1<br>at Compound<br>Interest | 2<br>Accumulation<br>of $1<br>per Period | 3<br>Sinking<br>Fund<br>Factor | 4<br>Pres. Value<br>Reversion<br>of $1 | 5<br>Present Value<br>Ord. Annuity<br>$1 per Period | 6<br>Instalment<br>to<br>Amortize $1 | n<br>YEARS |
|---|---|---|---|---|---|---|---|
| 1 | 1.100000 | 1.000000 | 1.000000 | .909091 | .909091 | 1.100000 | 1 |
| 2 | 1.210000 | 2.100000 | .476190 | .826446 | 1.735537 | .576190 | 2 |
| 3 | 1.331000 | 3.310000 | .302115 | .751315 | 2.486852 | .402115 | 3 |
| 4 | 1.464100 | 4.641000 | .215471 | .683013 | 3.169865 | .315471 | 4 |
| 5 | 1.610510 | 6.105100 | .163797 | .620921 | 3.790787 | .263797 | 5 |
| 6 | 1.771561 | 7.715610 | .129607 | .564474 | 4.355261 | .229607 | 6 |
| 7 | 1.948717 | 9.487171 | .105405 | .513158 | 4.868419 | .205405 | 7 |
| 8 | 2.143589 | 11.435888 | .087444 | .466507 | 5.334926 | .187444 | 8 |
| 9 | 2.357948 | 13.579477 | .073641 | .424098 | 5.759024 | .173641 | 9 |
| 10 | 2.593742 | 15.937425 | .062745 | .385543 | 6.144567 | .162745 | 10 |
| 11 | 2.853117 | 18.531167 | .053963 | .350494 | 6.495061 | .153963 | 11 |
| 12 | 3.138428 | 21.384284 | .046763 | .318631 | 6.813692 | .146763 | 12 |
| 13 | 3.452271 | 24.522712 | .040779 | .289664 | 7.103356 | .140779 | 13 |
| 14 | 3.797498 | 27.974983 | .035746 | .263331 | 7.366687 | .135746 | 14 |
| 15 | 4.177248 | 31.772482 | .031474 | .239392 | 7.606080 | .131474 | 15 |
| 16 | 4.594973 | 35.949730 | .027817 | .217629 | 7.823709 | .127817 | 16 |
| 17 | 5.054470 | 40.544703 | .024664 | .197845 | 8.021553 | .124664 | 17 |
| 18 | 5.559917 | 45.599173 | .021930 | .179859 | 8.201412 | .121930 | 18 |
| 19 | 6.115909 | 51.159090 | .019547 | .163508 | 8.364920 | .119547 | 19 |
| 20 | 6.727500 | 57.274999 | .017460 | .148644 | 8.513564 | .117460 | 20 |
| 21 | 7.400250 | 64.002499 | .015624 | .135131 | 8.648694 | .115624 | 21 |
| 22 | 8.140275 | 71.402749 | .014005 | .122846 | 8.771540 | .114005 | 22 |
| 23 | 8.854302 | 79.543024 | .012572 | .111678 | 8.883218 | .112572 | 23 |
| 24 | 9.849733 | 88.497327 | .011300 | .101526 | 8.984744 | .111300 | 24 |
| 25 | 10.834706 | 98.347059 | .010168 | .092296 | 9.077040 | .110168 | 25 |
| 26 | 11.918177 | 109.181765 | .009159 | .083905 | 9.160945 | .109159 | 26 |
| 27 | 13.109994 | 121.099942 | .008258 | .076278 | 9.237223 | .108258 | 27 |
| 28 | 14.420994 | 134.209936 | .007451 | .069343 | 9.306567 | .107451 | 28 |
| 29 | 15.863093 | 148.630930 | .006728 | .063039 | 9.369606 | .106728 | 29 |
| 30 | 17.449402 | 164.494023 | .006079 | .057309 | 9.426914 | .106079 | 30 |
| 31 | 19.194342 | 181.943425 | .005496 | .052099 | 9.479013 | .105496 | 31 |
| 32 | 21.113777 | 201.137767 | .004972 | .047362 | 9.526376 | .104972 | 32 |
| 33 | 23.225154 | 222.251544 | .004499 | .043057 | 9.569432 | .104499 | 33 |
| 34 | 25.547670 | 245.476699 | .004074 | .039143 | 9.608575 | .104074 | 34 |
| 35 | 28.102437 | 271.024368 | .003690 | .035584 | 9.644159 | .103690 | 35 |
| 36 | 30.912681 | 299.126805 | .003343 | .032349 | 9.676508 | .103343 | 36 |
| 37 | 34.003949 | 330.039486 | .003030 | .029408 | 9.705917 | .103030 | 37 |
| 38 | 37.404343 | 364.043434 | .002747 | .026735 | 9.732651 | .102747 | 38 |
| 39 | 41.144778 | 401.447778 | .002491 | .024304 | 9.756956 | .102491 | 39 |
| 40 | 45.259256 | 442.592556 | .002259 | .022095 | 9.779051 | .102259 | 40 |
| 41 | 49.785181 | 487.851811 | .002050 | .020086 | 9.799137 | .102050 | 41 |
| 42 | 54.763699 | 537.636992 | .001860 | .018260 | 9.817397 | .101860 | 42 |
| 43 | 60.240069 | 592.400692 | .001688 | .016600 | 9.833998 | .101688 | 43 |
| 44 | 66.264076 | 652.640761 | .001532 | .015091 | 9.849089 | .101532 | 44 |
| 45 | 72.890484 | 718.904837 | .001391 | .013719 | 9.862808 | .101391 | 45 |
| 46 | 80.179532 | 791.795321 | .001263 | .012472 | 9.875280 | .101263 | 46 |
| 47 | 88.197485 | 871.974853 | .001147 | .011338 | 9.886618 | .101147 | 47 |
| 48 | 97.017234 | 960.172338 | .001041 | .010307 | 9.896926 | .101041 | 48 |
| 49 | 106.718957 | 1057.189572 | .000946 | .009370 | 9.906296 | .100946 | 49 |
| 50 | 117.390853 | 1163.908529 | .000859 | .008519 | 9.914814 | .100859 | 50 |
| 51 | 129.129938 | 1281.299382 | .000780 | .007744 | 9.922559 | .100780 | 51 |
| 52 | 142.042932 | 1410.429320 | .000709 | .007040 | 9.929599 | .100709 | 52 |
| 53 | 156.247225 | 1552.472252 | .000644 | .006400 | 9.935999 | .100644 | 53 |
| 54 | 171.871948 | 1708.719477 | .000585 | .005818 | 9.941817 | .100585 | 54 |
| 55 | 189.059142 | 1880.591425 | .000532 | .005289 | 9.947106 | .100532 | 55 |
| 56 | 207.965057 | 2069.650567 | .000483 | .004809 | 9.951915 | .100483 | 56 |
| 57 | 228.761562 | 2277.615624 | .000439 | .004371 | 9.956286 | .100439 | 57 |
| 58 | 251.637719 | 2506.377186 | .000399 | .003974 | 9.960260 | .100399 | 58 |
| 59 | 276.801490 | 2758.014905 | .000363 | .003613 | 9.963873 | .100363 | 59 |
| 60 | 304.481640 | 3034.816395 | .000330 | .003284 | 9.967157 | .100330 | 60 |

Reprinted by permission, from *Ellwood's Tables for Real Estate Appraising and Financing* (Ridgewood, N.J.: published by the author, 1959).

MANAGEMENT DECISION SIMULATIONS

## TABLE OF RANDOM NUMBERS

| Line/Co. | (1) | (2) | (3) | (4) | (5) | (6) |
|---|---|---|---|---|---|---|
| 1. | 10480 | 15011 | 01536 | 02011 | 81647 | 91646 |
| 2. | 22368 | 46573 | 25595 | 85393 | 30995 | 89198 |
| 3. | 24130 | 48360 | 22527 | 97265 | 76393 | 64809 |
| 4. | 42167 | 93093 | 06243 | 61680 | 07856 | 16376 |
| 5. | 37570 | 39975 | 81837 | 16656 | 06121 | 91782 |
| 6. | 77921 | 06907 | 11008 | 42751 | 27756 | 53498 |
| 7. | 99562 | 72905 | 56420 | 69994 | 98872 | 31016 |
| 8. | 96301 | 91977 | 05463 | 07972 | 18876 | 20922 |
| 9. | 89579 | 14342 | 63661 | 10281 | 17453 | 18103 |
| 10. | 85475 | 36857 | 53342 | 53988 | 53060 | 59533 |
| 11. | 28918 | 69578 | 88231 | 33276 | 70997 | 79936 |
| 12. | 63553 | 40961 | 48235 | 03427 | 49626 | 69445 |
| 13. | 09429 | 93969 | 52636 | 92737 | 88974 | 33488 |
| 14. | 10365 | 61129 | 87529 | 85689 | 48237 | 52267 |
| 15. | 07119 | 97336 | 71048 | 08178 | 77233 | 13916 |
| 16. | 51085 | 12765 | 51821 | 51259 | 77452 | 16308 |
| 17. | 02368 | 21382 | 52404 | 60268 | 89368 | 19885 |
| 18. | 01011 | 54092 | 33362 | 94904 | 31273 | 04146 |
| 19. | 52162 | 53916 | 46369 | 58586 | 23216 | 14513 |
| 20. | 07056 | 97628 | 33787 | 09998 | 42698 | 06691 |
| 21. | 48663 | 91245 | 85828 | 14346 | 09172 | 30168 |
| 22. | 54164 | 58492 | 22421 | 74103 | 47040 | 25306 |
| 23. | 32639 | 32363 | 05597 | 24200 | 13363 | 38005 |
| 24. | 29334 | 27001 | 87637 | 87308 | 58731 | 00256 |
| 25. | 02488 | 33062 | 28834 | 07351 | 19731 | 92420 |

a Reproduced from Interstate Commerce Commission, Bureau of Transport Economics and Statistics, *Table of 105,000 Random Decimal Digits,* Statement No. 4914, File no. 261-A-1 (Washington, D.C., May, 1949) pp. 1 and 2.

Random Normal Numbers[a]

$\mu = 0, \sigma = 1$

| | (1) | (2) | (3) | (4) | (5) | (6) | (7) |
|---|---|---|---|---|---|---|---|
| 1 | 0.464 | 0.137 | 2.455 | −0.323 | −0.068 | 0.296 | −0.288 |
| 2 | 0.060 | −2.526 | −0.531 | −1.940 | 0.543 | −1.558 | 0.187 |
| 3 | 1.486 | −0.354 | −0.634 | 0.697 | 0.926 | 1.375 | 0.785 |
| 4 | 1.022 | −0.472 | 1.279 | 3.521 | 0.571 | −1.851 | 0.194 |
| 5 | 1.394 | −0.555 | 0.046 | 0.321 | 2.945 | 1.974 | −0.258 |
| 6 | 0.906 | −0.513 | −0.525 | 0.595 | 0.881 | −0.934 | 1.579 |
| 7 | 1.179 | −1.055 | 0.007 | 0.769 | 0.971 | 0.712 | 1.090 |
| 8 | −1.501 | −0.488 | −0.162 | −0.136 | 1.033 | 0.203 | 0.448 |
| 9 | −0.690 | 0.756 | −1.618 | −0.445 | −0.511 | −2.051 | −0.457 |
| 10 | 1.372 | 0.225 | 0.378 | 0.761 | 0.181 | −0.736 | 0.960 |
| 11 | −0.482 | 1.677 | −0.057 | −1.229 | −0.486 | 0.856 | −0.491 |
| 12 | −1.376 | −0.150 | 1.356 | −0.561 | −0.256 | 0.212 | 0.219 |
| 13 | −1.010 | 0.598 | −0.918 | 1.598 | 0.065 | 0.415 | −0.169 |
| 14 | −0.005 | −0.899 | 0.012 | −0.725 | 1.147 | −0.121 | −0.096 |
| 15 | 1.393 | −1.163 | −0.911 | 1.231 | −0.199 | −0.246 | 1.239 |
| 16 | −1.787 | −0.261 | 1.237 | 1.046 | −0.508 | −1.630 | −0.146 |
| 17 | −0.105 | −0.357 | −1.384 | 0.360 | −0.992 | −0.116 | −1.698 |
| 18 | −1.339 | 1.827 | −0.959 | 0.424 | 0.969 | −1.141 | −1.041 |
| 19 | 1.041 | 0.535 | 0.731 | 1.377 | 0.983 | −1.330 | 1.620 |
| 20 | 0.279 | −2.056 | 0.717 | −0.873 | −1.096 | −1.396 | 1.047 |
| 21 | −1.805 | −2.008 | −1.633 | 0.542 | 0.250 | 0.166 | 0.032 |
| 22 | −1.186 | 1.180 | 1.114 | 0.882 | 1.265 | −0.202 | 0.151 |
| 23 | 0.658 | −1.141 | 1.151 | −1.210 | −0.927 | 0.425 | 0.290 |
| 24 | −0.439 | 0.358 | −1.939 | 0.891 | −0.227 | 0.602 | 0.973 |
| 25 | 1.398 | −0.230 | 0.385 | −0.649 | −0.577 | 0.237 | −0.289 |
| 26 | 0.199 | 0.208 | −1.083 | −0.219 | −0.291 | 1.221 | 1.119 |
| 27 | 0.159 | 0.272 | −0.313 | 0.084 | −2.828 | −0.439 | −0.792 |
| 28 | 2.273 | 0.606 | 0.606 | −0.747 | 0.247 | 1.291 | 0.063 |
| 29 | 0.041 | −0.307 | 0.121 | 0.790 | −0.584 | 0.541 | 0.484 |
| 30 | −1.132 | −2.098 | 0.921 | 0.145 | 0.446 | −2.661 | 1.045 |
| 31 | 0.768 | 0.079 | −1.473 | 0.034 | −2.127 | 0.665 | 0.084 |
| 32 | 0.375 | −1.658 | −0.851 | 0.234 | −0.656 | 0.340 | −0.086 |
| 33 | −0.513 | −0.344 | 0.210 | −0.736 | 1.041 | 0.008 | 0.427 |
| 34 | 0.292 | −0.521 | 1.266 | −1.206 | −0.899 | 0.110 | −0.528 |
| 35 | 1.026 | 2.990 | −0.574 | −0.491 | −1.114 | 1.297 | −1.433 |
| 36 | −1.334 | 1.278 | −0.568 | −0.109 | −0.515 | −0.566 | 2.923 |
| 37 | −0.287 | −0.144 | −0.254 | 0.574 | −0.451 | −1.181 | −1.190 |
| 38 | 0.161 | −0.886 | −0.921 | −0.509 | 1.410 | −0.518 | 0.192 |
| 39 | −1.346 | 0.193 | −1.202 | 0.394 | −1.045 | 0.843 | 0.942 |
| 40 | 1.250 | −0.199 | −0.288 | 1.810 | 1.378 | 0.584 | 1.216 |

From Churchman, Ackoff, & Arnoff, *Introduction to Operations Research,* John Wiley & Sons, New York, 1957.

[a] This table is reproduced in part from a table of the RAND Corporation.

MANAGEMENT DECISION SIMULATIONS

### An Introduction to Time-Sharing Basic

To get on the Time-Sharing System, turn on the terminal (and coupler if needed) and dial the computer's telephone number to get the connect tone. Place the receiver in the coupler and type in the sign-in sequence. The "Return" key is to be depressed after each line entered. You can now interact with an existing program by retrieving it by its name, i.e.: GET-PROG 1 or begin composing your own program by naming it (NAM-MINE) or whatever you wish in 6 or less characters.

Every program instruction must have a line number to identify it. The program will be executed in the sequence of the line numbers. Therefore it is advisable to leave an interval between line number assignments to permit insertions found necessary later.

| Ln. | Instruction |
|-----|-------------|
| 100 | REM MY VERY OWN PROGRAM FOR EOQ |
| 110 | PRINT "ECONOMIC ORDER QUANTITIES" |
| 120 | PRINT |
| 130 | READ I, S |
| 140 | PRINT "ENTER ANNUAL REQTS AND UNIT PRICE (150,2.50)" |
| 150 | INPUT A, C |
| 160 | Q = SQR (2 * A * S/(C * I)) |
| 170 | PRINT |
| 180 | PRINT "A="; A, "S="; S, "C="; C, "I="; I, "EOQ="; Q |
| 190 | GO TO 140 |
| 200 | DATA   .24, 25.00 |
| 300 | END |

Desire to add the following before running

| | |
|-----|-------------|
| 122 | PRINT "ASSUMES USUAL FORMULA OF SQUARE ROOT OF" |
| 123 | PRINT "TWICE REQTS X ACQUISITION COST PER ORDER" |
| 124 | PRINT "DIVIDED BY UNIT COST TIMES CARRYING PERCENT" |
| 126 | PRINT |

Typing RUN would execute the above program requiring you to input **A & C** (with comma separating them) from keyboard.

A summary of **BASIC** program statements is as follows:

Remember! Each statement must begin with a line number. All variables must be coded or represented by a single alpha, $c$, or one alpha and one number, $c_1$. Strings of alphameric characters are represented by alpha and $ character, C\$. Subscripted variables are represented by alpha and numerics such as B(1) or H(4,6).

| Statement | Explanation | Example |
|-----------|-------------|---------|
| REM | Any string of characters for remarks nonexecutable explanation statement | 10  REM STUDY THESE EXAMPLES |
| LET | Variable = expression (the word LET is not necessary) | 42  $X2 = Z + Y * W\uparrow 2$ |

| READ | Reads values of variables, sequentially from DATA entries | 16 | READ X,Y,W1,Q(I,J) |
|------|------|------|------|
| RESTORE | Resets the DATA file to beginning | 10 | RESTORE |
| DATA | Number, number . . . , "String," enters data into program | 90 | DATA 4,6,8,"FIX" |
| PRINT | Output of literals (in quotes) calculated variables or expression | 70 | PRINT "X";Z,(Y+3)↑2 |
| INPUT | Variable, variable, . . . enters data "on-line" | 60 | INPUT X,Y,A$ |
| GO TO | Direct transfer to a line no. | 82 | GO TO 60 |
| IF-THEN | Results of numeric or logical comparison directs program to next or alternate line | 92 | IF I > I THEN 42 |
| FOR-TO | Loops through a series of steps incrementing the counter each cycle | 45 | FOR I=I TO 9 |
| NEXT | Directs program back to beginning of loop | 75 | NEXT I |
| END | Final program stop | 99 | END |
| STOP | Terminates program at this point | 80 | STOP |
| DEF FN__( ) | Defines your own function | 15 | DEF FNA(Y)=I+SQR(X) |
| GOSUB | Directs main program to a sub-program | 65 | GOSUB 130 |
| RETURN | End of subprogram, directs it back to main program | 150 | RETURN |
| DIM | Size reservations of arrays & matrices (subscripted variables) | 05 | DIM A(12),B$(6) |

## MANAGEMENT DECISION SIMULATIONS

The so-called System Commands although different from system to system
require no line numbers:

| | | |
|---|---|---|
| 'Shift' "O," | key | Backspace Erasure |
| 'ESC' | key | Deletes statement being typed |
| 'BRK' | key | Stops execution of a listing |
| 'Cᶜ' | keys | Gets you "out" of a program at Input time |

The following require 'RETURN' key
after typing:

| | |
|---|---|
| 10  A – – – A | Originates or replaces entry on line 10 |
| 10 | Deletes or erases line 10 |
| NAM-MINE | Identifies a program as MINE |
| SAV | Saves the program under its name MINE |
| GET-MINE | Retrieves a saved program called MINE |
| KIL-MINE | Unsaves or destroys program called MINE |
| SCRATCH | Erases current program except for its name |
| CAT | Lists programs named and saved |
| LIB | Lists system programs or library |
| LIST | Lists current or retrieved program |
| LIS-M | Lists program beginning at line M |
| PUNCH | Punches out tape automatically |
| TAPE | Informs system to read from tape |
| KEY | Puts control back to keyboard |
| RENUM-M, N | Renumbers current program in multiples of N beginning with line M (If M or N are blank they are assumed as 10) |
| DELETE-M,P | Erases lines M through P |
| APP-MINE | Retrieves saved program called MINE and adds to end of current program if line numbers are higher |
| RUN-M | Executes from line M or beginning if M is blank. |